'*Joan Robinson* is a welcome and timely reminder of Robinson's intelligence, energy, passionate commitment to social justice, and tireless capacity for debate. It portrays two voyages of intellectual discovery: the evolution of Robinson's thinking, with a due appreciation for her successes and failures; and Harcourt and Kerr's own measured re-evaluation of the post-Keynesian revolution in which Robinson and they played central roles. The reconsideration of Joan Robinson's life and work is one important starting-point in the broad effort to understand the evolution of twentieth-century economics and to imagine a future for economic analysis outside the narrow confines of neoliberal dogma.'

—Duncan K. Foley,
Leo Model Professor, New School for Social Research,
External Professor, Santa Fe Institute, US.

'This is an outstanding book and is a joy to read. It provides a comprehensive guide to the development of Joan Robinson's ideas, ideas which have influenced almost every area of economics. It will also be of interest to anyone wanting to learn more about the economics of John Maynard Keynes and his circle. Thoroughly recommended for mainstream economists and not only post-Keynesians.'

—Robert Dixon,
Professor of Economics at the University of Melbourne.

'Joan Robinson was one of the most significant members of a group of younger economists working in Cambridge in the circle of Keynes. She went on to become a leading figure in the elaboration and defence of Keynesian ideas after WWII. This intellectual biography by Harcourt and Kerr is an outstanding effort. It manages to set all of those contributions in the context of a coherent picture of her intellectual formation and development. It does this, moreover, while doing full justice both to her analytical sophistication and her influence within the profession. There was scarcely a major economic debate to which she did not make a decisive contribution. One comes away from a reading of Harcourt and Kerr's *Joan Robinson* feeling as though one knows much more about her, and those interventions, than when one began.'

—Murray Milgate,
Queens' College, Cambridge, UK.

Great Thinkers in Economics Series
Series Editor: A. P. Thirlwall is Professor of Applied Economics, University of Kent, UK.

Great Thinkers in Economics is designed to illuminate the economics of some of the great historical and contemporary economists by exploring the interactions between their lives and work, and the events surrounding them. The books are brief and written in a style that makes them not only of interest to professional economists, but also intelligible for students of economics and the interested layperson.

Titles include:
Alessandro Roncaglia
PIERO SRAFFA

William J. Barber
GUNNAR MYRDAL

Paul Davidson
JOHN MAYNARD KEYNES

Peter D. Groenewegen
ALFRED MARSHALL

Michael Szenberg and Lall Ramrattan
FRANCO MODIGLIANI

Gavin Kennedy
ADAM SMITH

John E. King
NICHOLAS KALDOR

Gordon Fletcher
DENNIS ROBERTSON

G. C. Harcourt and Prue Kerr
JOAN ROBINSON

Forthcoming titles include:
Esben Sloth Anderson
JOSEPH A. SCHUMPETER

Michael A. Lebowitz
KARL MARX

Julio Lopez and Michaël Samuel Assous
MICHAL KALECKI

Gerhard Michael Ambrosi
ARTHUR C. PIGOU

J. R. Stanfield
JOHN KENNETH GALBRAITH

Warren Young and Esteban Perez
ROY HARROD

Roger Middleton
ROBERT SOLOW

Paul Mosley and Barbara Ingham
SIR ARTHUR LEWIS

Robert Dimand
JAMES TOBIN

Great Thinkers in Economics
Series Standing Order ISBN 978–14039–8555-2 (Hardback) 978–14039–8556–9 (Paperback)
(outside North America only)

You can receive future titles in this series as they are published by placing a standing order. Please contact your bookseller or, in case of difficulty, write to us at the address below with your name and address, the title of the series and the ISBN quoted above.

Customer Services Department, Macmillan Distribution Ltd, Houndmills, Basingstoke, Hampshire RG21 6XS, England

---

Joan Robinson

G. C. Harcourt

and

Prue Kerr

palgrave
macmillan

First published 2009 by
PALGRAVE MACMILLAN

Palgrave Macmillan in the UK is an imprint of Macmillan Publishers Limited, registered in England, company number 785998, of Houndmills, Basingstoke, Hampshire RG21 6XS.

Palgrave Macmillan in the US is a division of St Martin's Press LLC, 175 Fifth Avenue, New York, NY 10010.

Palgrave Macmillan is the global academic imprint of the above companies and has companies and representatives throughout the world.

Palgrave® and Macmillan® are registered trademarks in the United States, the United Kingdom, Europe and other countries.

ISBN-13: 978-1-4039-9640-4 hardback

This book is printed on paper suitable for recycling and made from fully managed and sustained forest sources. Logging, pulping and manufacturing processes are expected to conform to the environmental regulations of the country of origin.

A catalogue record for this book is available from the British Library.

A catalog record for this book is available from the Library of Congress.

10 9 8 7 6 5 4 3 2 1
18 17 16 15 14 13 12 11 10 09

Printed and bound in Great Britain by
CPI Antony Rowe, Chippenham and Eastbourne

Contents

Figures and Table

Figures

Table

Preface

Both authors had the privilege and pleasure of knowing Joan Robinson personally, GCH from 1955 on, PK from 1978 on. As we mention in the concluding chapter, Chapter 12, we have written over 100 essays on the themes pursued in the book. In GCH's case, the major intellectual reason for his return to Cambridge from Adelaide in 1982 was to write the intellectual history of Joan Robinson and her circle. The aim of this book is to bring our collective findings together in one volume, to set out in one place what we believe to be the substantial legacy of Joan Robinson. It is our tribute to a much-admired and loved teacher, colleague and friend.

In writing the volume, we have been greatly helped by the comments of Robert Dixon, Cristina Marcuzzo and the very detailed and careful reading of the manuscript by Tony Thirlwall, the General Editor of the Series, 'Great Thinkers in Economics'. We have not always followed his advice but we are extremely grateful to him for his support and encouragement. We would also like to thank Debra Armstrong, Janet Nurse, Jane Starnes and Hazel Yorke for their great help in preparing the many drafts of the manuscript, and the librarians of the Marshall Library at Cambridge and at the University of New South Wales for their courteous help in chasing up elusive bibliographical entries. Finally, colleagues and friends too numerous to name have greatly aided us in the task of evaluating the contributions of Joan Robinson to our 'miserable subject' (Keynes, 1971–9, C.W., vol. XIV, 190).

As always, GCH thanks Joan Harcourt for her great love and for her sustained support of a task which has taken more than a quarter of a century to come to an end! PK thanks Stephanie Blankenburg for her boundless generosity and Wesley Rigg for his patient faith throughout the writing of this intellectual biography.

Acknowledgements

Cambridge Political Economy Society Trust
Archives of Marshall Library, Faculty of Economics, Cambridge
Modern Archive Centre, King's College Cambridge
Archives of Wren Library, Trinity College Cambridge
Archives of London School of Economics
BBC Written Archives
Institute of Advanced Study, University of Bologna
Discipline of English, Communication and Cultural Study, University of Western Australia

Abbreviations

GCH	Geoffrey Colin Harcourt
JVR	Joan Violet Robinson
EAGR	Edward Austin Gossage Robinson
JMK	John Maynard Keynes
RFK	Richard Ferdinand Kahn
NK	Nicholas Kaldor
C.E.P.	*Collected Economic Papers* of Joan Robinson (five volumes plus Index)
C.W.	*Collected Writings* of John Maynard Keynes
EIC	*The Economics of Imperfect Competition*
EME	*An Essay on Marxian Economics*

Joan Robinson, (1903–1983), is widely considered to be amongst the greatest economists of the twentieth century. After the success of her first book, *The Economics of Imperfect Competition*, Joan Robinson shifted her attention to Keynes's work. She was one of Keynes's circle of trusted colleagues, studying the theoretical possibilities offered by his *General Theory*.

This comprehensive study of Joan Robinson recounts her intellectual development and her major contributions, examining; her role in the making of *The General Theory*, her sympathetically critical interest in Marxian economics, her contributions to Labour Party policy in the 1930s and 1940s, her writings on development in China and India and her critique of the conceptual foundations of mainstream economics. Joan Robinson's story is intricately entwined with the story of Cambridge economics in the twentieth century, taking in major changes in the way economics was thought about, done and taught.

This book is not only indispensable reading for all interested in the history of Joan Robinson's life and work, but also to those studying Keynesian, Post-Keynesianism and economic development

1
Introduction

This volume is an intellectual biography of Joan Robinson (1903–83) who was undoubtedly one of the greatest economists of the twentieth century and the greatest woman economist.[1] In its pages we recount her intellectual development and her major contributions from her first publication in the early 1930s to her last, which was published posthumously in 1985. Her story is intricately entwined with the story of Cambridge economics in the twentieth century, taking in major changes in the way economics was thought about, done and taught, changes to which Joan Robinson and her circle, the first generation of what may loosely be called Keynes's pupils, made major contributions, from the 1920s until well into the post-war years. Most of the major players remained active until their deaths, most of which (apart from Keynes's, of course, who died in 1946) occurred in the 1980s and 1990s.[2]

With the intertwining of reason and identity, it seems pertinent to offer some glimpses into Joan Robinson's life. To understand the passion which she brought to the theoretical developments with which she was associated, we believe it is necessary to begin with a description of her background, of her forebears and upbringing. We discuss this in the next part of this chapter. We then present these glimpses which we hope will give some insight into the intellectual life of the woman who wrote the remarkable body of theory and analysis that forms the subject of this book. It is followed by a short outline of her career up until her death in August 1983, just over two months short of her eightieth birthday.[3]

Joan Robinson was born at Camberley, Surrey, on 31 October 1903, the third child in the family of four daughters and one son of Major General Sir Frederick Maurice and his wife, Helen Margaret Marsh. Joan Robinson came from a long line of radical dissenters (in a political, not denominational sense). Her paternal great grandfather was F. D. Maurice, the Christian socialist. Her paternal grandfather and her father were both professional soldiers and military historians. Her father was the central figure in the infamous Maurice debates in the House of Commons in 1918 (see below). Her mother was the daughter of Frederick Marsh, a surgeon who became Professor of Surgery at Cambridge and Master of Downing College, Cambridge. Her uncle was Sir Edward 'Eddie' Marsh, art connoisseur, literary critic and private secretary to a succession of notable politicians, including Churchill. Joan Robinson's father was a man of high, if quixotic, principles, traits which he passed on to his daughter. He was an excellent professional soldier, passionately loyal to his fellow officers and his men. When he felt that the government, and especially Lloyd George, were trying to blame the military for some ghastly errors on the Western Front in early 1918, he wrote a letter to leading newspapers stating that ministerial statements were false and provided the evidence. The disagreement was over the strength of British forces in the face of a fierce German assault and also over who had decided the troop numbers, the politicians or the army commanders. Though Maurice's arguments and behaviour were on the whole vindicated (Lloyd George was never to admit this), he nevertheless had to leave the army in April 1918 – it was 'bad form' for a serving officer to 'whistle blow', as we would say now. He subsequently became the Principal of East London (later Queen Mary) College, London.[4] Joan Robinson has said that until, as a 14-year-old schoolchild, she became known as Maurice's daughter, her life in her mind was more real to her than life in reality.[5] She did a switch at this juncture and we conjecture that her childhood fantasy life may be one clue as to why she was such a powerful theorist and a remorselessly logical writer and critic.

Joan Robinson went to St. Paul's Girls' School (her father had been to the boys' equivalent) and then to Girton College, Cambridge, in 1922. She had studied history at school but she chose to read for the Economics Tripos at Cambridge because she wanted to understand the causes of poverty and unemployment. She did not think her teachers and especially her supervisor at Girton, Marjorie Tappan-Hollond (there was mutual intellectual dislike between teacher and student), provided satisfactory answers.[6] She obtained a 2.i in both parts of the Tripos in 1924 and 1925, respectively (see Turner, 1989, 17–18). She could not, though, be awarded a degree because this right did not come to women in Cambridge until 1948. She did say that getting a second was 'a great disappointment' and we suspect that the fact that John Hicks also got a second in PPE at Oxford at about the same time was never of much comfort to her.

In 1926 she married Austin Robinson (E. A. G. Robinson) who was then a Fellow of Corpus Christi, its one unmarried fellow, having graduated in 1922. Shortly before his marriage Austin Robinson received an offer of a job as tutor to the Maharajah of Gwalior in India, a boy not yet ten years old, whose father had recently died. Cairncross (1993, 30) reports: 'Joan brought the proposed appointment to Austin's attention.' Joan was a close friend of the daughter of an associate of the Maharajah's family. Austin was offered a generous, tax-free stipend for an anticipated eight-to-ten-years appointment. Just two months after their marriage, Joan and Austin sailed for Bombay.

Their accounts of life in Gwalior reflect the privileges taken by the British in India at that time. Details of their life were recorded by both Joan and Austin in short memoirs of particular aspects of their daily routines. Austin records the day as beginning at around 6.30 a.m. with a tray of tea, followed immediately by him and Joan riding or perhaps driving through streets straggling with bullock carts, to the parade ground, where the Maharajah and his sister would be having their riding lesson and drill; Joan and Austin would ride as they pleased. At 7.30 a.m., everyone would assemble to ride back to the palace, with Joan and Austin and the four boys, who were educated with the Maharajah, trailing at the back. At home, after bathing in a tin bath, there would be breakfast and then Austin would go for three hours to the schoolroom. Joan occupied herself writing book reviews for the local papers (notes from a review of E. M. Forster's *A Passage to India* reveal a qualified assessment of the book), or critically reading Austin's writing; Austin was already writing analytical papers on the Indian experiences. After lunch together and a siesta, there were Hindi lessons, and then Austin played cricket with the boys and Joan took the girls to play badminton and another palace game at which she was not very skilled. They exercised themselves and the children for several hours. In the early evening, perhaps at 6.30 or 7 p.m., they motored to the Club where they met other expatriates; Joan would have a gin and lemonade, read out-of-date newspapers, socialise with the other members, perhaps take a swim or play a game of tennis. Austin notes that some 'conversation is conducted in a low tone as it savours of the intellectual and is therefore not really suitable for the Club' (EAGR 7/1/2/23). The Robinsons would return home and bathe and dress for dinner. Joan recounts a dinner one night at the palace. Her awkwardness and inability to generate small talk and her discomfort in such socially precious situations are apparent even then. Joan describes her 'flagging spirits' at one dinner and her dismay 'when I take a bite, I find it is full of meat, which unluckily I dislike' (EAGR 7/1/2/41). She continues to say '[M]y brain is quite congealed. I cannot think of a word to say to anyone' and she politely waits until it is 'seemly for us to go' (EAGR 7/1/2/46).

While in Gwalior Austin drafted a substantial portion of a review of the relations between the Indian states and the British Crown for the Prince. Cairncross (1993, 30) reports: 'At the end of June [1928] the group acting for the Princes met in Delhi and came to the conclusion that there was "a lot more to the economic case than they had thought". They invited Joan, who had gone to Delhi to help finish the case on the spot, to accompany them to London to assist in its presentation, and she travelled with them early in July' (ibid., p. 30). In London she helped with the presentation of the Princes' case. While she was in London, Austin resigned from his post and prepared to return to England (see also Tahir, 1990a, Ch. 1).

Austin and Joan also drafted substantial portions of a book on population. They discussed the optimal population of India, given the existence of alternatively diminishing, constant and increasing returns to industry. The optimum population was that at which there was maximum welfare per head and at which the various industry-types were in balance. Joan continued to work on the manuscript after she reached London while waiting for Austin to return. But once their new life in Cambridge began, she was distracted by new interests and the drafts were abandoned.

Cambridge became the base for both of them for the rest of their lives (Austin died in 1993). Austin Robinson was appointed to a university lectureship in 1929 and elected to a Fellowship in Sidney Sussex in 1931. Joan Robinson had to wait until 1934 for her first university post, as an Assistant lecturer. She was never a teaching fellow at any college but she did give supervisions to pupils from various colleges. She came to know Cambridge people – Keynes, and especially Richard Kahn, Keynes's favourite pupil who was elected to a Fellowship at King's in 1929; Piero Sraffa who came to Cambridge in 1927 and to whose lectures on advanced value theory she almost certainly went; Maurice Dobb who was to become the UK's foremost Marxist economist and who had graduated in the same year as Austin; Gerald Shove to whose lectures she had gone as an undergraduate; James Meade from Oxford who spent a year at Cambridge in 1930–1 and who was a member of the Cambridge 'Circus'; Dennis Robertson, again to whose lectures she had gone but with whom she had a hostile relationship, increasingly so from the 1930s on;

and, of course, the Professor of Political Economy, A. C. Pigou who we think liked Joan Robinson enough to vote her an 'honorary man' (his misogyny became marked after the First World War).

Joan Robinson's close relationships with her colleagues were intense and in some cases endured for the more than 50 years of her life in Cambridge. Her confidante and most trusted critic was Richard Kahn. To him she presented her ideas and work-in-progress which he read with an unsparing eye. In a planned but unpublished 'Introduction' drafted for a collection of Kahn's essays, she revealed: 'I remember in particular, as important steps, the recognition that there could be a self-sustaining short-period equilibrium at *any* level of employment and Kahn's suggestion of drawing cordons round the investment and consumption good industries and studying the interchange between them (of course, none of us had heard of Marx's schema of reproduction)' (JVR/i/8/4). Of him, she wrote: 'The question is bound to be raised, why such a powerful and energetic mind never expressed itself in any large-scale publication. The answer is partly to be found in the rare generosity with which Kahn gave his time, not only to Keynes and to me, but to innumerable pupils, colleagues, and strangers who submitted work to him' (JVR/i/8/6).

The other friendship dating from the late 1920s was with Piero Sraffa. 'Piero is my most precious jewel' (RFK/13/90/3/249). The two had an affectionate relationship which is reflected in his teasing letters to her while she was in hospital. In response to her pamphlet, *Economics is a Serious Subject,* in which she caricatured 'a continental economist', he replied: 'I know of course that you are pulling my leg, but it is nice to have it pulled that way'; and while she was in hospital convalescing, he wrote to her prior to a visit (31.1.39): 'We shall talk about history forecasts provided we keep clear of the prophets with whom I am sorry to hear you are getting so intimate' (JVR/vii/431/25). A few weeks later, Sraffa confides in her the agony he is in on being offered a fellowship at Trinity: 'I have failed to equate the marginal utilities [of the advantages and disadvantages], I wish I knew where they are' (JVR/vii/431/28). But Joan Robinson became aware of his reluctance to engage with her on analytical aspects of her written work. On her proofs on *The Economics of Imperfect Competition* (*EIC*) he wrote: 'I have avoided raising "broad issues" – it would be of no use to you at this stage, or indeed at any stage' (JVR/vii/431/6). And in 1953, when she had written the three essays, *On Re-reading Marx,* partly triggered and inspired by Sraffa's Introduction to Ricardo's *Principles*, (elsewhere she remarked how reading Sraffa's Introduction had suddenly enlightened her about the meaning and conceptualisation of the 'rate of profits' (*C.E.P.*, vol. IV, 1973,

247)), she referred to the essays as 'ideas one has been brooding over for years [which] suddenly take shape. The quality of the thought depends on the early brooding but the quality of the *prose* depends on the flash of inspiration. The faster written the better. ... It will be very interesting to see Piero's reaction. Of course, the whole thing is really aimed at him' (RFK/13/90/5/378) (28.10.52). She also sent the essays to Isiah Berlin in Oxford[7] and was anxious about the opinions of David Champernowne and Eric Hobsbawm (RFK/30/90/5). She saw these essays as highly provocative to both Marxists and Bastard Keynesians and said: 'I want to have the family joke about Piero. I cannot pinch twenty years of his life's work without acknowledge[ment] and acknowledgement in a joke is the only way I can do it' (RFK/13/90/5/381). Yet '[Piero] very well may prefer to pretend that he has never read the stuff, as he does over my Marx book. His attitude to the whole thing is very complicated' (RFK/13/90/5/370)(1.11.52). She understood Sraffa (1960) as a critique of marginal productivity theory and, incidentally, a solution to the transformation problem. 'I must insist that this is only my own view. Piero has always stuck close to pure unadulterated Marx and regards my amendments with suspicion' (Robinson, 1977b, *C.E.P.*, vol. V, 1979, n2, 285). She recognised Sraffa's 'model' as an abstraction from social and historical forms, but seemed not to then identify its categories with the very basic requirements of a system of production and exchange underlying the productive systems she recommended for replacing orthodox theories. Her own abstractions were institutional or social, and her mode of thinking was to pursue all the logical possibilities of a situation at that level of abstraction in a deductive chain, thereby reaching implications which a less inquisitive mind would fail to find, meanwhile finding contradictions and logical limits. Sraffa's system was spare yet far-reaching.

It is also telling of their relationship that Joan Robinson wrote to him: 'I have always been baffled because while your ideas are just what I want (apart from a few that are above my head) you do not like mine' (Sraffa/D3/12/111/337) (31.5.60). She subsequently wrote: 'All the work that I have been doing the last 10 years has been very much influenced by you – both our conversations in old days and by your Preface. ... I have a very deep feeling of gratitude to you. The fact that you reject it doesn't affect the case at all' (Sraffa/D3/12/111/340–1) (18.6.60).

Nicky Kaldor was a colleague from before the war but it was after the war, when Kaldor moved from LSE to Cambridge, that Joan Robinson became a good friend of the family. In 1941 the pair had submitted a proposal for a joint project to the National Institute of Economic and

Social Research (NK/3/10/118/30). The friendship had a sharp edge of rivalry, already in the 1930s (see King, 1998) but especially around the mid-1950s to the 1960s, when both were responding to Harrod (1939, 1948) and working out their respective Keynesian theories of growth and distribution. Joan Robinson was alert to the fact that Kaldor, although remarking that he was impressed with (the existence of) her manuscript (of 1956a), claimed not to have read it in order to keep his mind clear for his own ideas, but she was pleased to find that he subsequently studied her book (1956a) with his group of research students. A heated exchange of views took place through correspondence between the two as Kaldor and Joan Robinson worked on constructing a Keynesian treatment of the behaviour of an individual firm in the context of different sets of assumptions about the firm's decisions. One aim was to demonstrate that the choice of technique did not determine the real wage rate or the rate of profits. The letters reveal a rivalry which only became constructive later in the correspondence (NK/3/30/177).

Her attitude to the nature and dynamics of academic work was partly formed by her participation in the 'Circus'.[8] Referring to the 'Circus', she wrote: 'It would not have occurred to us at the time to think in those terms [of ownership of ideas]. Keynes, and all of us, thought that [it] was a great and serious importance to get the argument right; taking credit for it was quite a secondary matter. ... It did not need any motive of vanity or personal prestige for Kahn to contribute to the great task ...' (JVR/i/8/5). In 1962, she wrote to Kaldor: 'I value very much the work gang and I think that we all do each other more good working as a team than any one can by having "priority" or "all my own unaided work"' (NK 3/30/177/27). But otherwise there was a wide gulf between herself and Kahn in their approaches to publishing their ideas. She wrote to him (in 1952), 'I have not at all the same objection to you of making a fool of myself in what I believe is a good cause. Why should I care what people think? This is the profound disagreement between your and my reaction to life' (RFK/13/90/5/380).[9] At the same time, in November 1952, Joan Robinson wrote: 'I have realised more than ever after this [illness] how much one's whole personality is involved in one's "purely intellectual" work. I think the reason I have done so much more with a much weaker brain than any of us is because of my extremely simple-minded attitude' (RFK/13/90/5/354). She was known for her aversion to the formalisation of economic theory and earlier commented to Kahn: 'I did a bit of calculus but decided that it would be more painless to go through it all with you. ... We might sit on the hillside in Austria and do it' (RFK/13/90/3/130). She reacted to a letter from Kaldor in response to her article 'What is perfect competition?' (Robinson, 1934): 'Of course the proof [of the distribution between industries of a factor to which the elasticity of supply differs] is very simple by Nightmare methods' and repeated this sentiment: '[Kaldor] is really weaving the conclusions of my Objections chapter into the Nightmare, which we omitted to do at the time' (RFK/13/90/2/72, 80). This does not mean that she also rejected the use of statistics: 'I have been talking to [Brian Reddaway] about the idea of having small high power discussion groups on particular projects with a view to evolving ideas about what can and cannot be done with figures getting the phoneyness out of the statistical work and at the same time finding how to frame theory in terms that can be given meaning' (RFK/13/90/5/177). Her development work was based on examinations of (perhaps inadequate) statistics.

Joan Robinson started publishing papers in the early 1930s and wrote *EIC*, which was published in 1933. No doubt its reception was influential in her university appointment in 1934. She was made a university lecturer in 1937 in, it has to be said, a grudging and ungracious way (see below), a Reader in 1949 and a Professor in 1965, succeeding Austin. She 'retired' in 1971, remaining active into the last year of her life, despite poor health in her later years, a fact which her indomitable spirit always refused to accept.

Joan Robinson did not want to be known as a '*woman* economist' (see note 1 to this chapter). But there were situations where her gender posed obstacles to her. In 1933, Gottfreid Haberler wrote to Kahn: 'Who is Joan Robinson who wrote [in the last *Economic Journal*]? The Christian name sounds like a woman's but the article seems to me much too clever for a woman. ...' (JVR/vii/171). In 1935, C. R. Fay expressed his hostility towards her to Pigou. He objected to her being given a one-year lectureship instead of a one-term position: 'Mrs Robinson should be definitely informed that we desire from her a course on money of one term only. ... The point that she would thereby not qualify as a fulltime lecturer is difficult, but this change in her status was sprung upon us, as has indeed every change [in her position] from the time when she asked permission to give occasional lectures. The assumption has always seemed to me to be that if she wants it, of course she can have it' (RFK/14/99/209 et seq; 2/3/35). Fay even 'wrote to [Austin] Robinson as an old friend and pupil [about] ... the necessity of ensuring that his wife's work should be supplementary and not rival to the third year course' (RFK/ 14/99/211). Pigou, who was in general supportive of Joan Robinson, nevertheless asked her not to be controversial in her lectures. Keynes supported her: 'it would be very strong measures, even unprecedented, ... to veto a course which a lecturer greatly wanted to give in a case where there is no question as to the quality and popularity of the lectures. From what I hear, her lectures are exceedingly good and amongst the most successful with the men' (RFK/14/99/212).

Joan Robinson, however, had 'modern' views on the roles of women. On their return from India, she wrote to her husband: 'Please I don't want you to earn money to send me round the world. I am a strong believer in the economic independence of married women, and only ask to be allowed to earn some myself' (EAGR/2/1/13/59). Nearly ten years later, at last appointed to a university lectureship, she remarked: '[I] now share a cheque book and pay my own bill[s,] I feel the shackles are finally removed' (RFK/13/90/3/230); she referred to Virginia Woolf's *A Room of One's Own*. But the process of academic women being acknowledged as equals was slow. Soon after the outbreak of war, Austin Robinson received a request from the Offices of the War Cabinet for the names of some 'highly educated women who might be taken on in a subordinate capacity' (EAGR/2/1/17/62). Many years later, George Catephores reported that 'Two secret policemen, assigned to cover the meeting where [Joan Robinson] spoke, were overheard to say, after talking between themselves, "Just imagine: such a respectable-looking old lady. How can she utter such things?"' (JVR/vii/94; 5.5.72). In contrast, she received a letter from a listener in response to a BBC debate in which she participated: s/he (the gender of the listener is not known), described the 'clear definition of all you had to say, in contrast to the deliberate "woolliness" of your opponent. ... It is sad, but true, that if you want to hear either the truth, or some Common Sense, spoken clearly in discussion, you have to wait until a woman speaks' (JVR vii/443/1–2) (January 1945).

Though Cambridge was her base, she never lost the schoolgirl enthusiasm for travel. She took a great joy in the people she met, from the high officials and the academics to the younger students, and her interpreters and 'nursemaids', in the political and economic organisation of the place she was visiting, particularly at the ground level, in the history of the place and its monuments, in the many cultural displays and sites and in the natural surroundings of the countryside. She remarked on the splendour of the Bolshoi Ballet performing Prokofiev in Moscow, and on the 'genius' of Piero della Francesca, whose paintings she saw as 'the only thing in European art that equals Budhist sculptures' (RFK/13/90/5). In later years she spent part of each year in Kerala State in India; she visited China eight times in the post-war years; and her first visit to America was in 1961, an event which is still remembered with awe – and sometimes with affection – by those at MIT and elsewhere at the time (see Turner, 1989, Ch. 14).

Over her professional life, she was incredibly productive. Cristina Marcuzzo, who has produced six versions of Joan Robinson's bibliography, records 444 items in its latest incarnation in volume 1 of the Archive editions of Joan Robinson's writings (Marcuzzo, 2002). She wrote many books, many articles in both brownie-point journals and obscure ones, and was a prolific reviewer, writing both review articles and often cryptic, critical shorter ones. She could also write favourable reviews, for example, her review in the *Economic Journal* of Luigi Pasinetti's 1974 volume of essays in economic theory (Robinson, 1975a). Initially she was a critical Marshallian, taking issue with the master's findings but content to adopt (and adapt) his methods and to work on what was then called value theory (see Ch. 2). But once *A Treatise on Money* (1930) was published and the Cambridge 'Circus' met to discuss and criticise it, she quickly became a pioneering Keynesian, contributing both articles and books which expounded and added to the new ideas that Keynes was developing. She not only wrote on employment theory in the short and long period but also contributed seminal ideas to the theories of money and international trade (see Ch. 5).

When Michal Kalecki came on the scene in the mid-1930s, they quickly became friends and a sea change occurred in her approach. She came to frame issues within a Marxist analytical setting increasingly, stressing the importance of history while not accepting his or the Marxist ideology. She was much more a democratic socialist finding a niche on the left of Labour Party politics and policies. Many of her writings in the 1930s and 1940s were directed towards the formation of Labour Party policies in the light of Keynes's and Kalecki's findings (see Ch. 5). During the Second World War she thoroughly investigated Marx's *Capital*, to see what his economic theory had to teach orthodox economists and Keynesians (see Ch. 4). In the post-war years, Kahn and Joan Robinson both wrote innovative papers on monetary theory in the light of Keynes's 1936 book. While Joan Robinson was to increasingly give pride of place to Kalecki's approach to analysis, she always conceded that Keynes's monetary analysis was the most fundamental and deep of all approaches.

In economic theory in the post-war years she was associated with two major developments: what she dubbed the generalisation of *The General Theory* to the long period (though again Marx and Kalecki dominated the framework she adopted) (see Ch. 6) and the parallel critique of neoclassical theory of income distribution and of what she took to be its predominant method. Most of this latter development may be placed under the rubric of the Cambridge–Cambridge debates in capital theory (see Ch. 7). Opinions vary as to whether Joan Robinson or Piero Sraffa made the most fundamental critiques of the conceptual foundations of neoclassical theory. In our view their contributions are much more complementary than competitive, though it is doubtful if either of those authors would accept such a judgement; Joan Robinson suggested that Sraffa was appropriate for the long period while her contribution was for the short period.

A very large part of her post-war writing was concerned with development issues, not only those specifically concerning China, but also generally. Joan Robinson wanted to admire the Chinese experiment; it represented what seemed to her to be a relatively peaceful implementation of a planned economy, both rural and urban. She was observing and interpreting very complex events and translating them into an advocacy to offset what she believed to have been the unsympathetic critiques of Chinese policies which emanated from orthodox circles. She ultimately acknowledged her sometimes uncritical stance. Her last book, published in 1978, was titled *Aspects of Development and Underdevelopment* (Robinson, 1978c), in which she considered the development paths taken by both socialist and non-socialist developing countries and their difficulties in the face of increasingly globalised production (see Ch. 9). She also wrote three books for a more popular audience in which she explored the meaning of 'economics' (see Ch. 11), and with John Eatwell, an alternative textbook in which the authors tried to pass on to those beginning economics what she had learnt over her active writing and teaching life (see Ch. 10).

A theme which appeared often, particularly in her post-war work, is her intolerance of war and of the arms industry. The military sector is often drawn upon as an illustrative example of misplaced Keynesian expenditure and as an insidious use of aid expenditure. Perhaps her sensitivity to war was a response to the military nature of her family background. In 1938, she became very ill. She was vehemently opposed to Britain entering the war with Germany. Her father was being brought into Chamberlain's scheme to try and negotiate with Hitler, while in conflict with this her sister was working through a group of conservative MPs to get the ultimatum to Hitler immediately (RFK/13/90/3/30–1, 33–6). Out of loyalty to her family, Joan Robinson was forced into impossible compromises where her own views regarding the proper position Britain should take towards Germany had no support. Austin Robinson told

Kahn that he too was in favour of war. Kahn wrote to Austin Robinson: 'I have been coming ... to the view ... that one is in danger of minimising the part played in all this by Joan's thoughts about the war. ... Bearing in mind Joan's acutely sensitive feelings about persecution and hypocrisy and bearing in mind the state of acute neurosis into which the whole country was driven [ten?] days ago, I am inclined now to grant more importance to the superficial view' (6.10.38) (RFK/13/90/3/106). Keynes echoed these views although he added an extra factor: 'The strain of combining babies with so much intellectual work is at the bottom of it. ... The *conflict* between the desire to avoid war and the desire to defeat fascism has torn many people's feelings to pieces' (RFK/13/90/3/101–2) (4.10.38). She, herself, identified as the cause underlying her illness, the 'deep rift between my political and my tribal loyalty [which] had been a continuous and growing strain all these years' (Keynes's emphasis) (RFK/13/90/3/226). In 1941 she gave a lecture against war to students which focused on their moral responsibility as relatively privileged in their distance from the effects of the war. She urged them not to hate the Germans: 'To hate them leads nowhere. ... The needs of the present moment were always sown in the past and if our nation had power in the past we cannot be free of responsibility for what happens now' (JVR/iii/1). Subsequently, she expressed her frustration and anger at both the waste and the destructive nature of armaments, as well as their opportunity costs, both of social infrastructure and private investment, and, particularly where developing countries, otherwise impoverished, used aid for building up a weapons arsenal and a military industry. Her last public lecture was a criticism of the nuclear arms race in which she argued in terms of economics but also appealed to the audience's morality (Robinson, 1982; Kerr, 2008; see Ch. 12). This appeal was evident in Robinson (1962b, 119–20):

> The enormous strides made by production under the regime of international competition have brought us to the paradoxical situation that we are in today. Never before has communication been so complete. Never before has educated public opinion in every country been so conscious of the rest of the world. Never before was it worth while to think about poverty as a world problem; it is only now that it seems possible, by the application of science to health, birth control and production, to relieve the whole human race from its worst miseries.
>
> Yet never before has so great a proportion of economic energy and scientific study been devoted to means of destruction.

Marjorie Turner records Joan Robinson as saying that 'I don't think that I am at all a suitable subject for a biography as the outward flow of my life has been conventional and uninteresting' ('Preface' in Turner, 1989). Yet here is a woman whose writing another reviewer (of *Economic Philosophy*) saw as 'provocative, deliberately outrageous, sometimes almost capricious, witty, irritating but penetrating' (JVR/xv/12.10). Her interests were wide-ranging and her reading strayed beyond her specialist areas. She published in *The Royal Society of Arts, The Royal Statistical Society, Fabian Quarterly, Time and Tide, The New York Review of Books* and many other publications, both prestigious and obscure, reaching an audience beyond her academic colleagues. She was generous in supporting new journals with articles for founding issues. And she supported, with her articles, journals from many countries including Brazil, Chile, Pakistan, India, Japan, USSR, Greece and others. She reviewed widely; in 1958, for example, while working on her Keynesian theory of growth, on development in USSR, and on Mao's approach to development in China as well as on the progress of planning in India; she published a review of Lionel Robbins, *Robert Torrens and the Evolution of Classical Economics*. She also took an interest in local, Cambridge, affairs and wrote articles for the *Cambridge Review* and the *Cambridge Quarterly*; she patronised the Cambridge Arts Theatre as well as student productions of Shakespeare in the colleges' gardens during the summer twilight. Her relationships were not all professional ones. Turner describes friendships Joan Robinson developed with three girls from a Settlement School while a pupil at Saint Paul's and whom she continued to meet well after they had left their schools. And her openness to society is evident in another encounter. Abroad, a girl in the embassy, also called Joan Robinson, invited her, as her namesake, for tea. She wrote to Kahn that she was quite 'pleasantly surprised ... [when] the embassy girls took me round to their digs and we had a nice chat about this and that. ...' (JVR/i/4). And in the 1940s, she referred to her 'normal after-lecture chat with Lydia' (RFK/13/90/4). Another insight into Joan Robinson is revealed in a correspondence to her from the poet and surgeon Altounyan E. H. Riddall who was working in Syria during the 1930s. In it he discusses his torment in writing his poetry and his despair at his circumstances; there are no letters from Joan Robinson in the collection but it is clear she kept up a weekly correspondence with him at that time. Perhaps her imaginative powers can be seen at an early age: in her later years at school Joan Robinson disclosed that 'I have been informed, on credible authority, that I used to spend my time with the greatest enjoyment, sitting on the bench of a greenhouse, pretending to be a flower pot ...

that delight of escape into an unexpected existence' (JVR/v/1). It has been rumoured sometimes that Joan Robinson was not a 'good' mother. Affectionate mention of her daughters appear at many places in her papers. At the end of a letter to Nicholas Kaldor, in 1937, after discussing an article about perfect competition, she couldn't resist adding: 'My second daughter is five weeks old and very fat' (NK/3/30/177–8). And to Kahn she wrote after an outing: '[the children] behaved extremely well and the whole visit passed off almost without a tear or a puddle. They really are extremely charming' (RFK/13/90/4/7).

During her life she sought to find, perhaps help to create, a more just and equitable society than the ones she had grown up and lived in. This led her to make some howlers in her assessments of actual societies, for example, North Korea and, for a time anyway, aspects of the Chinese experiment. She was critical of the excesses, wastages and injustices of modern capitalism. Nevertheless we concur with Paul Samuelson's judgement that her utopian idealism, a search for that 'true socialism [which] was her first and ever love, not the pretenders that took its name in vain [about which] who is to say that her value judgements were wrong, or other than noble' (Samuelson, 1989, 136).

In early 1983 Joan Robinson suffered a massive stroke; she went into a coma and died in August 1983. Joan and Austin had two daughters and five grandchildren. Though Joan said she was not a good mother but was a good grandmother, her family thought she was good at both roles (see Harcourt (1995d, 2001a) and Ch. 12).

2
The Economics of Imperfect Competition

When Joan Robinson came to write *The Economics of Imperfect Competition* (Robinson, 1933a), she also began her long intellectual friendship with Richard Kahn. At much the same time, Kahn was writing his extraordinary fellowship dissertation for King's, *The Economics of the Short Period* (Kahn, 1929; 1989), after only one year of studying economics (see Harcourt, 1991; 1993). She almost certainly attended some of Piero Sraffa's remarkable lectures on 'Advanced theory of Value' (see Marcuzzo, 2005), which were given at the end of the 1920s and the beginning of the 1930s. As an undergraduate in the early 1920s she became familiar with the contents of A. C. Pigou's, Dennis Robertson's and, especially, Gerald Shove's, lectures and writings (in Shove's case, writings were rare) on Marshallian and Pigovian value theory. Joan's supervisor at Girton, Marjorie Tappan-Hollond, with whom she did not get on (but see Ch. 1, p. 3, n6), was also a staunch Marshallian. Austin Robinson was working on his *The Structure of Competitive Industry* (1931), ostensibly a textbook for the Cambridge Economic Handbook series, but in reality an original and innovative monograph on the theory of the firm (as John Whitaker (1989) points out; see also Harcourt (1997a; 2001a)), probably even before she started her book, certainly simultaneously with it. (As we saw, Joan and Austin had married in 1926 and went to India for two years, returning to Cambridge in the late 1920s.)

As we know now, Sraffa's lectures were extremely challenging to the views on which Joan Robinson had been brought up. Yet they were also much restrained as far as Sraffa himself was concerned. There is evidence that, at the same time as he was preparing the lectures – a much protracted period as it turned out – he was also beginning to take the steps that would lead him to his lifetime project of, in effect, the revival of the approach of classical political economy and rejection of the approach of neoclassical economics of which Marshall and Pigou were his principal Cambridge targets. Much of the contents of his lectures took in the arguments of his 1925 and 1926 articles, which grew out of his own training in Marshallian theory as it had come to him through its Italian interpreters. But Sraffa, partly through the influence of Gramsci, was simultaneously absorbing the teachings of the classical political economists and Marx on value and distribution theory, and other continental European influences, especially Walras and Pareto. His lectures contain an exposition of Pareto on indifference curves and on the move from cardinal to ordinal utility. The concept of utility was already abhorrent to Sraffa as he concentrated on quantitative measurement and physical existence in value theory, at least in principle, especially the meaning of costs in the two traditions, and in economic theory generally.[1] But as he was still so unsure as to how exactly he would develop his new departures, they did not make much of, even an embryonic, appearance in the written version of the lectures as such.

He was clear though about his views on the extremely limited application of partial equilibrium analysis to an understanding of price formation in actual circumstances, that is to say, how rare it was that actual situations satisfied the stringent conditions that made the method logically coherent by ensuring the independence of supply conditions from demand conditions. (This was a principal theme of his 1925 and 1926 articles.) This led him to his unequivocal statement in the 1930 symposium in the *Economic Journal* on the representative firm and increasing returns that Marshall's theory should be abandoned (Sraffa, 1930, 93). His knowledge of classical writings on the nature of the laws of returns under competitive conditions had by then led him to reject Marshall's, and especially Pigou's, attempts to take the concepts of increasing and decreasing returns, which occurred in different compartments of classical theory, and combine them together in the emerging, indeed emerged, neoclassical theory of value.

His 'pregnant suggestion' that had so much influenced Joan Robinson, that monopoly rather than pure (or perfect) competition should be the starting point for the theory of value, that we should consider a world of mini-monopolies set in a competitive environment, so that falling demand curves rather than rising cost curves were the ultimate constraint on both current output and future expansion, was for him an aside. He told GCH that he put the suggestion in the 1926 *Economic Journal* article because it would interest pragmatic Brits as opposed to philosophical continentals.

This contrast between British and European continental approaches in economics is fully reflected, if not always completely understood, in Joan Robinson's first major publication *Economics is a Serious Subject* (1932a), subtitled *The Apologia of an Economist to the Mathematician, the Scientist and the Plain Man*. Joan Robinson wrote it, we suspect, to clear her mind on, or at least justify, the method she followed in *The Economics of Imperfect Competition* itself. She did draw back in some important respects from her conclusions in the 1932 publication when she came to write the introduction[2] to the 1933 book (see Harcourt, 1990a; 1995b, 73–4).

In the December 1932 *Economic Journal*, Joan Robinson published an article, 'Imperfect competition and falling supply price' (Robinson, 1932b), which gave a tantalising preview of her forthcoming attraction, *The Economics of Imperfect Competition*. It contained her principal apparatus – marginal revenue and marginal cost curves – and her exposition of the tangency conditions of the average revenue and average cost curves for long-period equilibrium. She refers to the 1930 *Economic Journal* symposium on increasing returns and the representative firm, and Harrod (1930, 1931) and Sraffa (1926) as the context for posing her central proposition that 'While the presumption that average costs to the firm will be falling is far stronger than those critics suggest, the presumption that supply price will be falling is far weaker than they suppose' (544).

She ignores time and concentrates on imperfect competition. She makes explicit the assumptions which make the analysis tractable (but far from reality, as she readily admits). She draws diagrams which show equilibrium for the firm but with abnormal profits, that is, $MR=MC$, $P>AC$. The tangency condition whereby $P=AC$ implies that average costs must be falling.

She then analyses what happens when demand in the industry and for each firm increases. She shows that whether the equilibrium price is greater, less or stays constant (Joan Robinson writes rises, falls or stays constant, language that she would later repudiate) is related to the value of the price elasticity of demand at the new equilibrium position and how average costs 'move' as new firms enter the industry in response to the initial abnormal profits. If the demand curve 'returns' to its initial position, the new price equals the old: if it is less elastic in the new situation, price will be greater and vice versa if it is more elastic.

She then examines the cost and supply side. She concludes that

> an increase in the total demand for the commodity, when the market is imperfect, is far more likely to lower the average cost curves of the firms than when the market is perfect.

> It therefore appears ... to be highly probable that falling supply price is a result of imperfect competition.
>
> (544)[3]

Joan Robinson certainly regarded her book as a box of tools to be used to clear minds by making explicit both the assumptions on which the analysis was built and, in general, the great limitations of its applications. It was a very Marshallian book, though the box of tools analogy came from Pigou. Its central organising concept was, of course, the marginal revenue curve (alias the first derivative of the total revenue function).[4] It was used not only to analyse the demand for products – mostly intermediate rather than final products, it turns out, though this is usually ignored in the subsequent text-book expositions – but also for the services of the factors of production. Indeed, some of the reviewers singled out for special praise her analysis of the monopsony of buyers of the services of the factors of production meeting the countervailing power of their suppliers. She, both at that time and with greater emphasis later on, stressed the implications of this sort of analysis combined with that of Pigovian exploitation, on which she built and developed, as an internal critique of the marginal productivity theory of distribution, to which she was to take more and more exception with the passing of the years. She ultimately claimed that this criticism, and the demonstration that in a slump, firms could survive, albeit with excess capacity, rather than either produce at full capacity or shut down completely, as was implied by Marshallian/Pigovian analysis, were the two most damning criticisms of the functioning of modern capitalism, up to Keynes's demonstration of the possibility of sustained under-employment rest states.

Keynes's report on the book to Harold Macmillan (25 November 1932; Macmillan was later to be the British prime minister in the second half of the 1950s and the early 1960s) was, as is to be expected, perceptive in several dimensions. Evidently, the manuscript was originally entitled *Monopoly*. He suggested – though the suggestion was not eventually taken up – a more accurate title: *The Theory of Value under Monopoly and Competition*. As Kaldor (1934a; Kerr with Harcourt (eds.), vol. I, 2002, 153) pointed out, 'of "imperfect competition proper," [as opposed to monopoly[5]], of the problems peculiar to the type of situation presented by her at the beginning, there is little to be found; and such as there is is too tautological to improve our insight very much'. Keynes saw her book as a thorough synthesis, 'the cream [taken] off a new movement', with a central organising concept of ideas that had been in the air in the leading centres of economic theorising for the past few years. He thought that it would 'be for a little while to come an essential one for any serious student of the modern theory of value'. He also felt it would be pretty much free of errors because 'it had been very elaborately and carefully criticised by R.F Kahn, ... a long way the ablest and most reliable critic of this type of work to be found' (Keynes, 1932; Kerr with Harcourt (eds.), vol. I, 2002, 150).

As we noted, some reviewers pointed out that imperfect competition was just what most of the book was *not* about. This was mainly because her explicit assumptions about the nature of the firm's demand curve made the resulting apparatus inappropriate for the analysis of duopoly and oligopoly, that is to say, her assumptions ruled out the treatment of interactions between firms due to their perceptions of what rivals' reactions would be to changes in their behaviour with regard to the prices they set. Her treatment of selling costs was also perfunctory and unsatisfactory.

It is interesting to note that Kahn, by starting from the 'stylised facts' (as we would call them now) of the UK textile industry of that time at least, *was* able to tackle duopoly, though his findings took a long time to enter the public domain in an article (see Kahn, 1937).[6] Just as it is still something of an unsolved puzzle as to why Kahn did not persuade Keynes to use microeconomic foundations of imperfectly competitive or oligopolistic structures in *The General Theory*, so it is a similar puzzle as to why he did not suggest to Joan Robinson that she follow his own method when writing her book. Her approach was very much the axiomatic procedure especially of Pigou. Pigou assumed profit-maximising and cost-minimising so as to make more rigorous and precise the more loose, more vague insights in the narrative in the text of Marshall's *Principles*. (Marshall's footnotes and mathematical appendices are another matter as far as presentation is concerned.) Marco Dardi (1996, Kerr with Harcourt (eds.), vol. I, 2002) has wise words to say about how Kahn was torn between the conflicting demands of his two greatest friends, which led him not to press his own inclinations as revealed in *The Economics of the Short Period*. Dardi also has wise things to say concerning Marshallian procedures in tackling short-period and long-period interactions. He felt Keynes would have worked within them and Joan Robinson too, even though she denied this towards the end of her life by leaving the short period to Keynes and Michal Kalecki and the long period to Sraffa (see Bhaduri and Robinson, 1980).

When Joan Robinson was writing her book, long-period analysis was central, indeed pivotal in Marshall's work. Kahn had noted this when he called 'the theory of long-period value, ... the real business of the *Principles*' (Kahn (1929; 1989, xxiii)). Sraffa, too, took 'a point of view embracing long periods' in his 1926 article (539). Yet there is considerable evidence that like Kahn, and influenced by the stagnation in the staple UK industries in the 1920s, Joan Robinson was more concerned with the short period, what Kahn (1929; 1989, 2) called 'the long end of the short period from which [those industries were] suffering'.

It is striking how many fundamental and difficult issues, which Joan Robinson was to tackle later, are at least signalled in the responses to her book. The book had distinguished reviewers and well thought out reviews: Gerald Shove in the *Economic Journal* (1933; Kerr with Harcourt (eds.), 2002, vol. I), Joseph Schumpeter in the *Journal of Political Economy* (1934; Kerr with Harcourt (eds.), 2002, vol. I), Kaldor in *Economica* (1934a; Kerr with Harcourt (eds.), 2002, vol. I), Corwin Edwards in the *American Economic Review* (1933; Kerr with Harcourt (eds.), 2002, vol. I), for example. Overall, the book was very well received by the reviewers and the profession, thoroughly justifying the delightful story about Mary Paley Marshall embracing Joan at a party, warmly congratulating her and saying, sternly, that when she saw Alfred (dead then for nine years), she would tell him that he was quite wrong to say that women could not do economic theory.

As Joan Robinson was to recognise very clearly soon after publication and to state with authority in the preface to the second edition of the book in 1969, her approach in the book could not handle time, in so far as it differed from space, at all.[7] She was to call this a 'shameless fudge' – the assumption that the ultimate equilibrium price and quantity would wait patiently, unmoving, 'out there' while individual business-people tried by trial and error, groping, to find the equilibrium price to set. That is to say, as she was to point out forcefully, when 'lecturing' as a Cambridge economist at Oxford in 1953, path-dependence of equilibrium (or lack of equilibrium) had been ruled out by assumption. She blamed Marshall who had implicitly and sneakily implied a generality when setting out fully a most atypical situation in which path-dependence could be ignored legitimately. She refers to his 'remarkable intuitive genius ... he knew by instinct the one case where you can say something without [the space/time distinction] getting you all mixed up. The short period supply curve, under strictly perfect competition, when demand always rises, never falls. ... He worked out [this case] with great lucidity and then he filled the book with tear gas, so that no one would notice he had fudged the whole of the rest of the argument.' (Robinson, 1953; *C.E.P.*, vol. IV, 1973, 258–9). It is no surprise that it was Shove who made this point most clearly, but it is also to be found, well understood, in Kaldor's and Schumpeter's reviews.[8]

In his review, Kaldor drew attention to the fuzzy nature of the concept of the industry in her approach because, once differentiated products are taken into account, *which* other firms are making products which compete with the product of the firm under consideration depends on the particular firm and its product from which the analysis started. That is to say, there are, in principle, as many industries clustering around firms as there are firms themselves. Joan Robinson notices this and other limitations, but usually then carries on to present the detailed technical analysis putting the new tools through their paces as formal exercises. To her credit, she progressively backed off from such a procedure in her later work, putting more and more emphasis on the need to get clear the conceptual basis of problems before proceeding, so flowing increasingly against the tide of approach and presentation in modern economic theory.

The problem of the meaning and measurement of capital within the neoclassical approach is also noted by reviewers in their discussion of her treatment of the demand for the services of the factors of production. Shove and Schumpeter especially commented on this.[9]

Needless to say, Edward Chamberlin also had many points to make as an independent developer of the implications for price theory of differentiated products in monopolistic competitive structures. (He started earlier than Joan Robinson, but their books were published in the same year (Chamberlin, 1933).)[10] He was at pains then and ever after to show how different, and better, his product was. Joan Robinson very quickly was to say that he was welcome to first place if it meant so much to him. The conventional wisdom increasingly became that it was rightly his. At the beginning of the 1940s, Robert Triffin (1941) made the most explicit 'compare and contrast' analysis of the approaches and results of the two books. He concluded marginally in favour of Chamberlin, but it was a close-run thing. Chamberlin had the edge partly because he tackled oligopoly with his small group case, even though the bulk of his analysis concerned the large group case. There, albeit by a different route, he established, as had Joan Robinson, the tangency solution of average revenue and average cost curves in full equilibrium with normal profits ruling, accompanied by excess capacity in the sense of scope for lower costs if further expansion had not been limited by demand conditions. Triffin himself went in a different direction by adopting a general, as opposed to a partial, equilibrium approach to the problem.

One reason why Joan Robinson so readily ceded the field to Chamberlin, as it were, was because she was already deeply involved with Kahn, James Meade, Austin Robinson and Sraffa in discussions on, and criticisms of, *A Treatise on Money* (1930) through the formation of the 'Circus' in 1930–1. This quickly became exchanges to and fro with Keynes's emerging take on the causes of sustained unemployment and the interrelationship of monetary and real factors in the analysis of overall output and employment in capitalist economies, as Keynes simultaneously lectured on and wrote *The General Theory* (see Ch. 3).[11]

3

Joan Robinson and her Circle in the Run-up to and Aftermath of the Publication of *The General Theory*

In the Michaelmas term of 1930, Piero Sraffa formed the 'Circus' in order to discuss *A Treatise on Money* (Keynes, 1930). The 'Circus' consisted of Austin and Joan Robinson, Richard Kahn, James Meade (who was in Cambridge for a year before teaching economics at Oxford) and Sraffa. It ran until March 1931.[1] Keynes did not attend in person. Margaret Meade described him as akin to God offstage in a morality play with Kahn, the go-between, the 'Messenger Angel' from God taking messages from the mortals' discussions and criticisms 'to Heaven' and returning with God's responses (see *C.W.*, vol. XIII, 1973a, 338–9).

Some members of the 'Circus' also attended Keynes's lectures in the 1930s as he started to make what became *The General Theory*, partly as a response to the criticisms and queries of the 'Circus' (and after) but also, and principally, in response to both criticisms by the profession generally and, most crucially, in response to the changed circumstances of the capitalist world as the Great Depression emerged. Not only did Keynes begin to rethink on theory, he also changed his emphasis on policy, becoming more and more sceptical concerning the ability of monetary policy alone to tackle the malfunctioning of the economies of the UK and the US in particular. In *A Treatise on Money* and beforehand, monetary policy had been directed principally at maintaining a stable general price level.

The 'Circus' concentrated especially on Keynes's assumption that there could be a change in the voluntary desire to save without there being any effect on the output (as opposed to the prices) of consumption goods and so on employment in those trades and, indeed, overall. Keynes was subsequently to say that they – he wrote to Joan Robinson even though it was Austin Robinson who initially latched onto the 'Widow's cruse' fallacy, as the above argument was dubbed – were 'a little hard on [him]' because it was only a provisional assumption which an author was entitled to make in proceeding, allowing the dominant forces at work in a given situation to be seen and understood more starkly and clearly before complications were introduced in a fuller, more comprehensive and realistic analysis. '[O]nly at one particular point [had he] assumed constant output ... [he had made] this absolutely clear ... one must be allowed at a particular stage of [an] argument to make simplifying assumptions' (Keynes, *C.W.*, vol. XIII, 1973a, 270).

Hayek was Keynes's foremost critic when *A Treatise on Money* was published, with his review articles in *Economica* (Hayek, 1931b; 1932a) and exchanges with Keynes (Hayek, 1931c; Keynes, 1931a). Keynes's reply (1931a) drifted in to his own review of Hayek's *Prices and Production* (1931a) and may be coupled with Sraffa's review article of *Prices and Production* in the *Economic Journal* (Sraffa, 1932a), and Sraffa's subsequent exchange with Hayek over it (Sraffa, 1932b; Hayek, 1932b).[2]

Joan Robinson wrote an article about the Hayek/Keynes exchanges in 1931; however, it was not published in *Economica* until 1933 (Robinson, 1933b). The article was called 'A parable of savings and investment'. The author assumed familiarity with the terminology, definitions and approach of *A Treatise on Money*, including knowledge of the paragraphs on the widow's cruse and Dainard jars.[3] It is addressed to the 'simple minded reader' within which class she included herself. She set herself to explain why in Keynes's view (and as theoretical propositions only) there could be a depression while maintaining full employment and a trade boom without an increase in output. This was still very much an argument within the framework of *A Treatise on Money* by someone brought up in the quantity theory approach; that is to say, Keynes's Marshallian training meant that in both his great books, he used Marshall's three-period approach: the market period with a given supply, the short period with short-period flows constrained by given stocks of capital goods and skilled labour forces, and a long period in which both capital and labour were variable (but changes in technical methods, once the analysis had begun, were confined within the *ceteris paribus* pound), all suitably adapted to a macroeconomic setting. Keynes tells us explicitly in the preface to *A Treatise on Money*, the principal analysis he has in mind. Market-clearing prices for the existing stock of commodities are set in the market period, they induce changes in output (and so in prices) in the short period, and the consequential short-period equilibria converge over 'time' on the long-period position, the full stock/flow equilibrium in which normal profits and wages are received. All this is the background to Joan Robinson's discussion.

But her article also contains embryonic ideas of great importance for understanding later developments in the thoughts and contributions of Keynes and his followers. In particular, there is concern with the process of price formation in, first, markets where flows dominate stocks, and, secondly, in markets where stocks dominate flows and, thirdly, the vital importance of having a class of speculative traders who take views on the future course of market prices while not being producers of the commodities concerned themselves.[4] In the context of the exchanges between Hayek and Keynes, it is the consumption goods trades that are characterised by the first sort of market, the capital goods trades, by the second, and the market for securities, by the third factor.

The discussions by both Keynes and Joan Robinson of the second sort of market are somewhat masked by the fact that the stock of existing securities (which are backed by the stock of physical capital goods created by past investment) dominates the determination of the prices of securities *and* capital goods, newly created and old. In post–*General Theory* times, this seems a confusion. In *The General Theory*, Keynes assumes explicitly that free competition is usually the characteristic of the markets for *all* types of commodities. Thus, marginal costs of production dominate the determination of the prices of new capital goods, given the demand for the services of *all* capital goods and the supply of existing capital goods in a given short-period situation, as Paul Davidson brilliantly makes clear in *Money and the Real World* (Davidson, 1972).

As for the market for securities, Joan Robinson points out that if there were *not* a divergence of views concerning the course of their prices in the future, so that any moment of time, every market participator, or potential participator, was either a bull or a bear, the prices of securities would fluctuate between infinity and zero, respectively. With divergent views, the equilibrium prices, which are established, bring about at least momentary truces between bulls and bears in the special class of speculators/traders identified above. The infant theory of liquidity preference of *The General Theory* may be discerned here.

In her other 1933 article, prophetically entitled 'The theory of money and the analysis of output' (Robinson, 1933c), which has often been reprinted,[5] Joan Robinson, like Keynes, seems still to be suspended between two worlds. For she tells us that Keynes without batting an eyelid has provided us with a *long-period* theory of overall output and employment in a setting initially established to analyse the determination of the general price level in a theory of money. Keynes 'had failed to notice [when he wrote *A Treatise on Money*] that he had incidentally evolved a new theory of the long-period analysis of output'. (1933c; *C.E.P.*, vol. I,

1951, 56). Moreover, 'he completely overlooks [its] significance [and does not pause] to remark that he has proved that output may be in equilibrium at any number of different levels, and that while there is a natural tendency towards equilibrium between savings and investment (in a very long run), there is no natural tendency towards full employment of the factors of production' (Robinson, 1933c; *C.E.P.*, vol. I, 1951, 56).

Joan Robinson also points out how Keynes, as with other quantity theorists, was often bamboozled by what the manipulation of identities could do and could not do. She argues that it 'is idle to say that ... abnormal profits *cause* ... new investment [as they are but] a symptom of a situation in which new investment ... will take place'. Also to regard them as a direct cause of a rise in output is misleading and, moreover, as there are no abnormal profits in long-period equilibrium (especially on *A Treatise on Money* definitions), 'a theory which regards [actual] profits as the mainspring of action is incapable of dealing with long-period analysis', (Robinson, 1933c; *C.E.P.*, vol. I, 1951, 57–8, emphasis in original).

She noted, too, that Keynes was inhibited by feeling that writing a treatise on money required him to concentrate on issues concerned with the general level of prices, and neglect output and its changes in disequilibrium *and* equilibrium. Keynes was well aware of this, of course. Here are typical statements in Keynes's letter of 28 November 1930 to Ralph Hawtrey after the publication of *A Treatise on Money* but in reply to Hawtrey's comments on the proofs: 'The question *how much* reduction in output is caused ... is important ... not strictly a monetary problem. [Keynes had] not attempted to deal with it ... [he was] primarily concerned with what governs *prices*.' Again, 'I am not dealing with the complete set of causes which determine the volume of output ... this would have led [him] an endlessly long journey into the theory of short-period supply and a long way from monetary theory ... [He agreed] that it will probably be difficult in the future to prevent monetary theory and the theory of short-period supply from running together' (Keynes, *C.W.*, vol. XIII, 1973a, 145–6, emphasis in original).

Joan Robinson partially confirms this in the conclusion of her article: 'The Theory of Money, relieved of its too-heavy task, can be confined to its proper sphere, and become indeed a theory of money, while the Analysis of Output can continue to develop an analysis of output' (Robinson, 1933c; *C.E.P.*, vol. I, 1951, 58). We write 'partially' because she is still accepting the classical dichotomy between the real and the money, which Keynes was to overthrow in *The General Theory*.

Kahn was in the US for the early part of the 1930s. Before he went, he had published his famous article on the multiplier (Kahn, 1931), in which, under carefully specified conditions, he had put an exact figure on the overall rise in employment that could be captured from a given increase in primary employment. This removed the fuzziness surrounding the arguments of Keynes and Hubert Henderson concerning the impact of public works in their 1929 pamphlet 'Can Lloyd George do it?' (Keynes, 1931; Keynes, *C.W.*, vol. IX, 1972, 86–125). It was also noted for James Meade's contribution, 'Mr Meade's relation', in which the multiplier was estimated by using leakages into saving (see Meade, 1993). Kahn's article played a key role in Keynes's subsequent specification of the consumption function and his own chapters on the multiplier in *The General Theory*.

Kahn was much missed by Keynes as Keynes started on his journey to *The General Theory* (1936) and by Joan Robinson as she was writing *The Economics of Imperfect Competition* (1933a). (He did correspond frequently with them, especially with Joan Robinson.) Kahn, in turn, was worried about being the sole or at least the principal recipient and critic of Keynes's writings. He urged Joan Robinson to come on board as well. In a letter of 2 March 1933, he wrote: 'Naturally you cannot raise the point, but if Maynard hints that he would like you to look at his stuff I do wish you would ... I am a bit appalled at the prospect of having the sole responsibility thrust on me after my return' (quoted in Rosselli, 2005, 270). She was more than willing to do so and she did, so enthusiastically, that by September 1934 she wrote to Kahn (5–6 September 1934) to ask whether Keynes would 'like [her] to write him a Preface for the new work showing in what respects his ideas have altered?' (quoted in Marcuzzo and Sardoni, 2005, 176). This was not the only time when she misjudged what another author's feelings could be, especially those of Keynes. Though he ultimately was to welcome her 'told-to-the-children' version of *The General Theory*, her *Introduction to the Theory of Employment* (1937a), by writing (20 November 1937) 'You have been very successful ... in simplifying and have skated round the complications beautifully', initially he was lukewarm about the project, to say the least (see Marcuzzo and Sardoni, 2005, 177). Piero Sraffa, too, was sometimes irritated by her interpretations and applications of his writings, though it did not harm their deep, caring and supportive friendship with one another (see Harcourt, 1990b; Sardoni (ed.) 1992, 300–1).

Moreover, Keynes came increasingly to appreciate her comments and responses and not least her fierce loyalty to the new ideas against the antagonistic 'doubting Thomases' among Keynes's previous supporters and even collaborators and friends: Robertson, of course, Hawtrey, Pigou and Hubert Henderson, for example. As volume XIII of the

Collected Writings shows (and this is reinforced by Cristina Marcuzzo's and Annalisa Rosselli's new (edited) volume, 2005), Joan Robinson became an integral part of the criticisms and support of the emerging *General Theory*. In particular, Joan Robinson and Kahn supported Keynes's use of a Marshallian approach in *The General Theory*, despite Sraffa's trenchant critique of it at the level of the firm and industry in the 1920s and 1930s.[6]

Simultaneously, she, Kahn, Meade and Austin Robinson were debating with the younger stalwarts of Hayek and Robbins at the LSE, especially Abba Lerner. Lerner was to become, for a while at least, one of Keynes's most fervent disciples; and this, despite efforts by the doubters to keep him on the straight and narrow when, following one of the meetings of the young, he showed signs of wobbling. At an inn halfway between London and Cambridge (in Bishops Stortford), Meade and Kahn explained the multiplier to the LSE band. 'Next day ... with some help, Lerner repeated it correctly and seemed to be convinced. His companions were quite shocked and were seen afterwards walking up and down the lawn, trying to restore his faith' (Robinson, 1978d, xv). Lorie Tarshis, who was an affiliated student and then a PhD student in Cambridge at the time, also played a key role in Lerner's conversion with their post–Marmite sandwich luncheon discussions of the respective merits of their two heroes.[7]

As with Kahn and Keynes, see Harcourt (1994; 1995b), by the time *The General Theory* was published, Joan Robinson too emphasised that the short period in its own right was the setting both for Kahn's work on prices (Kahn, 1929; 1989), and Keynes's on employment. This is witnessed to, first, by Keynes's list of what is locked up in the *ceteris paribus* pound (Keynes, 1936, *C.W.*, vol. VII, 1973, 245), and by Joan Robinson's own excursions into long-period analysis in her *Essays in the Theory of Employment* (Robinson, 1937b). She did this mainly in order to see whether the results of *The General Theory* were robust even though she regarded the exercise by then as very much economics for the economists and certainly not the province of *The General Theory* itself (see her letter (19 June 1935) to Keynes about her long-period analysis in Keynes, *C.W.*, vol. XIII, 1973a, 647–8).[8] Nevertheless in her exposition of the new theory in her *Introduction* she remained distinctly old-fashioned when considering long-period propositions: 'For the discussion of problems involving broad changes over the course of generations, in population, the rate of technical progress or the general social forces influencing thriftiness, it is possible to regard fluctuations in employment as secondary consideration and to conduct the discussion in terms of a self-regulating system' (Robinson, 1937a, 84).

As far as the development of *The General Theory* is concerned, it is, as we noted above, her essay on the long period that is most relevant. She uses the concept of the elasticity of substitution between capital and labour, then at the height of fashion,[9] and differential saving behaviour at the margin for wage-earners and profit-receivers to tease out many of *The General Theory* propositions established for the short period. Her long period is a very Marshallian concept, what Dennis Robertson (1956, 16) dubbed 'the never-never land of unrealised tendency' of pure theory, for net investment is zero as the optimum stock of capital goods in the given situation has been established and only normal profits are received. Hawtrey (1937) in his review of the *Essays*, but not Harrod (1937) in his review, was sceptical about the value of such an elaborate analysis. It is true that it is a hybrid of the old and the new but it does make the positive contribution of showing that effective demand makes theoretical sense in a long-period setting and that a full employment equilibrium is not necessarily a long-period outcome. (This was confirmed yet again and many years later by Colin Rogers in his contribution to a 'second edition' of *The General Theory* (Rogers, 1997).) In the 1983 special issue of the *Cambridge Journal of Economics* in honour of Joan Robinson, there were a number of articles about her 1937 long-period theory.[10] Jan Kregel (1983) represents her as producing a long-period theory of effective demand based on the orthodox theory of distribution which captures both the effect of saving on the capital stock and the importance of relative factor prices in acting as part of a self-adjusting mechanism to create equilibrium. John Eatwell (1983) and later Pierangelo Garegnani (1996) also interpret her argument as neoclassical – and flawed. Eatwell establishes the non-Keynesian nature of her essay by showing that in order to reach unorthodox results she had to operate where the elasticity of substitution was less than unity. Terry O'Shaughnessy (1988; Kerr with Harcourt (eds), (2002) vol. II, 73–99) develops her 'neoclassical' reasoning to achieve non-neoclassical results, disputing the flaw which Eatwell and Garegnani claimed to exist in her explanation.

Joan Robinson also developed the concept of disguised unemployment, so ultimately bringing together her observations while in India in the late 1920s with her understanding of and contributions to the new theory emerging in Cambridge. Her 1937 *Essays* also contain her exposition of what was later to be known in the literature as the Harris–Todaro model of internal migration (1970). Pervez Tahir (1990a; 1999) has documented this in telling detail, illustrating, yet again, how dangerous it is to be too far ahead of your time. (Tahir referred to her as 'a neglected precursor'.)

Keynes and Joan Robinson had extensive debates over her chapter on the foreign exchanges and he probably still had some reservations about its final form when the volume was published. In commenting on the proofs, he considered 'the book as a whole a bit uneven ... but the general effect ... splendid, full of originality and interest' (12 November, 1936; *C.W.*, vol. XIV, 1973b, 147).

She had reservations about *his* definitions of full employment and wrote a very long first chapter about the concept itself. To our mind, Keynes's discussion and definitions of full employment and involuntary unemployment were exactly what was needed for the purposes Keynes had in mind when writing a 'book chiefly addressed to [his] fellow economists, ... [the] main purpose [of which was] to deal with difficult questions of theory and only [secondarily] with ... applications of theory to practice' (Keynes, 1936; *C.W.*, vol. VII, 1973, v). As is well known, Keynes defined involuntary unemployment on p. 15 of *The General Theory* as follows:

> *Men [*sic*] are involuntarily unemployed if, in the event of a small rise in the price of wage-goods relatively to the money-wage, both the aggregate supply of labour willing to work for the current money-wage and the aggregate demand for it at that wage would be greater than the existing volume of employment.* (emphasis in the original)

He argued on p. 26 that in the classical system (we know now that he meant Pigou's version, see Ambrosi (2003)), 'effective demand ... is an infinite range of values all equally admissible' so that the marginal disutility of labour sets an upper limit when further increases in the value of effective demand will no longer be associated with greater output. This gives rise to a definition of full employment equivalent to the one on p. 15: aggregate employment is inelastic in response to an increase in effective demand for its output.

We know that Keynes was willing to accept, for his theoretical purposes, the first classical postulate of the equality of the real wage with the marginal product of labour (assuming freely competitive market structures) but not the second postulate regarding labour supply and the real wage. A simple diagram (see Figure 3.1), illustrates what he had in mind and his equivalent definitions of full employment (in the sense of absence of involuntary unemployment).

On the vertical axis, we measure the marginal product of labour (mpl) and the real wage (rw). (We assume that the relative prices of wage- and non-wage-goods do not change when production of them does.) On the horizontal axis, we measure employment (N). We show on the D-curve,

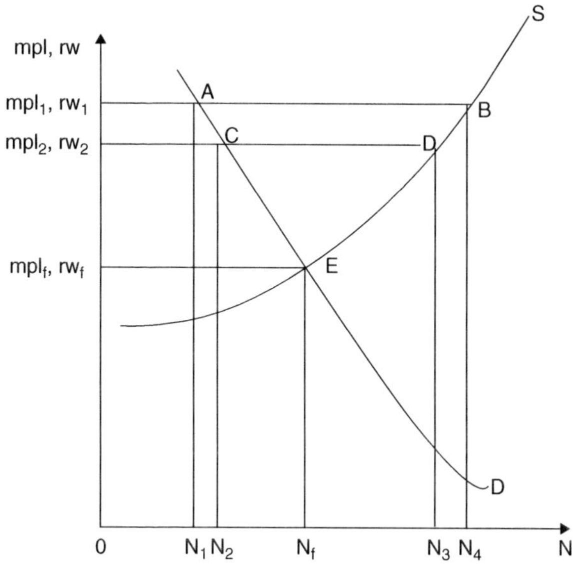

Figure 3.1 Full employment and involuntary unemployment in *The General Theory*

possible points of effective demand; on the S-curve, voluntary supplies of labour services associated with each level of the real wage and its associated money-wage and price level of wage-goods. The intersection of the two curves at E corresponds to *both* of Keynes's definitions of full employment.

If we consider point A on the D curve, mpl_1 A is the amount of labour demanded and it is less than the supply, rw_1 B. Suppose now that the prices of wage-goods are greater relative to the money-wage so that C is the new point of effective demand CD ($=N_2N_3$) is the amount of involuntary unemployment. We see that both the aggregate supply of labour at the current money-wage (ON_3) and the aggregate demand for labour (ON_2) exceed the existing volume of employment (ON_1).

Joan Robinson's analysis was much more detailed and practical, discussing possible trade union, employer and government behaviours. She concentrated on the likely effects on money-wages in given situations, identifying three possible ranges of employment: those so low that money-wages would tend to fall, an intermediate range where they would tend to remain constant and a range of higher levels where they would tend to increase. She thought that the intermediate range would have levels of employment well below the level of full employment, both on Keynes's definitions and on her own, more loosely defined one. Similarly, she defines involuntary unemployment as 'the amount of work which, in existing conditions, the population is willing but unable to perform' (Robinson, 1937b, 7). She adds that '[N]o absolutely precise measure of this quantity can be found but for all practical purposes a common-sense definition will suffice. [Moreover,] [i]n this sense unemployment may exist even when money wages are rising' (ibid.).[11]

Harrod (1937) wrote an extremely favourable review of her 1937 *Essays* in the *Economic Journal*; a 'volume of great distinction ... [While never departing] from a high level of precise thinking ... she has occasion to apply her finely wrought analytical tools ... to problems of the hour ... the interplay of her fine mind with the slipshod constructions of popular thought makes a delightful entertainment' (Harrod, 1937, 326; Kerr with Harcourt (eds.), 2002, vol. II, 11).

It is also notable for Harrod signalling issues that were to dominate discussions in later years: what is meant by a quantity of capital (and its marginal product) in long-period conditions. (Keynes had alerted Joan Robinson to the incoherent nature of capital and its marginal product in macroeconomic analysis, especially when using the concept of the elasticity of substitution of capital for labour in situations when technical progress was occurring. She dodged by saying that Sraffa was 'devoting his life to the question [of the meaning and measurement of capital], and we cannot expect an answer quickly' (28 September 1937; quoted by Marcuzzo and Sardoni, 2005, 184).

Harrod also signalled his subsequent debates with Joan Robinson concerning the nature of technical progress. In particular, what were the definitions of labour-saving and capital-saving inventions and what should be held constant when the definitions are set out? He suggested the rate of interest. Finally, while admiring how much she was able to get out of the static method, he nevertheless called for a move to dynamic methods, a foretaste of what he was to present explicitly in his 1939 'Essay'.

Be that as it may, what was to radically change her focus and emphasis in the later years of the 1930s was the beginning of her intellectual friendship with Michal Kalecki in 1936 and her introduction to Marxian thought, initially through her review in the *Economic Journal* of John Strachey's 1935 *The Nature of Capitalist Crisis* (Robinson, 1936a) (the first part of the review is reproduced in her 1937 *Essays*) and then in the early years of the war, her first systematic reading of Marx's writings (see Chapter 4).[12]

4
Marx in Joan Robinson's Argument

> It surely should be possible to adopt a language in which the two parties could talk to each other. Neither party really wants to, for each fears that their hold on ideology might be lost in the process of translating the familiar language in which each has been accustomed to recite the creed.
>
> Robinson (1973b, 247)

4.1 Introduction

This chapter examines the formation of Joan Robinson's early views on Marx through a dialogue with Maurice Dobb, and then the reception of these views at the time by Kalecki, Keynes and some reviewers. It considers also her enduring views on Marx's economics. *An Essay on Marxian Economics* (*EME*)[1] (Robinson, 1942b) is an important book. It is one of the few serious attempts by an economist to reconcile Marx's economic theory with orthodox and Keynesian economic theory. The predominant area of engagement between orthodox and Marxist economists had for some time been the issue of the transformation of values into prices. Joan Robinson's book argued that 'value' was not necessary to Marx's overall argument. Perhaps this was her strategy of redirecting attention back onto the other aspects of *Capital*. It was unusual for a prominent academic economist to take Marx seriously (although some of her colleagues, Maurice Dobb and Piero Sraffa, took Marx very seriously, as did Paul Sweezy). Joan Robinson's intuition was that there was a certain sympathy between Keynes's theory of employment and effective demand and Marx's theory of crises, and that his presentation of the relevant questions to be posed was pertinent.[2] Another element of her enquiry was her attempt to escape Marshallian orthodoxy. Thus, her book contains a critique of the orthodox theory of the normal rate of profits. Her instruction in Marxian economics underlay her move to a more classical approach in, for example, Robinson (1951a) and Robinson (1956a) as she was seeking a way to move away from Marshall. Her interest in Marx also reflected her attempt to make her economics more 'real', to address the inequities of the capitalist world. The book was, however, researched and written over a period of less than six months; she had little time to deliberate or reflect on her interpretations (which could partly account for her simplistic reading of *Capital*, although not of Marshall). The dialogue between Joan Robinson and Dobb, and the subsequent appraisal of *EME* by its Marxist reviewers, should also be seen in the context of intellectual debates in Britain at that time. The dominant intellectual frame of mind was logical empiricism. At the same time there was a tradition of English radicalism, which was opposed to the theoretical structure of Marxism. In Cambridge, even among the Left, there was a divide between the liberal radicals and the Marxists. Among the Marxists were Joan Robinson's colleagues Maurice Dobb and Piero Sraffa, the latter also a close friend.

In 1935, Dobb delivered an (unpublished) lecture to the Economics Society in Copenhagen entitled 'A Criticism of Some Trends in Modern Economic Theory'.[3] He remarks upon the nature of abstractions and relationships entailed in orthodox economics, arguing that their misrepresentation or the absence of fundamental social concepts and events meant that no conclusions or implications about the material, social and economic world could be drawn from such theories. His regard for the realism of concepts and of processes, and his extension of theory beyond deductive logic, underlay his responses to Joan Robinson's interpretation of Marx. By this time, Sraffa was developing his own criteria for a satisfactory theory which included methodological realism with respect to both concepts and processes. For Sraffa, deductive logic, while indispensable to scientific argument, was insufficient on its own to analyse social and economic reality and to arrive at a coherent theory equipped with explanatory power. Hence, deductive logic was inadequate as an argument as were abstractions not based on observed reality.[4] Sraffa's deliberations gave Dobb's propositions some formal basis.

4.2 Joan Robinson and Dobb on Marx

In February 1939, Maurice Dobb wrote to Joan Robinson telling her that a research student who 'sat at your feet last year ... is now determined to find parallels between Marx and Keynes' (Dobb: CB 22 (1)). In December 1940, Joan Robinson wrote to Richard Kahn that 'My next project is to make a dictionary to [*sic*] Marx so that he can be read by economists. Value = man hours. Surplus value = product–real wages etc. I had some conversation with Dobb but he is really useless – always running with the hare and hunting with the hounds' (RFK\13\90\4\376–7). In March 1941, she wrote to Kahn that 'I am now spending my spare time reading *Capital*. I think it will be fun to lecture on'. And a week later, she again revealed her continuing interest in Marx in another letter to Kahn: 'These pencil marks are due to a discussion with some young Marxists. There is a lot of excellent stuff in Marx, eg, that the quantity of money is determined by prices, not vice versa. But none of the Marxists seem to understand him' (RFK\13\90\4\400). In May, she wrote that on her usual Monday night firewatch, 'I spent the time putting in footnotes to the first chapter of my book on Marx. I am having a regular orgy on Marx this week – this evening I am opening at the [secret?] seminar. ... I have discovered one intelligent Marxist at LSE. I think he is a Czech or perhaps Hungarian. I hope to exploit him to the full as I need to get the orthodox reaction to my views' (RFK\13\90\4\422). Later in May, she continued: 'I am working on my book on Marx. Its chief purpose is to show that economics is no good – either Marxist or ours – except for short-period analysis. This ought to please Maynard' (RFK\13\90\4\424).

These letters reveal a number of Joan Robinson's traits, her tendency, for example, to reduce an argument to a simple form and to attribute to anyone who disagreed with her views, ignorance or confusion, but also, the process of her introduction to Marx.

Despite her disparaging remarks about Dobb at the beginning of her undertaking on Marx, she maintained an intense correspondence and conversation with him about points of Marx's arguments in *Capital* during the writing of the book, in the first half of 1941. 'The purpose of this essay is to compare the economic analysis of Marx's *Capital* with current academic teaching' (*EME*, v). In her 1941 article on Marx and unemployment, she stated as her objective to convert Marx's analysis of unemployment and put it into a language intelligible to academic economists; to bridge the gap. In the 1965 preface to the second edition of *EME*, she stated her aim as being to 'apply academic modes of analysis' to Marx's economic work. Her method of proceeding was to equate terms from Marx with candidate counterparts from orthodox theory. Dobb was sceptical about the project itself. Dobb and Joan Robinson seem to have discussed this methodology at the outset of her investigation. He wrote to her on 31 January 1941:

> I think my trouble about this translation business you spoke of the other night is twofold. First, I feel that in the case of writers who have something important to say, it is much *more* important (at any rate, of prior importance in time) to learn their language than to translate *{*I'm assuming of course that by 'translate' something more radical is meant than simply substituting a few words here and there, like utility for 'use-value' etc}; and the more important the more one's own conventional ways of thoughts and modes of expression diverge from theirs. Otherwise, unless one has really got inside t'other chaps head *and* his skin (ie felt problems within the context that he viewed them), one is almost sure to miss, or even distort, the meaning in translation, as is so commonly done by historians of thought. Secondly, I feel that the 'poetic' element – shades of meaning inherent as it were in style, construction, emphasis – is important in all economic languages certainly, and perhaps in all languages outside the rarest and most refined discourses of Logical Positivists. This is just what gets lost in translation from one poetic convention into another. And most of it, I suggest, is *not* just irrelevant 'moral' stuff, but is concerned with the *slant* that theory has on reality – with the completeness or incompleteness of the picture of the real world it affords, with the perspective and 'projection' and dimensions it is employing, with what it throws into relief as causally important and what it relegates to the shade. Whether these meanings could or could not ultimately be reduced to a propositional system I don't feel competent to say. But I feel quite sure they usually can't be rendered in half-a-dozen or a dozen simple propositions. All of which means that I think I'd plump for Marx, inter alia, being approached and studied so far as possible in the original language, despite its inconveniences, rather than in modernised translation [originally 'translation'] (without, of course, ruling out the virtue of translating special points for purposes of elucidation).
>
> (JVR\vii\120\11–3; emphasis in original)

Dobb makes a number of points here, which Joan Robinson failed to acknowledge in her project. First, there is the doubt that one *can* actually translate terms from one methodological system of ideas to another which, in a sense, is its opposition. Secondly, those aspects of this system that are not reducible to precise or finite concepts are not, thereby, irrelevant to that argument, nor are they discardable 'moral stuff'. Thirdly, because a theory has many dimensions to it, it is not reducible solely to a set of deductive propositions. Nevertheless Joan Robinson persevered in her attempt to 'translate' Marx into orthodox or alternatively Keynesian terms and relationships; she interpreted 'the slant that theory has on reality' as an irrelevant, moral dimension, and she strove to transform Marx's dialectical argument by reducing it to a propositional system based on static concepts and deductive logic. Dobb reiterated his disapproval of the latter exercise in another letter on 11 March 1941: 'I'm afraid I've never been able quite to see the fuss about this stock-flow problem – or, rather, to see how the difficulty of it is capable of solution by a trick of analysis' (JVR\vii\120\19–20).[5] Elsewhere, he states: 'This strikes me as a perfectly straightforward answer (and to my mind realistically correct in broad outline), even if he didn't get as far as setting out the algebra of it' (JVR/vii/120/19).

He returns to one of his first points, again trying to persuade Joan Robinson that 'the "poetic" element, shades of meaning inherent as it were in style, construction, emphasis – is important in all economic languages'(JVR/vii/120/12). He makes the point that the formal system of argument is only part of the story: 'I don't think I'm really concerned to "give marks to Marx": merely to try and see the problem as he saw it, as a prerequisite of understanding him, and to emphasise, perhaps, that the mode of expression he used may itself be an essential key to seeing what he was driving at' (14 March 1941: JVR\vii\120\23)[6]:

> It seems to me, therefore, that Marx's way of explaining it (which I agree with you comes *formally* to the same thing as yours) is the more realistic picture of the actual mechanism.
>
> (15 March 1941: JVR/vii/120/25–6)

And then he goes further to argue that in appreciating these other dimensions to a system of argument, one might actually develop different arguments from those which are the outcome of a more reductionist methodology.

'The difference, surely, is that the different emphasis of each of the two expositions implies a different causal story?' (18 March 1941: JVR\vii\120\28).

Dobb then becomes more specific. Joan Robinson cannot see any point to Marx's labour theory of value and its associated notion of the rate of exploitation. Although she observes that Marx 'used [the labour theory of value] ... to express certain ideas about the nature of the capitalist system', she continues her interpretation 'and the importance of these ideas in no way depends upon the particular terminology in which he chose to set them forth' (*EME*, 20). She may be correct in saying that the terminology is in some sense arbitrary but the nature of the concepts chosen is crucial. For example, are they exclusive concepts or are they dialectical, able to convey transitions of meaning? Are they abstract or do they rely on the senses? Is knowledge only authentic if it can be integrated into a deductive theory? She concludes her chapter 'The Labour Theory of Value' as follows: 'no point of substance in Marx's argument depends upon the labour theory of value' (ibid., p. 27). But the argument of volume I of *Capital* is not so easily reduced to deductive propositions.

Dobb wrote to JVR on 21 March 1941:

> But so far as what is here is concerned, there does seem to be one crucial omission. It seems to me to be misleading to launch into a comparison of Marx's structure and the 'orthodox' without emphasising what Marx meant by 'exploitation'; seeing that this is a large part of the point of his Vol I and the crucial distinction between him and others. This I feel is specially important in view of the fact that in your introductory bit about the ways in which Marx and economists have differed in the past, you seem to imply that this part of Marx is just irrelevant moral stuff on a par with 'reward of enterprise', and that modern economics which is purified of such moral tones can be reconciled with Marxism if the latter agrees to give to its notion of 'surplus-value' no more than a formal meaning (namely the difference between total product and wages). Here I think we're back at one of our earlier oral arguments. ... At any rate, Marx's theory of s.v. and exploitation is in my opinion (1) more than a tautological statement (Lerner's – 'the capitalist gets what labour doesn't') (2) this additional statement is a description of fact and *not* a moral judgement (3) this description is true of capitalist society, whereas all the 'abstinence' stuff (as well as the 'amoral' approach which makes no distinction between the return to one factor of production and another) is false and obscurantist. I'm not quite sure whether you would agree here or not. But I think it is clearly fundamental. If you don't, may I put this question? In a slave economy, there is, surely, a quite positive meaning to be given to the statement that the source of slave owners' income is the exploitation of the slaves' labour – that it is *derived* from the slaves' labour and is not 'produced' by any economic activity of the slave owner?

> Whether it is ethical or not for such a form of income to exist is then a quite distinct question, depending on some norm of ethical conduct. But as a factual characterisation of a slave economy some such statement is surely fundamental to any study of a slave society, and an economics which omitted it or slurred it over would, surely, be very inadequate, if not actually misleading.
>
> (JVR\vii\120\31–2, emphasis in original)

What Dobb was emphasising was the nature and scope of the explanatory role of Marx's use of the classical labour theory of value in the analysis of capitalism. Marx used the notion of exploitation to represent a real relationship, and to develop his analysis of the production of surplus value and then of its appropriation – its distribution between wages and profits. From here it led into a theory of exchange values. The two aspects are essentially linked. But Joan Robinson was insistently reductionist. In *EME*, she claimed: 'Whatever inward meaning the conception of *value* may have for a student of Hegel, to a modern English reader it is purely a matter of definition. The *value* of a commodity consists of the labour-time required to produce it, including the labour-time required by subsidiary commodities which enter into its production' (*EME*, 15). Formally, this may be correct in certain circumstances, but it is incomplete, as Dobb remarked above. Marx was not primarily interested in a theory of relative prices[7] but in the origins and behaviour of surplus value in aggregate, in its evolution both in the short and the long run, in the role of wage labour as a class in producing this surplus value and in the capitalist class receiving an average rate of profit. Joan Robinson selected out the deductively arguable elements of *Capital*. So what the labour theory of value has to say about production she considered trivial or irrelevant, and what it says about exchange, wrong. She tries to equate the concept of value with the orthodox concept of price, concluding 'According to Marx's own argument, the labour theory of value fails to provide a theory of prices' (*EME*, 20).

But consider this example more closely. Joan Robinson saw a disjuncture between volume I and volume III of *Capital*, seeing most of volume I as unnecessary. The point of volume I was to elaborate on the classical labour theory of value, to develop a theory of the production and appropriation of surplus value, and so ultimately of profits. In volume III, Marx turns to exchange and to prices of production and the equalisation of the rate of profits, to which Joan Robinson can relate with orthodox notions; so it is only volume III which, she sees, provides the possibility of a basis for comparing Marx and orthodox economics, viz., in a theory of relative prices, which is the primary object of the orthodox enquiry. In volume III, Marx comments: 'under capitalist production, the general law of value enforces itself merely as the prevailing tendency, in a very complicated and approximate manner, as a never ascertainable average of ceaseless fluctuations' (Marx, 1909b, vol. III, 190). Joan Robinson sees the difficulties reconciling values with prices of production and, seeing value only in its exchange sphere, instead states: 'none of the important ideas which [Marx] expresses in terms of the concept of value cannot be better expressed without it' (*EME*, 24). Her alternative is to express the variables in terms of money prices where her arguments against the concept of value are clearly as applicable to these concepts in terms of money (ibid.). Instead of recognising the different spheres of analysis, of production and exchange, and the different forms of expression of Marx's circuits of capital (outlined clearly in volume II of *Capital*), she reduces all economic activity which, she understands, can be theorised, to the exchange process to the exclusion of production. For, it was in the latter that Marx identified the sphere in which surplus value has its origins rather than in the spheres of circulation (both in terms of labour and output) which is affected primarily by ephemeral conditions of relative scarcity rather than by those persisting in the realm of production itself. Marx remarked: 'If the rate of surplus-value is known ... then the rate of profit expresses nothing else but what it actually is, namely a different way of measuring surplus-value. ... But in reality, in the world of phenomena, the conditions are reversed. Surplus-value is given, but only as an excess of the selling price of commodities over their cost-price. And it remains a mystery where this surplus is originated, whether it is due to the exploitation of labour in the process of production, or to overcharging the purchaser in the process of circulation, or to both. ... If the rate of profit is made the point of departure, there is no basis on which to make any conclusions regarding the specific relations between the surplus and the variable capital invested in wages' (1909b, vol. III, 60–1). Dobb adds similarly that 'under capitalism it is value-considerations and not "the satisfaction of the national wants" that rule production' (JVR\vii\120\43). Paradoxically, this was a sentiment that Joan Robinson frequently expressed in the 1940s and continued to do so into the 1960s and 1970s but she had no way of arguing this 'scientifically'.

Perhaps Dobb felt some exasperation with Joan Robinson's reductionist and deductive approach to Marx and a theory of capitalist activity. In 1932, he had written *On Marxism Today* and gone on to write his 1937 book, *Political Economy and Capitalism*; he stated these views clearly.[8]

> The only way in which the historical process can be conceptualised and held in thought is not as logically continuous, but as a dialectical process – a process in which at each stage the contemporary activity of making history introduces a new and contradictory element, which is only reducible to logical order when it has already become, in contemplation, a dead item of the past. ... It is of the essence of Marxism that it cannot be expounded as a set of propositions and that it cannot be learned as a dogma. ... Precisely because activity can only be comprehended in a concrete and not an abstract manner, Marxism can only be understood in its application.
>
> (Dobb, 1932, 21–2)[9]

But this was precisely what Joan Robinson had attempted to do, viz., to determine from the three volumes of *Capital* a set of concepts and of definitions, of deductive propositions. Because she proceeds to 'translate' Marx's historical materialism and dialectical reasoning into deductive logic, much is distorted or lost, the conceptualisation of causality is inverted and its pattern is changed; its relationship to history is lost.

For example, the deductive process, 'followed to its logical conclusion' and treated ahistorically, cannot accommodate the transformation of a quantitative change into qualitative change (e.g., see *EME*, 96). The distance which this takes Joan Robinson from Marx's argument is apparent.

> There is no reason why the rate of exploitation should be treated as either logically or historically prior to the rate of profit. Logically, what is important is the total amount of surplus which the capitalist class succeeds in acquiring. ... And there is no virtue in dividing that total by the amount of labour employed, to find the rate of exploitation, rather than by the amount of capital, to find the rate of profit. Historically, it is natural to suppose that different industries are developed with widely varying rates of exploitation, varying rates of profit, and varying ratios of capital to labour. The push and pull of competition then tends to establish a common rate of profit. ... The movement from an equal rate of exploitation towards an equal rate of profit is not a process in the development of capitalism, but a process in the development of economic analysis, from the primitive labour theory of value towards a theory of the interaction between relative demands and relative costs.
>
> (*EME*, 19–20)

This statement reveals several aspects of her interpretation of Marx's *Capital*. Once again, she is focused on exchange to the exclusion of production.[10] Second, Marx pursued a methodology which led him to develop concepts which represented elements of capitalism in its primitive state and which could then trace the transformation of the forms these concepts took as the stages of capitalism evolved. Third, he followed the uneven course of development as the social, economic and political relationships initiated and adapted to change in a historical process of shifting power. History was a succession of phases which developed their internal contradictions and gave rise to new forms. As the historical phases evolved, so too did the analytical concepts and analysis. Joan Robinson acknowledges the historical elements of Marx's writing as a comment on a context which itself does not offer conceptual categories or enter into her analysis. She fails to appreciate the analytical point of distinguishing between the rate of exploitation, the organic composition of capital and the rate of profits. Consequently, analysis of production reveals a set of universal laws while analysis of distribution and exchange is historically contingent (see Shove, 1944, 52). She seems to be unaware of the benefit of a material basis for economic theory.[11]

Marx, on the contrary, in discussing the equalisation of the rate of profits and the establishment of prices of production, states: 'Aside from the fact that prices and their movement are dominated by the law of value, it is quite appropriate, under these circumstances, to regard the value of commodities not only theoretically, but also historically, as existing prior to prices of production' (Marx, vol. III, 1909b, 208–9). And, as if in answer to Joan Robinson's above statement, Marx continued: 'The competition of the capitals in the different spheres then results in the prices of production which equalises the rates of profit between the different spheres. This last process requires a higher development of capitalist production than the previous process [of equalising market-values and market-prices]' (Marx, vol. III, 1909b, 212).[12]

A corollary of treating Marx's analysis as a set of deductive propositions is that the concepts tend also to be of a static (i.e., not with intrinsic properties to change) nature. Her ahistorical analysis means for example, that she interchanges the relationships between s/v, c/v and $s/c+v$ as if they were rigid symbols of deductive logic.[13] Hence, she can claim that they reveal only 'tautological' relationships (*EME*, 42). Dobb (1951) illustrates what this implies: 'Mrs Robinson, for example, speaks of Marx's "drastic inconsistency" in assuming that the rate of profit can fall in conditions of "constant real wages" (*EME*, 42–3). But this "startling contradiction" (as she also calls it) disappears if technological change applies to non-wage-goods industries only.' Dobb continues, to point out that Marx 'only considered this relevant to the determination of total profit if it affected the production of ... wage goods, and thereby lowered wages (in value). Only then could it raise what he termed "relative surplus value" by reducing the proportion of the labour force of society required to produce wage goods. ... Without a change in this crucial ratio, total profit or surplus value could not alter, whatever change in other non-wage goods might occur' (1951, 20). Dobb contradicted Joan Robinson: 'I can't really see that you can say that M. simply forgot all about this point [of increased productivity in wage goods industry] and was misled by a tautology and *assumed* simply that the rate of surplus value was unchanged; when he explicitly refers to two "opposite movements" as joint products of the same cause' (Dobb's emphasis; JVR\vii\120\36).

Similarly, while Joan Robinson (*EME*, 45–6) acknowledges that there are counter-tendencies to the rate of profits to fall, she remains adamant that Marx insists on a constant rate of exploitation and that with rising productivity and constant wages this cannot happen. Dobb, on several occasions, had disputed her interpretation of Marx on this issue of the production of relative surplus value. 'On P.274 he [Marx] says; "on an average the same causes which raise the rate of relative s.v., lower the mass of the employed labour-power. It is evident, however, that there will be more or less in this *according to the definite proportion in which the opposite movements exert themselves*"' (Dobb's emphasis; JVR\vii\120\35). Dobb continues in the same letter to quote Marx on the issue of the raising of the productive power of labour: 'he has referred to two ways in which increased productive power shows itself – in "raising the relative s.v. or reducing the value of the constant capital, so that *those commodities which enter either into the reproduction of labour-power or into the elements of constant capital are cheapened.* Both of these ... go hand in hand with a relative reduction of the variable as compared to the constant capital. *Both imply a fall in the rate of profit and both of them check it*"' (Dobb's emphasis in the quote from Marx, 1909b, vol III, 291) (JVR\vii\120\35–6). These relationships occur in the context of specific social, political and technological processes, and cannot be understood apart from these. The separation of the 'economic' from its context mirrors Joan Robinson's separation of the 'moral' from the 'scientific'. Dobb tries to point out to her that these are processes which cannot be represented by ahistorical variables and deduction; this separation then restricts her interpretation of Marx.

Directing her attention to the realm of exchange, Joan Robinson was more generous-spirited towards Marx. One aspect on which she was prepared to grant Marx credit was the achievement by him of nearly developing a theory of effective demand in the style of Kalecki and Keynes. Although in her book she did not identify Kalecki's use of the schema of reproduction of Marx, she did remark on the fact that using the schema Marx could clarify crises of realisation as well as crises of disproportional production. She had already applauded Marx for his recognition of the disruptive effects of an inequitable distribution of income and its associated deficiency of effective demand (Robinson, 1941). She credits Kalecki with demonstrating how Marx's method provided the basis for an analysis of effective demand (ibid., p. 240).[14] In her chapters, 'Effective Demand' and 'The General Theory of Employment', she remarks on 'Marx's analysis of reproduction in terms of the balance between the consumption-good and capital-good industries. ... In particular, Marx's contention that the excess of surplus value over capitalists' consumption (the rate of saving) is limited by the sum of outlay on new capital goods (home investment), the excess of exports over imports (foreign investment) and production of gold' (*EME*, 79). Although the subject of the schema did not come into the letters between Dobb and Joan Robinson, Dobb had remarked upon their use in Dobb (1937, 1940). He wrote: 'The main purpose of these *schema* was two-fold. First, they showed clearly the difference between the gross and the net product, between the total of commodity transactions and the revenue or income of individuals. ... Secondly, they postulated the relationships which would need to hold between the capital-goods industries and consumption-goods industries, on the one hand, and, on the other hand, the replacement demand of industries for equipment and raw materials, and the division of income between consumption and investment. This implicitly afforded an answer to the crude under-consumption theory: it showed that capital accumulation could proceed without causing any problems within the sphere of exchange, provided that these relationships were observed' (ibid., p. 101–2). (Dobb acknowledged here, in his revisions in the second edition of his book, Kalecki's reference to the schema in his *Essays in the Theory of Fluctuations* (1939a).) Within the simple structure of the schema, the precarious balance of realisation could be understood. Joan Robinson interpreted Marx as having an embryonic theory of effective demand (see Sardoni, 1987).

But Dobb also emphasised that this was only one aspect of a contradictory force; there were also the conditions for the production of surplus value to be realised. Dobb wrote to Joan Robinson: 'he [Marx] clearly thought that it was *both* the problem of demand *and* the limitation of investment by profit considerations (ie a periodic falling-profit tendency) that caused crises' (JVR\vii\120\40–1). He suggests that 'the "contradiction" that you say there is between Marx's treatment in the places where he is and is not talking about "realisation" would, I think, have been regarded by M as contradictions that existed in the real world of capitalism. In this sense: that capitalist policies were constantly concerned with improving the conditions for *producing* a large profit (eg reducing wages in order to increase *s*/*v*), while at the same time the very conditions that were favourable to a *production* of a large s.v. made the problem of *realising* s.v. more difficult' (JVR\vii\120\39–40, emphasis in original). Perhaps this was why Joan Robinson interpreted the tendency for the rate of profits to fall as absolute, without understanding the various other forces on the production of surplus value which counteracted it.[15] She did not yet see the schema as a circuit. Her judgement of Marx as being 'contradictory' is, as Dobb points out, because capitalism *is* contradictory.

4.3 Kalecki and Joan Robinson on Marx

As we have seen, in her new Preface to the second edition of *EME*, written in 1965, Joan Robinson stated: 'Piero Sraffa teased me, saying that I treated Marx like a little-known forerunner of Kalecki.' In 1939, she ran a discussion class on Kalecki's 1939 book; she took his work very seriously. She referred to Kalecki in several places in *EME*. The first instance is to compare Marx's and Kalecki's analyses of the turning point of a boom. In Marx's terms, at the turning point of a boom, there is an absolute overproduction of capital; total profits are constant and the new capital can only gain a share of the profits at the expense of existing capital. The competition between capitals means that capital is underemployed (*EME*, 47). Kalecki's model shows investment as constant so profits are constant but the capital stock is increasing. Again, (imperfect) competition distributes the profits so that capital is variously employed in different plants at different levels of capacity, generating a lower average rate of profits. The two similar descriptions are compatible and follow different steps in the same causal analysis. In Marx's scheme, the turning point might come because, for example, higher wages associated with higher demand for labour relative to the reserve army reduces the share, and the rate of profits and investment declines. For Kalecki, there is failure of effective demand due to a slump in investment in response to a falling rate of profits which itself gives rise to lower profits.

Joan Robinson argued that Marx's cycle was much longer than the trade cycle which responds simply to effective demand and that 'The operation of Marx's long-period cycle has not been detected by the statisticians, for, if it exists, it is swamped by the more violent movements of the trade cycle, and disturbed by bursts of invention, due to the progress of science, as well as by wars, geographical discoveries and other large-scale accidents, which are not directly connected with the scarcity of labour, or which, at any rate, cannot be reduced to a simple relationship with it' (*EME*, 103–4).[16] This is precisely the point: the relationship is not reducible to a simple proposition.

Joan Robinson addresses the long-period factors affecting the rate of surplus value and argues that long-period productivity growth will more than offset these factors, and that the only way for the rate of profits to fall is for the organic composition of capital to rise more rapidly than productivity. Kalecki's is a short-period theory as compared with Joan Robinson's long-period objections to Marx. Later in the book (*EME*, ch. 10), she distinguishes between the two situations, seeing a 'confusion between this long-run cycle, which might be found in a world subject to Say's Law, and the short-run cycle of effective demand' (*EME*, 104). Marx, she argued, suffered from this 'confusion' in his theory of crises.

She again draws on Kalecki (1939a) in another context, viz., to illustrate 'an empirical law of distribution' which is 'a remarkable constancy in the proportionate share of labour in output as a whole' (*EME*, 97). She regards neither the Marxian nor the 'academic' approach as a satisfactory explanation. (The neoclassical theory based on the Cobb–Douglas production function does not merit attention.)[17]

Her third reference to Kalecki is to his observation that a higher proportion of wages at the margin is consumed than that of profits. The context is the issue of whether a growth in money-wages will increase real wages and whether this will reduce employment. Dobb had tried to persuade her, in a letter, that the reduction in investment and capitalists' consumption that would follow the cut in profits would exactly offset or even more than outweigh the increase in consumption out of wages: 'Capitalists' income is smaller *because* they have economised in consumption (*this* is balanced by an equivalent rise of wage-earners' consumption), and *in addition* investment declines because of the narrowed margin between selling-price and wage-cost. In other words, if *real* wages (and not only money wages) rise, must not both the marginal efficiency of capital and the propensity to consume of capitalists *fall in terms of wage-units?* And if not, why not?' (JVR/vii/120/34; emphasis in original). In *EME* (109), Joan Robinson suggests that investment in long-lived projects like house-building, might decline with the rise in costs, but investment in consumer-producing machinery would increase and offset this. Perhaps this short discussion in her text was to answer to Dobb's objection.

Kalecki wrote to Joan Robinson soon after the book appeared, on 30 July 1942. His general comment was: 'I think that your analysis of Marx is very valuable because it has shown that one conception in his writings is a quite consistent theory; while Marxists who wanted to show that everything is right and consistent failed to show even that. The book although written in a simple language does not make an easy reading; and I do not think there is much hope of it being understood by Marxists' (JVR/vii/232/9). Kalecki comments on her references to the 'law of motion' of capitalism as if this were Marx's expression. Rather, he claims, this expression was a metaphor of classical political economy. (Harrod (1942), in a brief note on the book, made the same point; and in an exchange in *Tribune* (30.10.42; 2.11.42: 20.11.42 (JVR); 27.11.42) she also debated the uses of this expression.) Kalecki's more specific responses were: 'p.40 and p.97. On Marx's assumptions as you put them one *can* construct a complete theory of profits.[18] [...] ... Marx's assumptions are, of course, wrong; but if they are accepted they do provide us with a theory of profits' (Kalecki's emphasis; JVR/vii/232/11).

Joan Robinson did not accept that Marx, and classical economics, had a coherent theory of profits until after reading Sraffa's Introduction to the Ricardo volumes (Sraffa with Dobb (eds.) 1951). Neither did she retract her statement that the share of wages in the national product had been approximately constant over the long run. In fact, she reiterated it in her 1966 preface to the new edition of *EME* (xvii) with data and explanation to support her case. Relative shares, she argued, were the outcome of the struggle between trade unions and employers, but she extended this proposition into its price and exchange implications.

4.4 Keynes's response to *An Essay on Marxian Economics*

Keynes, too, had a guarded response to her book, offering that it was 'as well written as anything you have done. This in spite of the fact that there is something intrinsically boring in an attempt to make sense of what is in fact not sense. However, you have got round it by making no undue attempt in this direction' (Keynes; 20 August 1942; JMK/L/42/102–3). He goes on to make two more specific points, one about Marx's value theory and prices, and one a reaction to her reference to his own work. 'On page 29, could you not have made still more sense of his system of values by pointing out how comparatively well it would work if we were to suppose that capital is not scarce. In this state of affairs, which we may hope to reach sooner or later, depreciation, if we forget about risk, would be the only cost of capital, and quite a pack of Marx's theoretical difficulties would have disappeared' (Keynes, ibid.). (That capitalism would also have disappeared is overlooked.) Joan Robinson responds to this letter, conceding Keynes's point about capital (21 August 1942; JMK/CO/8/246). In the preface to the 1966 edition, she acknowledges this point again (*EME*, 1966, x).

Keynes then corrects her misinterpretation of him in his use of wage units as a measure of output: '[y]our footnote on page 23: – I do not plead guilty here. Certainly I never intended to suggest that the wage unit is a stable measure of real output for purposes of comparison between periods widely different in other respects'.[19] Joan Robinson seemed keen to placate Keynes but Keynes was not appeased. He replied on 27 August 1942: 'I still do not plead guilty about the footnote on labour as the only factor of production. For my units to work, two conditions must be fulfilled, namely, that labour in some sense is the only factor of production and that we are functioning in short-period conditions. I stated both of these conditions explicitly. You seem to be arguing that only the second condition is necessary and appear to be accusing me of saying that only the first condition is necessary. I said in the book and still think that both are required' (Keynes: JMK/CO/8/249–50).

C. R. Fay, in his review of *EME*, remarked on the same footnote and defended Keynes before dismissing her book as immature (Fay, 1942). The offending footnote to Keynes was removed in the 1947 reprint although Kalecki's objections were ignored.

Various other figures recorded their responses to Joan Robinson's book. Schumpeter stated, in the context of a discussion to the effect that no one in their right mind would be a Marxist, particularly 'in the sense that they actually try and revitalise Marx's pure economics [that]. ... [t]he outstanding examples are P.M. Sweezy and J. Robinson. (f/n. Still more remarkable [than Sweezy's belief in the use of Marx's economics], and something of a psychological riddle, is Mrs Robinson's *Essay on Marxian Economics* (1942)' (Schumpeter, 1954, 884–5). He did not elaborate.

She also received letters from Hans Singer and Harold Laski. The latter wrote enthusiastically: 'I should be ungrateful indeed if I did not thank you for your "*Essay on Marxian Economics*". I have found it illuminating and exciting – perhaps the beginning of a new and exciting development of the relation of the labour movement to academic economics.

I do warmly congratulate you, if I may, on a masterly argument' (JVR/vii/252/1).

An Essay on Marxian Economics was widely reviewed. Harrod (in the *Observer*) sums up the estimate of the more conservative reviewers: 'on the whole our regard for Marx is not increased but our regard for the old orthodoxy is somewhat diminished' (Harrod, 1942). This would particularly apply to Gerald Shove who wrote perhaps the most considered review, in *The Economic Journal*. He objected to her representation of the Marshallian theory of profits. Keen to defend Marshall, he rejected her depiction of orthodox theory as harmonious, eternal and following some 'inexorable natural law'. The particular target of her attack on orthodoxy was the role of the rate of interest as the supply price of capital; that it was the justification for 'waiting'. Shove argues that since Marshall did not clearly distinguish saving from investment, his treatment of the interest rate and accumulation was obscure. In Marshall, he argues, it is a decrease in the *demand* price of capital (i.e., its marginal productivity or rate of return obtainable by investment) which tends to reduce its stock; a fall in its *supply* price (i.e., the interest rate at which funds are available for investment) has the contrary effect. It would seem that the rate of interest has an important bearing on the stock of capital, a conclusion which, he claims, Joan Robinson herself draws. In outlining the 'modern tendency in academic theory', she remarks that 'the rate of interest, though its movements tell in the right direction, is too weak an influence adequately to regulate the level of investment' (*EME*, 83–4). In extending Keynes's case, she observes that 'the lower the authorities succeed in setting the rate of interest, the larger the stock of capital is likely to be. Thus the notion of the rate of interest as an element in the necessary supply price of capital is deprived of its foundation' (*EME*, 85).

In criticising Marshall for failing to develop a dynamic theory, Joan Robinson argues that for equilibrium, the rate of accumulation would have to be zero. This would be a static state ('The equilibrium rate of profit is that rate which induces zero net investment' (*EME*, 72)). Shove points out that 'There is no *logical* inconsistency between an expanding system and the maintenance of an "equilibrium" rate of profit. So long as the expansion of demand (or supply) is correctly estimated, the supply of capital and the demand for it keep in step, and the actual rate of profit ruling at any given moment is equal to the supply price of the stock of capital existing at that moment' (Shove, 1944, 60, emphasis in original).[20] Joan Robinson referred to the issue in 1951, as unresolved (Robinson, *C.E.P.*, vol. II, 1960, 23, 25). In her 1966 preface to *EME*, she again referred to this issue and blamed Marshall's lack of clarity over the 'normal rate of profits'; she left her original statement about zero net investment in the text.

Some reviewers associated her interest in imperfect competition with her interest in Marxian economics, perhaps supposing that a political link implied a consistency in the theoretical bases of each, although they did not themselves offer a theoretical link. The recurrent Marxist criticisms were of her failure to understand Marx's labour theory of value, of misrepresenting the theory of the falling rate of profits, and in general of not understanding Marx's method and argument. T. A. Jackson, writing in the journal, *The Plebs*, wrote: 'She fails completely to grasp what Marx was aiming at when he sought for "the law of motion of capitalist society". To her, the end is attained in a mathematical formula, which to Marx expressed at best only one side of a complex three-dimensional relationship. To her, the goal is mathematical; to Marx, "there is only one science, the science of history"' (Jackson, 1943). He continues on this theme: 'Joan Robinson seeks for, and complains when Marx does not provide rigid definitions capable of algebraic expression. Marx, since he is analysing a process, knows that all definitions are of necessity provisional only; at best, of service only to be superseded' (ibid.). Joan Robinson's method is subjectivist and idealist whereas Marx's is realist, materialist and dialectical. Her methods are as inappropriate for critical evaluation of his 'as a quart pot would be for measuring an electric current' (ibid.). It is the problem of reducing ideas to rigid categories and to a set of simplistic deductive propositions which Dobb had warned her against. Jackson also commented on her confusion over value and price. Joan Robinson seems not to see that price is a form which value takes in the exchange circuit and instead strains at Marx's use of value to demonstrate that it does not *equal* price. Jackson states: 'Unless price is, what Marx thought it was, the "money-name" of a quantity of value, which in turn was, in Marx's words, "a relation between men expressed as a relation between things" – unless price is this, it is an insoluble mystery' (ibid.).

E. M. Chossudowsky, in *Economica* (November 1943), also commented on her treatment of value as 'but "a matter of definition". ... [Yet] coupled with [Marx's] theory of the class struggle the theory of value gives rise to the remaining body of his analysis.' He too remarked on her rigid interpretation of the tendency for the rate of profits to fall. In particular, he drew attention to her interpretation that 'Marx's argument fails to establish a presumption that the rate of profit tends to fall, when the problem of effective demand is left out of account' (*EME*, 47). Furthermore, she understands the problem of effective demand to arise out of a maldistribution of income. Chossudowsky objects that the implication of her argument is that if the problem of effective demand is resolved, the disruptions of the cycle would be smoothed away. He quotes Dobb: 'Marx considered the contradictions within the sphere of production – the contradiction between growing productive power, consequent upon accumulation, and falling profitability of capital, between the *productive forces* and the *productive relations* of capitalist society – as the essence of the matter' (Dobb, 1937, 1940, 121; emphasis in original). Joan Robinson focused her analysis on exchange. He also remarked on her 'dogmatic' treatment of the rate of exploitation echoing Dobb's warning to her. Finally, he makes the point, along with Flanders (1943) and echoing Marx's Eleventh Thesis on Feuerbach, that academic economists aim only to interpret society while Marxists aim to transform it and 'so long as academics remain but disinterested onlookers of the social scene the similarities between their analysis and that of Marx will continue to be but formal and the gulf that separates them from Marxism will remain unabridged' (Chossudowsky, 1942).

4.5 After *An Essay on Marxian Economics*

Joan Robinson continued to comment on Marxian economics for the rest of her life. In 1951, she wrote the introduction to the English translation of Rosa Luxemburg's *Accumulation of Capital*. Her emphasis on the exchange process and her attraction to Keynes's theory of effective demand as an explanation of crisis, possibly directed her to Luxemburg's Marxism as a subject of study. In this, she drew on the reproduction schema to demonstrate the possibilities of disruption to the process of accumulation. She exhibited considerably more openness to Marx's arguments, acknowledging that some of the ambiguities in his concepts could be overlooked, or even clarified, and when interpreted in sympathy with their intended purpose, could be seen to present a feasible and coherent argument about the contradictory tendencies in a capitalist economy. She was open to the interactive nature of the relationships. In 1953, she published the essays, *On Re-reading Marx*. These were polemical essays, celebrating her interpretation of the meaning of the 'rate of profits' in classical theory (including Keynes) inspired by Sraffa's Introduction to the Ricardo volumes (Sraffa with the collaboration of Dobb (1951)). Here, she declared herself a Left-wing Keynesian, thereby placing herself in relation to her writing on Marx. In Robinson (1954), on the labour theory of value, she acknowledges the role of Marx's theory in explaining the rate of surplus value, but nevertheless focuses only on its role in explaining relative prices. While she accepts that, in principle, it provides a sound basis, she nevertheless maintains that it neglects the short-period influences, for example, of restricted supplies of factors on prices. Furthermore, she argues, it does not allow for the role of money-wages in determining prices – she introduces the index number problem associated with using aggregates with changing composition – nor the role of trade unions in improving labour's share. She concludes that 'the failure of the assumptions required by the analysis to be fulfilled in reality means that it provides a very inaccurate picture of how capitalism works and a very feeble guide for investment in a planned economy, but within its own limits there seems nothing to object to about it, either from the right or from the left' (Robinson, 1954; *C.E.P.*, vol. II, 1960, 58). At least some of her complaints again arise from her focus on the form of capital in the exchange process, while others are based on her attempt to build a short-period analysis onto Marx's long period.

By the time *EME* was reissued (1966), Sraffa's profound work, (Sraffa, 1960), had been published and much discussed. With her interpretation of his contribution being initially limited to solving the transformation problem and also to demonstrating the logical flaws in the conceptual basis of neoclassical capital theory, she revisited Marx's labour theory of value. In her new preface, she restates her arguments about the irrelevance of 'value' for Marx's process and once again concludes that it is, on its own, an inadequate concept for explaining relative shares; instead, one needs to look at relative bargaining strength of labour and capital. She argues that it is inadequate as an account of exploitation. For example, the division of the product between capital and labour is explained by Marx by reference to a historically determined subsistence wage and to the size of the reserve army of labour relative to the current state of accumulation and so demand for labour. The latter relation depends also on the nature of technical progress and the amount of profits available for investment. Joan Robinson subsumes all of these relationships into the confrontation in the market place between capital and labour. Once again, it is in the sphere of exchange that she conducts her analysis. Although her account may be consistent with Marx's, it is partial. There is no place to explain and analyse changes in productivity of labour as employment increases, for example, nor changes in the value of wages as productivity of labour progresses; there is no scope for the productive relations to interact with the productive forces. Everything is subsumed into exchange. But Joan Robinson defers to the historical evidence to illustrate her case that arguing in terms of values does not clarify, but unnecessarily obscures, Marx's scheme. Her own method began at the empirical level and the subsequent abstractions tend to be of institutional forms, generally sympathetic to Marx's aim, but less political. Joan Robinson saw that while Sraffa may have used the word 'value' interchangeably with 'price', he was in fact presenting a way of resolving some of the analytical obscurities (as she saw them) in Marx's argument, present, because Marx did rely on 'value'. In effect, Sraffa's solution was based upon an alternative labour theory of value.[21]

It is interesting that around this time she made several remarks about her own understanding of the role of *EME*. Joan Robinson (1977b, *C.E.P.*, vol. V, 1979, 289–97) (a review of Ronald Meek's *Essays in the Labour Theory of Value*) states: 'I did not intend my *Essay on Marxian Economics* (1942) as a criticism of Marx. I wrote it to alert my bourgeois colleagues to the existence of penetrating and important ideas in *Capital* that they ought not to continue to neglect. ... (In fact, that book was the first round in the 'Cambridge criticism' which, with the aid of Piero Sraffa, finally pulverised equilibrium theory twenty years later.)' (ibid., p. 280). In this review of Meek, she continues to say: 'The theories that Marx put forward in terms of *value* are the indispensable basis for a treatment of the economics of capitalism, which the orthodox school fails to provide. ... The Marxian concept of the nature of an economic system, characterised by the manner in which production is controlled and a surplus extracted from it, is more important than ever. ... The central topic in teaching economics ought to be the nature of productive systems. ... To interpret history, the interplay of the forces of production and the relations of production is an invaluable clue.' (ibid., p. 282–3, emphasis in original). Her reading of Marx had become far more open-minded and sympathetic.

In 'The organic composition of capital' (Robinson, 1978a), she again translates Keynesian ideas into Marxian analysis. But still, she is cautious about the term 'value'. In (Robinson, 1978b) she states: 'Steedman[22] points out that when we have a description of capitalist production and distribution in terms of physical processes and flows of payments, a description in terms of *value* adds nothing at all. (The present reviewer pointed this out in 1942 and has been treated as an enemy by the professed Marxists ever since)' (Robinson, 1978b, 276, emphasis in original). But her statement, 'The answer must be found not in terms of value but in terms of history' (ibid., p. 278), is too glib and reflects her limited interpretation of the nature of abstraction in Marx's history. Nevertheless she interpreted Marx's abstract 'model' of volume

I of *Capital* as being about early stages of capitalism and of volume III as being about later, developed stages of capitalism (Robinson, 1966b, ix) as reflected by different phases in the development of that abstract 'model'. But she came to suggest that Marx's abstract concepts could be given approximate operational categories so that their historical counterparts could be understood in the light of his theories.

In 'Ideology and Analysis' (Robinson, 1973a), she undertakes a task similar to that she set herself in *EME*. 'A Marxian analysis of the historical evolution of the rate of exploitation provides the setting, in broad terms, for a theory of profits; some detail can be fitted into it with the aid of Kalecki. ... It is possible also to work out a long-period version of the theory, in which accumulation is going on at a steady rate. This, however, is only a first step which should not be given much weight' (Robinson, 1973a; *C.E.P.*, vol. V, 1979, 261). Perhaps, here, she is identifying, or at least finding compatible, her own theoretical work (Robinson, 1951a, 1956a, 1962e) with the Marxist tradition. This theoretical construction of analyses apparently linked by a common methodology and basic assumptions, represented a step in a succession of movements against her Marshallian heritage. It paralleled a gradual shift in her methodological ideas about value and science (see Chapter 11). She identifies Kalecki's work with progressive Marxism: 'Michal Kalecki, also reviled by dogmatists, has analysed the process of realisation of the surplus ... [and] linked it to the principle of effective demand and the instability of capitalism, to class war in the North and to quasi-feudalism in the South, as well as developing the analysis of expanded reproduction in capitalist and planned economi[e]s' (Robinson, 1978b; *C.E.P.*, vol. V, 1979, 279). She cites Kalecki's 'value-free' treatment of these issues. Kalecki worked at a different level of analysis to that which Joan Robinson identifies with Marx, applying his arguments and extending them to practice. Her uncompromising stand had been against the use of the concept of 'value'. Instead, she now attempts to replace 'value' by the specific forms it takes at different stages in the circulation of capital, understanding that it will therefore be represented by different categories – empirical and abstract. In this way, she can bring together Marx, Kalecki and Sraffa, each contributing in a methodologically consistent way to an overall picture of capitalism. She still rejects 'the' (i.e., Marx's) labour theory of value as an obstruction to clear thinking. Yet Sraffa's system is also a labour theory of value as is, with a different set of abstractions, Pasinetti's natural system (e.g., Pasinetti, 2007).

In 'Who is a Marxist' (Robinson, 1979; *C.E.P.*, vol. V, 1979, 248–53) she illustrates the use of *P*/*W* (where *P* stands for profit and *W* for wages), instead of Marx's *s*/*v*; the former can be roughly observed in the national statistics, while *s*/*v* can be distinguished only in the abstract (see f/n 14); she also uses this argument in 'Ideology and Analysis' (Robinson, 1973a, *C.E.P.*, vol. V, 1979, 254–61). In Robinson (1979), Joan Robinson returns to Sraffa's 'model': 'Sraffa offered this argument as a battering ram to knock down orthodox theory and clear a space in which the Marxian theory of distribution and of prices could be elaborated' (Robinson, 1979, *C.E.P.*, vol. V, 1979, 250).

In 1977, she wrote: 'Sraffa provides a clearly specified one-technique model which shows the meaning of *value*, the labour-time directly and indirectly required to produce a commodity, and he shows how *values* are systematically related to prices by the level of the rate of profit[s]. This gives a simplified picture of how exploitation works in a capitalist economy which is producing output at a steady rate, without crises.

Incidentally, it has the great advantage of having knocked out the academic theory of profit as the measure of the "productivity of capital"' (Robinson, 1977a; *C.E.P.*, vol. V, 1979, 296). Bhaduri and Joan Robinson (1980) extended this position, elaborating Sraffa's 'model' to include 'distribution according to Marx and realisation according to Kalecki', following Marxian abstractions and relationships. Joan Robinson is satisfied that Sraffa has resolved Marx's transformation problem while remaining true to his tradition. Kalecki then resolves the realisation problem on the basis of volume II of *Capital*, using the reproduction schema. 'With the light that Sraffa has thrown on the theory of value and Kalecki on the process of realisation of the surplus, we can develop a complete system, not of *neo* Marxism but of *intelligible* Marxism, and, what is more important, adapt it to the analysis of contemporary problems of capitalism, socialism and so-called "development"'(Robinson, 1979; *C.E.P.*, vol. V, 1979, 253, emphasis in original). Sraffa's work seemed somehow to enable her to accept Marx's arguments, if not his choice of abstractions, on a neutral ground.

Despite the misreadings and limitations of Joan Robinson's works, her interpretation of Marx was not of inconsequence. She was not unaware of the different approach she took to Marx. 'There is a terrible lot of stuff, it is true, that a "vulgar empirical English" mind like mine finds very unrewarding, but there is also quite plainly set out a simplified "economic model" which Marx used to analyse distribution in a static state, capital accumulation, technological progress, the trade cycle, and all the rest of it' (Robinson, 1957a). Joan Robinson relied upon deductive processes but also on contradictions or paradoxes. She was conscious of realism in the abstractions she made; her use of contradictions as a basis for a process, and her use of the schema of reproduction, introduced the possibility of interactive or circuitous processes. Although she wanted her theory to be relevant to selected aspects of capitalism – this was one of the attractions to Marx – by adapting 'academic modes of analysis' to Marx's theories, she adjusted his concepts to abstractions and representations with more convenient empirical counterparts. She became more aware of the need to ground her concepts in history, even if, subsequently, she did not always do so successfully. She was not looking for a grand theory to embrace all aspects of capitalism which Kalecki hinted at in his comment to her that the law of motion of capitalism was the labour theory of value expressed in all its theoretical links (JVR/vii/232). Her study of Marx opened up other dimensions of economic theorising to her and it had implications for her subsequent post-Keynesian analyses of growth and income distribution, and of her interpretations of the national and international development of capitalism. Her writing on development, particularly on China but also on undeveloped capitalist economies, follows Marxist themes if not his direct theoretical approach (see Chapters 5 and 9).

One of her reviewers, Allen Flanders, asked: 'How far does the synthesis which she shows to be possible between Marxist and modern economic ways of thought provide a theoretical basis for a new and more realistic socialist programme?' (Flanders, 1943). Around the time she wrote *EME*, she was also writing on socialist planning in post-war Britain (see Chapter 5). In her programme for Britain, it was monopoly which had to be opposed and it was the theory of effective demand that dominated her analysis.

5

Joan Robinson and Socialist Planning in the Years of High Theory

> The problem of the balance of trade, the problem of raising the standard of life of our people, the problem of dealing with housing, dealing with employment, all these national problems must be solved on a central basis. If they're solved centrally they must be solved by the Government, that's to say they must be under ultimate democratic control and not by some businessmen you are getting together.
>
> 'Are cartels either desirable or necessary?', BBC broadcast, Joan Robinson (1945a)

5.1 Introduction

The poverty and misery of the 1930s were inescapably dire. The injustices of unemployment and of the distribution of wealth and income drove many to action. Elizabeth Durbin (1985) describes the British Labour Party in the 1930s as being concerned with the inequitable and unjust society, as manifest in general practical and also in theoretical issues. On the theoretical level, it had to define the proposed new socialist state and its rationales; on the practical level, it had to elaborate appropriate policies for introducing socialism into Britain through parliamentary democracy. The members of the Labour Party believed passionately in the ability to achieve a new society which was to be both more efficient and more just. The Soviet example served as a guide. The economic circumstances of the 1930s legitimised the intervention into the national and international economy which the Labour Party proposed to undertake when it came into office. The socialism of the Labour Party saw that there were two broad dimensions to the economy that were to be addressed: its allocative efficiency and its aggregative performance. It looked to the new economic theories of the 1930s to inform it on each of these problems. Joan Robinson's own direct theoretical interests in particular put her at the centre of both these bodies of analysis.

As we noted, Joan Robinson came to economics driven by an outrage at inequalities in the distribution of income and wealth, and the social injustice of poverty.[1] The plight of the masses of unemployed during the 1930s and then the onset of war, drew her into political engagement. She had worked in the early 1930s for the New Fabian Research Bureau and was among the most active members in the group. She participated in study and research groups into the war years (see King, 2005). But she did more than this; she took on the responsibility of educating the population in the basic arguments of the new theories and in their policies. If people understood the logic, she believed that they would be persuaded to its practice. She was a Fabian socialist but not a Marxist.[2] Joan Robinson was primarily a theorist – but she was driven by a moral, even political cause as she presented a theoretical basis for an all-embracing plan.

It was also an exciting period for economics. As we have seen, Sraffa (1926) had published a shattering critique of Marshallian marginalism and its method of partial equilibrium.[3] His 'pregnant suggestion' that monopoly rather than competition was typical of market structures was the insight and stimulus for Joan Robinson's first revolution – the theory of imperfect competition. Meanwhile, Keynes had rewritten monetary theory and transformed it into a theory of output and employment, of a monetary production economy, and Robinson immediately immersed herself in its implications. The period was one in which the British Labour Party committed itself to developing strategies for democratic socialism, adopting Keynesianism during the war years as a theoretical base.

The orthodox theory of the 1920s and early 1930s was one which justified free market capitalism, albeit with Marshallian/Pigovian qualifications. And now, the reassurances of this theory were losing their credibility. Instead of starting from the assumption of a perfectly competitive market structure, Joan Robinson's 'new' theory began with imperfect competition.[4] It was recognised that the economy was becoming increasingly influenced by monopolistic firms and groups of industrialists acting in concert. Joan Robinson, in *The Economics of Imperfect Competition* (*EIC*, 1933a), showed how this tendency to market concentration also tended to reduce levels of output of the firm and so employment. It could seem that monopolies were, partly at least, to blame for the mass unemployment. Pigou had shown that even with the assumptions of perfect competition, there were Marshallian market situations which did not behave in the prescribed way, viz. collectively consumed goods, goods with externalities; Sraffa had demonstrated the prevalence of goods, the production of which was characterised by increasing returns, and in particular by interdependent demand and supply curves. The new theory offered an explanation as to why certain particular industries should be run collectively under public ownership in order to be efficient. Joan Robinson appears to have taken her conclusions from *EIC* and attempted to extend them as a theory of output and distribution.[5] But as she continued to discuss monopoly into the 1930s and 1940s, it was increasingly in terms of the Keynesian and Kaleckian theory of output and employment and was less reliant on the partial mechanisms and marginalism of the analysis of *EIC*.[6]

In 1936, Keynes's *General Theory* was published. As we saw, Joan Robinson, as a member of the 'Circus', had already absorbed the early stages of the argument (Robinson, 1933b; 1933c) and went on to explore some of its implications (Robinson, 1937a; 1937b); she was immediately arguing for full employment policies although it took until 1944 for the Labour Party to finally adopt full employment as an objective. Orthodox theory could only account for unemployment in the short period and not in the long period, and now there was a tendency for theory to be more focused on the short period, following Kahn's influential (within a charmed circle) dissertation on the short period and imperfect competition (Kahn, 1929; 1989). In retrospect, Joan Robinson attributed a major part of Keynes's revolution to this shift. She moved from her nevertheless still axiomatic methodology in *EIC* to a method of adopting the apparently more 'realistic' premises and propositions of Keynes's theory, a methodological shift perhaps prompted by her understanding of Sraffa's 1926 critique. Joan Robinson responded at first to Sraffa's critique of the lack of realism in marginalism by modifying the apparatus; it was Sraffa's objection to the functional relations between costs and output which she came to interpret at first as descriptively inadequate.[7] It was only much later (Sraffa, 1960) that the generality of Sraffa's critique of marginalism emerged. Her failure to anticipate, at this point in time, the methodological nature of this criticism led to her holding simultaneously a theory of value of which she rejected the associated theory of output and distribution, and an alternative theory of output and employment whose basis was in the perfect competition she rejected (although Kalecki (1936, 1982; 1990) argued that the market structure adopted made no essential difference to the outcome of the theory of output and Keynes (1936) made a similar claim). She would only come much later to wholly reject long-period equilibrium theory.

Nevertheless it meant that the socialists in the Labour Party, ranging from Austin and Joan Robinson to Hugh Dalton to James Meade, now had two strands to their critique of capitalism, the imperfections in the market structure and the inefficiencies and waste thus created, and the tendency to unemployment on an aggregate level due to a lack of effective demand. They are not necessarily consistent explanations of the plight of the economy.[8] These two strands are mixed together in Joan Robinson's critique of capitalism and her proposals for a post-war alternative.[9]

5.2 Market structure

5.2.1 Laisser-faire

Joan Robinson wrote a number of pamphlets during the war as well as newspaper and popular journal articles and radio broadcasts, all of which followed a consistent theme: 'The criterion of profit fails to coincide with the criterion of what is socially desirable' (Robinson, 1943a, 7). This was the argument that *laisser-faire* capitalism had failed to provide full employment and a desirable allocation of labour and resources. While the war artificially kept everyone in employment, unless deliberate action were taken, unemployment would again reappear after the war. Fear of a slump post-war (while not excluding the possibility of post-war inflation – 'a successful employment policy, just because it is successful, entails a chronic danger of inflation' (Robinson, 1946b) – particularly of a US slump, threatened the much needed export market. *Laisser-faire* capitalism now needed intervention, to be modified or even replaced by some form of planning and an alternative economic structure with different rules to guarantee such full employment.

But what was *laisser-faire* capitalism? Which theoretical economy of perfect competition did she mean?[10, 11] Or did she mean Britain before the First World War? Keynes (1926; *C.W.*, vol. IX, 1972) demonstrated the opportune nature of the principle of *laisser-faire* in its rise out of the conjunction of political and moral philosophy, and the political and economic structure of the late eighteenth century. He observed that

> many of those who recognise that the simplified hypothesis does not accurately correspond to fact conclude nevertheless that it does represent what is 'natural' and therefore ideal. They regard the simplified hypothesis as health, and the further complications as disease.
>
> Keynes (1926; *C.W.*, vol. IX, 1972, 285)

Joan Robinson echoed Keynes's closing metaphor as she referred to the ideal state of the *laisser-faire* economy with its perfectly competitive market structure and no 'complications'.

> In the philosophy of laisser faire the activities of industry were reconciled with the public interest by the mechanism of competition. Competition, we were taught, ensured efficiency within each industry, subordinated production to consumers' demand and regulated the flow of resources into the most productive channels. Through competition, the self-interested pursuit of profit was harnessed to the common weal, and all individual activities automatically coordinated into a harmonious whole.
>
> Robinson (1942b, 401–2)

There were two dimensions to her rebuttal of *laisser-faire*: a theoretical and a political one. She was an opponent of the practice of *laisser-faire* capitalism. It rewarded greed and gave rise to an inequitable and unjust distribution of income; it had no way of acknowledging needs unless they were registered monetarily; it was inefficient in its reliance on advertising to create demands; and it was immoral in its wastage of resources which were left unemployed when people's needs are unmet. Her rejection of the theory of *laisser-faire* also had two elements: first, the many complications in the contemporary market structure which meant the theory was inoperable or irrelevant, that is, the issue of its realism and the construction of a more 'realistic' theory of imperfect competition which demonstrated the inefficiencies of *laisser-faire*; secondly, a fundamental flaw in *laisser-faire* that unless there is perfect price discrimination, *laisser-faire* will fail to provide the ideal selection of commodities. This, she adds, is only the case in firms with falling average costs, that is, imperfect competition, but since this describes most firms for the relevant part of their output, *laisser-faire*, she concludes, has no justification (Robinson, 1935).[12] And then, the further issue of Keynes's theory of effective demand which showed that a *laisser-faire* economy is likely to lead to unemployment equilibria.[13]

5.2.2 Imperfect competition

There was no longer a *laisser-faire* complex of numerous competitive firms, individually facing infinitely elastic demand curves. On the contrary, the economy was now characterised by industry groupings, trade associations – small groups of oligopolists acting together to further the interests of their particular group. Her main target was the Federation of British Industries (e.g., see Robinson, 1942b; 1943c; 1943d).

In an unpublished manuscript entitled 'Control of Monopoly' (JVR/iv/6; 15 March 1943), she set out some thoughts about the implications of monopolies. The ideas confirm that she maintained conclusions she had reached in the 1930s. There were five 'specific evils generally associated with monopoly'. The first is the tendency to maintain high profit margins. Sometimes this is done to protect the least efficient members of a trade association. Sometimes it exists as a tacit understanding against price-cutting. It does not necessarily indicate a high rate of profit if the industry is carrying excess capacity – an oversupply of capital. The effects of high margins are to keep the ratio of wages to prices down and to retain inefficient firms in the market. This adoption of a mark-up theory of pricing represents a departure from her neoclassical analysis of 1933. It is more consistent with the further implication she drew that high margins are associated with a distribution of income away from wages' share and the impact of this on effective demand.

The second 'evil' was the tendency for the monopolist or trade association to prevent new capital from entering the industry and so restricting investment. This compounded the tendency for a monopolistic industry to restrict output. The third was the inherent conservatism of owners of existing sunk capital towards new commodities or new methods of production. Monopolies were less likely to undertake investment in new technologies, as this would entail new costs in retraining labour and risks in new capital; they preferred to remain in safe markets in which they already had committed capital. Research, she argued, is directed in such a way that potentially useful discoveries are not made or are suppressed. Fourth, the presence of trade associations lends itself to the abuse of political power in the interests of private capital. Elsewhere, she refers to the power of business to restrict full employment policies and she also had in mind political favours.[14] Fifth, higher prices mean that Britain's exports are less competitive.

The conservatism, which she associated with monopolies, is compounded by the presence of agreements made between the corporations and their workers, whereby the employees agree to acquiesce to moderate wage claims in return for job security in the face of threats to their existing skills base and technological redundancy. Wage-sharing agreements discourage catch-up wage claims when the corporations raise their prices and are satisfactory to the workers if the prices of wage goods rise at the same rate or at less than the prices of the products they produce. The usual outcome of this practice is to redistribute income towards profits which again impacts upon aggregate consumption and investment. At the same time, these practices discourage labour mobility and innovation.

Next she asks: is it possible to return to a competitive market structure, and is it desirable? That is, even if such a state could be attained, does the theory of free competition actually deliver the optimal outcome? She adds to her earlier critique of *laisser-faire*, pointing out the inefficiencies surrounding non-price competition and the tendency for competition to drive down wages. Furthermore in the competitive economy, firms are unaware of their rivals' strategies, making for large-scale misdirection of resources. She suggests some measures to restore justice to competitiveness, including reform of the patent law, reform of the libel law (to prevent misleading advertising), the imposition of a minimum wage and stringent labour laws to encourage 'good employers', and control over some of the stages of production such as to allow other stages to be competitive. She is clearly in favour of markets which are, in some ways at least, regulated so that those which are competitive can operate freely and those that are not can be managed. It is an unsatisfactory theoretical compromise.

Joan Robinson acknowledges that 'The private profit system has to its credit stupendous achievements in the development of technique' (Robinson, 1943a, 20). A new economic system can be developed which makes use of all that knowledge: 'now that the advance has been made, some different system may ... hold out better prospects for the future' (ibid., p. 8). This can be done 'without sacrificing the technical complexity which capitalism has brought into existence' (ibid., p. 9). The centralisation of investment under a National Investment Board (NIB) would engender, she argues, better conditions for research and innovation, by overcoming the repressive effects on change of monopolies. She also airs a view that the era of single genius inventors is passed and that now science progresses more by collective research such as would be conducted under the auspices of the NIB (Robinson, 1943a).[15] '[T]he age of bright ideas is already gone. The modern scientist works as one of a team in an expensively equipped laboratory. ... under a planned system scientists and technicians, given adequate facilities, would supply a superabundance of new discoveries' (Robinson, 1943f, 23). She was not immune to idealising at times; to the above she added: 'no-one has ever suggested that scientists need the profit motive to keep their minds alive' (ibid., p. 24).

To create and sustain full employment, there needs to be control over investment and the direction of large industry groups gives that control to the state. To exercise control over monopolised industries, she advocates nationalisation, particularly where the monopoly exists for technical reasons of scale economies. Owners of firms to be nationalised should be compensated from a general fund made up, for example, from taxes on all forms of wealth.

It is interesting to note that Galbraith at around this time was developing completely different and more complex ideas about the method of understanding monopolies and their implications for economic dynamics (see, for example, Galbraith, 1948; also Rothschild, 1947). Joan Robinson's world seems to have been contained by the exigencies of war: where she associated stagnation of ideas with monopolies, Galbraith was suggesting a power in their heightened competitiveness.

5.3 Keynes and Kalecki

Another reason for the lack of employment in a capitalist economy, she argued, was the unequal distribution of income – this underlay her interpretation of Keynes's theory of effective demand. (Her booklet (Robinson, 1943h) is an introduction to Keynesian economics.) The distribution of purchasing power bore no relationship to the distribution of needs. As, she argued, under a monopolistic industry structure, income tends to be distributed towards profits and away from wages, a higher and higher portion of it is saved and not consumed. Nonetheless she saw that the lack of investment demand posed the fundamental threat to prosperity. First, low levels of effective demand resulting from an unequal distribution of income discouraged investment and secondly, the capacity-creating effect of investment and its tendency to reduce future planned investment together meant that bursts of investment expenditure tended to be followed by falling profits and subsequent slumps in output and employment. This mechanism she offered as a critique of *laisser-faire* theory itself as well as a critique of the system (Robinson, 1943a; 1943h). Nevertheless she differentiated her theory from that of Harrod (Harrod, 1936) in a letter to Kaldor:

> You seem to accept the Harrod point of view that the falling value of the multiplier [due to a secular rise in income and a consequent redistribution in favour of profits] is important and to neglect the main point, ie, the falling rate of profit per unit of capital as the amount of physical capital in existence increases. I hold that (a) probably in fact the multiplier alters very little over the ordinary range of fluctuations ...; (b) that even if the multiplier does fall appreciably this has quite a minor importance. It seems to me that the neglect of the very simple and very fundamental fact of capital accumulation lowering the rate of profit leads people to overestimate the importance of ... points such as falling value of the multiplier.
>
> (NK 3/30/177/12; 22 September 1937)

Indeed, it is Harrod's combination of 'The Multiplier' with 'The Relation' which Keynes failed to note,[16] which marks Harrod's contribution, but in her (Robinson, 1936b) review of Harrod's *Trade Cycle* she concluded that 'the essential part which is played by the accumulation of capital in curtailing the inducement to invest is not given its due prominence in Mr. Harrod's analysis'. This comment, together with her views on a falling rate of profits as capital accumulates, suggests Kalecki's influence. She met Kalecki in 1936 and read his work in English,[17] enough to see how it complemented and extended Keynes's theories. Kalecki (1936, 1939a) was presenting both a basis for a theory of distribution and pricing at the level of the firm and industry, and an aggregate theory of output, employment and distribution in a monopolistic environment. He developed a mark-up theory of pricing, arguing that simple profit-maximising is insufficient for understanding pricing behaviour. He, too, was responding to the fundamental criticisms that Sraffa had made of Marshall's theory[18] and was developing an analytical structure that differed from the 'new' theories of the 1930s, rejecting the singular use of equilibrium theory. Kalecki's work offered the possibility of a theory of output and employment which showed the likelihood of unemployment equilibria, combined with a theory of distribution within an imperfect market structure. Subsequently, Joan Robinson, as we saw, acknowledged that '[it] was Michal Kalecki rather than I who brought imperfect competition into touch with the theory of employment' (Robinson, 1969 (1933a), Preface, viii).

5.4 Planning

'Under free market capitalism, the institutions and agents of capitalism serve a number of functions: they initiate schemes which decide what is to be produced and by what capital equipment; they manage the day-to-day running of industry; they provide the savings which make capital accumulation possible and operate financial mechanisms which bring together lender and borrower. These functions, under latter day capitalism, are not very well fulfilled' (Robinson, 1943c). Capitalism requires planning if it is to meet the full employment objective. Planning can answer both elements of her objections to *laisser-faire* capitalism, its inefficient and unequal market structure, and its tendency to lack of effective demand. 'A Socialist system must evolve a method of administration that allows a large element of individual responsibility and initiative in matters of detail, within the general framework of the plan. But Socialism does require that the main decisions governing economic life should be taken consciously by the agents of the community' (ibid.).

To be successful, Keynesian policies required substantial institutional reform such as the introduction of an NIB. She had in 1933 contributed to a research group organised by Colin Clark for the Society for Socialist Propaganda and the New Fabian Research Bureau, on the problem of capital supply and of the form and powers of an NIB.[19] An NIB would be a central part of the overall economic plan. She argued (Robinson, 1943g) that the provision of capital goods need not be nationalised; it is the demand for capital goods which needs to be regulated. The NIB would make long-term plans to mobilise the capital resources available and ensure an efficient distribution of resources relative to needs. It could issue and raise loans. The Fabians proposed that state control over the sectors of fuel and power, finance, foreign trade and transport would give it the necessary power to address the problem of insufficient investment demand (e.g., Robinson, 1942a; 1943g). With the state controlling such a broad base of investment, there was little scope for remaining private investment to disrupt the economic plan. Nevertheless in one place she advocates complete nationalisation of the productive sector (Robinson, 1943a): 'So long as the general pattern of economic life is laid out by private property, a patch of national control here and there cannot make any great improvement in the design' (ibid., 19). She would leave some fringe consumer items in the hands of private production just to provide some choice. She looks, uncritically and idealistically, to Russia as an example of successful, rational planning (Robinson, 1943g, 15). The Soviet example was an inspiration to the socialists and Joan Robinson defended Stalin into the 1950s and 1960s.[20]

On the grounds that 'It is widely agreed that the fundamental cause of mass unemployment lies in the failure of consuming power to keep pace with productive power in an unregulated economy' (Robinson, 1943d), she proposed (her adaptation of) a Beveridge-style plan which would simultaneously redistribute income towards wage-earners and give 'control over a sufficient proportion of the demand for new capital equipment' (ibid.) to the state.

5.5 Budgeting: 'Deficit finance is a policy of reform not revolution' (Robinson, 1944a)

To give form to this plan, she outlines the elements of a budget which would best meet its objectives. The budget, she argues, expresses a view about the relations between the government and the rest of the economy, viz., industry and trade and individuals. Keynes (1933a) had suggested that 'the next budget should be divided into two parts one of which shall include those items of expenditure which it would be proper to treat as loan expenditure in present circumstances'. Some years later, he presented the national accounts in such a way that loans to the public and the private sectors could be distinguished, and budgetary and spending policies then based on achieving a full employment level of output: 'the purpose is to present a sharp distinction between the policy of collecting in taxes less than the current non-capital expenditure of the state as a means of stimulating *consumption* and the policy of the Treasury's influencing public capital expenditure as a means of stimulating *investment*. There are times and occasions for each of these policies; but they are essentially different and each, to the extent that it is applied, operates as an *alternative* to the other.' (Keynes, 1945, 406; emphasis in original) and 'one of the principal purposes of the Public Capital Budget was to balance and stabilise the investment budget for the national economy as a whole' (ibid., 409). This was Joan Robinson's view exactly. She also shared Keynes's later (1945) view that 'the outlets for public investment are not yet nearly saturated and ... for the time being, at least, we are more concerned with increasing the capital equipment of the nation than with raising the immediate standards of private consumption' (ibid., 409–10). Of course, to the extent that there were resources available, the public investment would generate higher levels of private consumption.

Joan Robinson (1944a) advocates a similar budgetary system with three separate accounts: an Ordinary Budget, a Social Insurance Budget or 'Beveridge Budget' and the Capital or Loan Account. While the first two should be such as to balance at full employment, the last should aim to maintain full employment. A minister of national development would have as her/his scope the whole economy, and the whole range of activity, including private and public investment, investment in social infrastructure, consumption, administration and defence. The minister could issue loans from the Capital Budget Account to public sector authorities, local authorities or the private sector. This minister's decisions should be in real terms, 'in terms of man-power, productive capacity and imported materials, as it is these which set the real limits to national production' (Robinson, 1944a) (although see Austin Robinson (1967) who was to warn in retrospect of the overriding concern with the aggregate position at the expense of coordinating structural details). The ordinary budget and the Social Insurance budget will both tend to be in deficit when there is unemployment. This will contribute to offsetting the slump and vice versa, the surplus on these budgets during a boom will be a brake on inflation. Inflation, like a depression, will probably need adjunct budgetary policies such as expenditure taxes. But expenditure taxes must be used selectively so that they are not effectively regressive.

5.6 Pricing and distribution

Another element of planning was the determination of prices. One basic feature of capitalism was its pricing system. Price control was one means of protecting or raising labour's share of the national income. The lack of a critique of the logic of the orthodox theory meant that there were some anomalies in the socialists' policies on the question of how to price, and a substantial group of economists including Joan Robinson believed that some form of marginal cost pricing was the way to ensure efficient allocation of resources while preserving consumers' freedom to choose. In some notes on 'The economic system in a socialist state', she stated: 'If private enterprise were abolished and all production controlled by a central plan, it would be possible to reproduce by artificial means the workings of the ideal competitive system, and to achieve the results which the actual system has failed to bring about. But how far does the ideal competitive system really provide a working model for a socialist system?' (Robinson, 1937c). She seems to accept the validity of the orthodox theory of value but is ambivalent as to its relevance, concluding that its sphere of application is quite limited. Elsewhere, she stated that 'if all business men lived up to the textbook postulates, always aiming to maximise profits and always producing in the most efficient manner available, private investment would regulate itself and productive capacity would automatically expand at the required pace' (Robinson, 1945b; *C.E.P.*, vol. I, 1951, 100). The role of the pricing mechanism was then a divisive issue among the socialists.[21] Lerner (1944), using general equilibrium analysis, showed that equating price to marginal cost would create an allocation of resources which would be efficient in terms of both production and consumption. The freedom to consumers, which this system allowed, complemented their political freedom in a democracy. Others were suspicious of using this orthodox theory for socialist policy and preferred planned central control over prices. Joan Robinson advocated some price control especially if there was to be a need for post-war rationing, with price subsidies for necessities (Robinson, 1943c; 1943d). In the market for commodities which were more optional, she advocated marginal cost pricing and for luxuries, an expenditure tax. Prices should be set so that profit margins are just enough to pressure firms to operate at near full capacity, thus eliminating inefficient firms while maintaining firms' total profits. She also leaves little room for private expenditure decisions, arguing that advertising and popular culture form consumers' preferences and these are at least as arbitrary as the provision by the socialist state, of basic needs. 'In minor matters the pricing system could be maintained' (ibid.). In Joan Robinson (1942b), she argues for the need for marginal values in pricing. Dobb (1941) pointed out to her that '[Marx] is contrasting the price-form with the social essence, and is saying that the latter could be *different* under socialism *even if* the price-form remained the same' (Dobb's emphasis; JVR vii/120/42).

Policies to address redistribution directly acted, for example, through minimum wage legislation, educational reforms, the social security system and progressive direct taxation, keeping in mind incentive effects, specific indirect taxes which targeted luxury goods, controls on prices and so on, profit margins and even, she suggests, extending the wartime provision of utility goods as a way to stop wastage from advertising and unnecessary differentiation (Robinson, 1943b; 1943g, 19–20). In general, she was impressed with the success of the wartime measures of rationing introduced to counter inflationary tendencies and stretch resources, and sees these as reasonably tolerated and so as politically feasible to extend to post-war readjustment (Robinson, 1943c), although she observes wryly towards the end of the war that the English are longing for their cream buns (Robinson, 2004). She seems undaunted by the associated bureaucracy or problems of compliance with such restrictions.

5.7 Monetary policy

Joan Robinson proposed through this period a cheap money policy. She argued that now it is clear that the rate of interest is more or less arbitrarily set by the Treasury and the Bank of England, it is no longer an economic instrument but a political one (Robinson, 1943g, 22–3). To pursue a cheap money policy after the war would mean abandoning the rate of interest as a means to counter inflation. It is not effective in this role, she argues, advocating low interest rates for accessible loans for consumer capital spending and for private investment, and also as a way to keep down government repayments on its debt (Robinson, ibid.; see also Robinson, 1944b; Howson, 1988). Low interest rates would also minimise the wealth of the rentier class (*op. cit.*, 22–3). Among her papers is a manuscript entitled 'The rate of interest' written during the war (JVR/ii/4/1–4). Here, she advocates the use of cheap money as a long-run development strategy. The rate of interest can be kept low because there is no limit to the amount of borrowing that the state can do.[22] If the public is not confident that bond prices will be maintained, the government can borrow from the banks to ensure that they are. A low long-run rate of interest encourages investment in projects with long-run time horizons, like railway electrification or industrial development, and it reduces rentier income. The addition to the value of income-earning assets could be neutralised by appropriate taxation. The apparent choice is between the short-run use of the rate of interest in an attempt to manipulate spending and the long-run use of cheap money to encourage economic development; it is the latter which is effective.[23]

5.8 The role of unemployment

Having solved the problems of unemployment and inequality by planning and redistributive budgeting, there is then the further problem arising from sustained full employment: '[unemployment] is part of the essential mechanism of the system, and has a definite function to fulfil. ... The first function of unemployment ... is that it maintains the authority of master over man' (Robinson, 1943e; also 1943b; see also Kalecki, 1943). Sustained full employment alters that balance. Furthermore, unemployment, by reducing the pressure on money-wages, keeps prices relatively stable. Sustained full employment puts constant upward pressure on money-wages. The industrialists respond by putting up prices. An arbitrary redistribution then occurs both between wages and profits and between groups of wage-earners. She suggests various responses to this pressure such as controlling profit margins or allowing wages to increase relative to prices (e.g., see Robinson, 1943c). Where unemployment or wage pressures are due to structural problems, she favours means to facilitate a flexible labour market. She is opposed to using wage differentials to attract labour out of one industry towards another more prosperous, arguing instead that workers will be attracted to new jobs as they appear. 'I believe that using relative wage rates to make the labour force respond to changes in supply and demand for commodities is not classical laisser-faire doctrine and is in fact of very dubious advantage' (letter to James Meade, 1947; Meade 3/5). If an industry needed to shed labour and it lowered its wages, why should those workers who remained lose the element of rent they were receiving in the initial wage? Alternatively, if this industry wanted to attract labour, does it have to raise the wages of all existing workers to those of the new labour? She argues that

> I think it is very doubtful if wage rates (a) can (b) should be used as part of the pricing system to regulate labour movements. Classical theory surely is that wages should equalise net advantages in some long-run sense, and that profits should reflect the [long-run] changes in supply and demand for commodities. Industries expand when profits are above average and this calls in the required labour. If Labour is in reality insufficiently mobile to make this happen it should be made more mobile – It is here that we have to look for the right kind of remedies.
>
> (ibid.)[24]

This letter is interesting for her uncharacteristic reference to classical long-period theory. Here she is following the argument that relative wages settle over the long period to reflect job characteristics, and the movements of labour will be in response to profitability and so the expanded availability of jobs in emerging markets. She is arguing tangentially to Salter (1960) that if wages are related to industry or firm productivity or productivity change, declining (and low) productivity industries will be sustained as their costs are low while high (and increasing) productivity industries will not expand as much as otherwise, or will be priced out by rising costs (see also Harcourt, 1997b; 2001b, ch. 17). Thus, the overall effect on the economy of industry-specific wage claims is to slow down investment, productivity change and growth. Nevertheless she maintains that 'a rational society would certainly not contain the enormous inequalities which exist in capitalist or feudal states, and would not recognise mere ownership of property as a source of income, but it would have to make use of differences in income as an incentive to work and to acquire knowledge and skill, so that complete equality could not be attained' (Robinson, 1943g, 16). There is a need for compromise in deciding on wage levels, she argues (ibid.); there are two separate principles: payment in response to need and in response to effort. She advocates a wage agreement of some kind as part of the programme of market reform; such as payment by results, profit-sharing and an extension of works councils which give the employees a voice in the daily running of the industry.[25] Such strategies could preserve relative shares and stable prices while allowing 'full' employment. There should also be a safety net of a minimum wage.

5.9 Balance of payments

In a BBC radio broadcast (Robinson, 1943h) and in a talk to the British Council in 1945 (Robinson, 2004), Robinson extends her argument to take into account Britain's desperate balance of payments prospects in the post-war period; Britain not only had massive war debts to the US but also to its own outposts, it had sold much of its foreign income-earning assets, and it had much diminished domestic productive capacity. Also fearing the loss of export markets, she urges the leading nations of the world to pursue full employment policies so that each can expand and provide markets for the other. There is as well an underlying fear that the US will not cooperate in this and in fact will experience a slump post-war and this will further damage Britain's exports prospects (Robinson, 1944b; letter to Keynes, JVR /vii/240/25–6). The post-war economy will be characterised by changing international and domestic markets and Britain will need a flexible labour force 'and some authority to take a world view and direct labour to where it is needed' (Robinson, 1943h; also Robinson, 2004). She cautions that post-war import spending will have to be restrained, Britain would be mobilising its resources for peacetime production as well as exports and its export markets were not certain as the US dictated the commercial policy of post-war international trade agreements. Pursuing a full employment policy will create a higher demand for imports. She suggests (Robinson, 1943d) that the wartime controls over foreign exchange and imported raw materials and domestic investment in import-replacement industries will provide the basis for a system that can regulate the balance of trade and allow for full employment. A corollary to this, she argues, referring to the collapse of the currency in 1931, is control over capital movements in order to prevent capital flights. Hot money destroyed the payments system in the 1930s when there was almost complete freedom of movement of all currencies,[26] and a new system of payments would need to have strategies in place to prevent this from recurring (Robinson, 1944b; 1944c): 'private owners of wealth ought to be deprived of the right to move their funds around the world according to their private fancies' (Robinson, 1944b, 247). She pursues the implications of a free market in currencies in several letters to Meade (Meade 2/4 107, 108) worrying about the plight of countries with relatively unsophisticated financial institutions.

There are two arms to international policy: the commercial and the currency plans. If Britain is to lose control over its commercial policy, that is, to surrender its Imperial Preferences system of trade and adopt a non-discriminatory trading policy, it must be free to decide on its currency strategy. 'The main question for Great Britain is whether it is possible to make ends meet under a system of non-discriminatory multilateral trade, or whether the only resort is to fix up bilateral bargains, buying imports only from those countries which are willing to take payment in British goods' (ibid., 249–50). This short-run strategy will be crucial, whatever the long-run procedures are. State monopoly of foreign trade might be necessary but this would entail setting prices as well.

Joan Robinson examined the proposals of the US and the UK for a stable system of international payments (Robinson, 1943i). The first requirement, she argued, was control over capital flows.

The second requirement was protection against the possibility of chronic disequilibrium in the balance of payments of a major trading country. She illustrates this, with little subtlety, by describing a major country running a persistent surplus against which its trading partners can only protect themselves by domestic deflation and contraction. A combined pursuit by all trading partners of full employment policies is necessary. The plan she is discussing is essentially Bancor[27]; it operates by having a central Fund which holds deposits in the central bank of each country. A chronic surplus country would therefore find reserves of its own currency held by other countries, scarce. The Fund then rations the scarce currency so that trade with that country is cut back, but other international transactions are not reduced. An international deflation and contraction are avoided. To avoid rationing of its own currency, a chronic surplus country could increase its foreign lending to cover its export surplus.

The third requirement is stability of exchange rates. Leaving each country to independently fix its own rates could lead to competitive devaluations, for example. The plan is for the Fund and the member nations to settle the exchange rates and then for countries to maintain these rates within a margin. The plan will not come into effect until a country feels it has readjusted from the effects of being at war, so discussion of it is, she muses, academic.

In a letter (7 April 1948) Meade cautioned against relying on the scarce currency clause as a method of containing the British deficit, suggesting that exports to the US and imports from them should be monitored through the price mechanism. Joan Robinson maintained that import controls were justified in the circumstances and that the US would not retaliate. Meade objected: 'you will never get a permanently scientific use of import controls' as countries successively impose protection in response to others (Meade 3/6.59).

Joan Robinson (1946a) examines the adjustment mechanism of classical trade theory under the assumption of full employment. She demonstrates that without the assumption of full employment, none of the structural adjustments need ever take place; that the outcome could easily be chronic imbalance with its resultant institutional implications. Further, the mechanisms by themselves do not work automatically; they may be confined to only a range of values or they may be, for various reasons, extremely unresponsive. '[I]t is necessary to recognise that the classical doctrine does not exclude starvation from the mechanism by which equilibrium tends to be established' (Robinson, 1946a, *C.E.P.*, vol. I, 1951, 189). Her conclusion is that adjustment could be possible only if there were conscious trading policies and if all trading partners undertook full employment policies in their domestic economies. Planning was necessary for both domestic and international trade balance.

5.10 Conclusion

Joan Robinson, along with many socialist economists, used the new orthodox economics and Keynes's theories as bases for intervention to maintain full employment with the micro-arguments for intervention in industry or activities where the market failed. This juxtaposition of the new orthodox theory with Keynes's analysis was popularly revealed by, for example, Meade (1936) and Lerner (1944). Durbin notes that this rationale was the precursor of the neoclassical synthesis after the war (1985, 276). Joan Robinson still maintained that theory was separable from politics during this period (Robinson, 1932a, 1933c). She chose political or moral objectives and then developed her theory 'scientifically' to produce policies which would achieve these. Her response to Sraffa (1926) was to develop what she saw as the more relevant theory of imperfect competition from which she could then draw policy. She had two branches of theory for two problems: imperfect competition theory for the problems created by monopolies and Keynesian theory for the problems of unemployment. The socialist movement was in its ascendancy and her ideas for socialist planning supported those popularly held. Within her many pamphlets and statements were the fragments of an overall economic plan which integrated a national investment policy with nationalisation, social security, wages policies, budgeting and external controls. It was idealistic and not well-informed by contemporary debates over planning and over the Soviet case; she did not heed Dobb's advice to move away from *a priori* argument and take notice of the historical changes in order to understand the economic process (Dobb, 1941). After the war, she returned to abstract theory; later, realising that her 'new' theory, her response to Sraffa, was not as she had originally perceived it, her critique became one of marginalism itself and her dualist approach ultimately gave way to a view that theory and ideology were essentially mixed in the economist's method (see Chapter 11).

6
The Making of *The Accumulation of Capital*

6.1

The Accumulation of Capital (1956) was intended to be Joan Robinson's *magnum opus*. It grew out of the advances she was making on many fronts in the years of World War II and afterwards.[1] The major influences on her were Keynes (of course), her work on Marx placed within a fruitful setting and approach by Kalecki,[2] Harrod's seminal work on dynamic theory just before (1939) and soon after the end of the war (1948), pressing real world problems associated with the post-war reconstruction of Europe and the emergence of consciousness about development in underdeveloped societies in the economics profession of the developed societies.

Keynes's revolution was increasingly being accepted in both academia and government. Attention was turning from the employment-creating effects of accumulation to its capacity-creating effects. Moreover, as Keynes had conquered the short period in a macroeconomic sense, at least as far as his immediate colleagues and disciples in Cambridge were concerned, so it was natural that they, when account is taken of these other influences as well, should turn their attention to the long period and so to 'the generalization of *The General Theory* to the long period'.

Piero Sraffa, virtually unknown to even his closest colleagues and friends, was following his own revolutionary new path in economic theory, criticising the conceptual and logical bases of the supply and demand theories in all their forms while simultaneously rehabilitating classical and Marxian political economy.[3] His influence would not come fully into the public domain until the publication of *Production of Commodities* in 1960. Hints of what was to come were in the 'Introduction' in 1951 to the Sraffa with the collaboration of Dobb edition of the works and correspondence of David Ricardo. Indeed, for Joan Robinson, the 'Introduction' to the Ricardo volumes brought a great flash of illumination about the nature and role of profits in advanced capitalist economies. When reprinting her 'Essays 1953' (originally published as 'a little known pamphlet ... by the Students Bookshop, Cambridge, in 1953' (*C.E.P.*, vol. IV, 1973b, v)) in volume IV of her *Collected Economic Papers* in 1973, she wrote:

> These essays were written in a hilarious mood after reading Piero Sraffa's Introduction ..., which caused me to see that the concept of the rate of profit on capital is essentially the same in Ricardo, Marx, Marshall and Keynes; while the essential difference between these, on the one side, and Walras, Pigou and the latter-day textbook writers, on the other, – is that the Ricardians are describing an historical process of accumulation in a changing world while the Walrasians dwell in a timeless equilibrium where there is no distinction between the future and the past.
>
> (*C.E.P.*, vol. IV, 1973b, 247)[4]

As well as these positive developments in the making of theory, there was also considerable attention given to methodological issues, again stimulated by Harrod's desire to replace static by dynamic analysis, or at least make the latter just as important, as a natural complement to the revived interest in distribution and growth over time, reinterpreted in the light of Keynes's and, in Joan Robinson's case, Kalecki's new theories. For Harrod, this new and exciting way of seeing and doing economics would make 'the old static formulation of problems [seem] stale, flat and unprofitable' (Harrod, 1939, 15). These concerns were, of course, the original province of classical political economy and Marx, suppressed by the rise of neoclassical economics with its concentration on price formation and resource allocation in mostly competitive settings, usually in static settings as well. Joan Robinson is typically forthright about this. In the preface to her 1956 volume (v), she writes:

> Economic analysis, serving for two centuries to win an understanding of the Nature and Causes of the Wealth of Nations, has been fobbed off with another bride – a Theory of Value ... deep seated political reasons for the substitution ... also a purely technical reason ... excessively difficult to conduct an analysis of over-all movements of an economy through time, involving changes in population, capital accumulation and technical change, at the same

time as an analysis of the detailed relations between output and price of particular commodities ... Economists for the last hundred years have sacrificed dynamic theory in order to discuss relative prices ... unfortunate [because] such a drastic departure from reality [makes verification of results impossible and rules out] discussion of most of the problems that are actually interesting [condemning] economics to ... arid formalism.

In Joan Robinson's thinking, this led her to reappraise what equilibrium meant in the short period and the long period, especially in a macroeconomic setting. She coupled this with her increasing dissatisfaction with both neoclassical concepts and methods, as she saw them, especially in the theory of distribution and its accompanying relevance for a discussion of the choice of technique in the economy as a whole in analysing the process of growth. The outcome was both a sustained attack on neoclassical and neo-neoclassical results and procedures, and the development of distribution and growth theory in a classical–Marxian–Kaleckian–Keynesian setting. All these developments may be judged as innovative, revolutionary in their effects, perhaps even so shocking that, now all the principal first-generation pioneers are dead, much of the profession, following good economic practice, is inclined to assume that they and their ideas never existed in the first place.

With such a background, it is not surprising that *The Accumulation of Capital* was published when its author was the same age as Keynes was when *The General Theory* was published. Again, just as she wrote *Introduction to the Theory of Employment* (1937a), her 'told-to-the-children' book (Keynes, *C.W.*, vol. XIV, 1973b, 148), to help explain the new theory, so she wrote her *Essays in the Theory of Economic Growth* (1962e) to explain *The Accumulation of Capital* to those who were mystified, or irritated, or both, by the 1956 volume. Certainly, the 1962 volume was a great help in extracting messages that had been overlaid or were not brought out as clearly in her 'big book' (though the *Essays* too are not always easy-going).

All the above themes may be found in a number of articles and chapters in books preceding the publication of *The Accumulation of Capital*. Thus, in *The Rate of Interest and Other Essays* (1952a), we are told immediately that

the THEME of these essays is the analysis of a dynamic economic system [- dynamic analysis in the sense] that it cannot explain how an economy behaves in given conditions, without reference to past

> history; ... static analysis purports to describe a position of equilibrium which the system will reach ... if the given conditions remain unchanged for long enough no matter where it started from.

She adds:

> Short-period analysis is concerned with the equilibrium of a system with a given stock of capital and ... given expectations about the future. Past history is thus put into the initial conditions, so the analysis is static in itself ... yet part of a dynamic theory. [Thus] Keynes' General Theory, [though] strictly static in form, ... opened the way for a great outburst of analysis of dynamic problems.
>
> (Robinson, 1952a, v)

After the introductory title essay, we have 'Notes on the economics of technical progress', 'The Generalisation of the General Theory' and 'Acknowledgments and disclaimers', in which Marx, Marshall, Rosa Luxemburg, contemporaries Kalecki and Harrod, and the acceleration principle and general, are named. The collection was preceded by her long introduction to the English translation of Rosa Luxemburg's *Accumulation of Capital* in 1951 (Robinson, 1951a). Following it were her very important 1953 essays, *On Re-reading Marx*, to which we have already referred and which contain her Cambridge economist's visit to Oxford essay where some of her methodological critiques about time and space in economic analysis are presented in a stark and compelling manner (especially when read with hindsight) and, of course, her 1953–4 *Review of Economic Studies* paper which brought the Cambridge–Cambridge debates in capital theory into the public domain for the first time.

There are in addition, an *Economic Journal* article, 'The model of an expanding economy' (1952b) and her Delhi School of Economics lecture on 'Marx, Marshall and Keynes'. These are reprinted in volume II of her *C.E.P.* (1960), the preface to which is dated December 1959. Significantly, the author writes that the essays belong 'to the field of what is sometimes called post-Keynesian economics' (v). To this must be added her difficult but profound essays, 'The philosophy of prices', 'Notes on the theory of economic development' and 'Population and development'. The second section of the volume, 'highly scholastic, ... consists of various chips from the block from which [she] hacked [*The*] *Accumulation of Capital*' (v).

It is, therefore, quite extraordinary on how many fronts she was advancing virtually simultaneously. (Just for good measure, she reprinted in the same volume two retrospective essays on imperfect competition and three on monetary matters, two on the rate of interest, one on full employment and inflation.) The interconnectedness between all of them was certainly clear in her own mind though, naturally, when taking stock at various points in time, she was to feel that clarity, emphasis, proportion and perspective had not always been attained. Especially, as we have noted, is this true of *The Accumulation of Capital* and her perception of its reception, which led her to publish *Essays* in 1962 in order to provide readers with a clearer perspective. In the Preface, she writes:

> The essays ... might be regarded as an introduction rather than ... a supplement to [her] *Accumulation* ... [which] was found excessively difficult. The main fault [was] too terse an exposition of the main ideas ... and a failure to mark sufficiently sharply the departure from the confused but weighty corpus of traditional teaching ... required when ... a Keynesian approach to long-period problems [was adopted]. [She offered] the present volume with apologies to readers whose heads ached over the earlier one.
>
> (v)

Nevertheless it could be argued that, as ever, she may have been too hard on herself; for, if we read Tibor Barna's review of the 1956 volume (Barna, 1957; Kerr with Harcourt (eds.), 2002, vol. III, 30–3), it is apparent that serious readers could absorb both the big picture, as it were, and the minutiae of what she presented. Barna wrote:

> The object of Mrs. Robinson's analysis is to clarify the consequences and the proximate causes of differences in, and changes in, the rate of accumulation ... Mrs. Robinson works with a dynamic two-sector linear model, and in ... Book II, without the use of mathematics or diagrams, squeezes all the answers out of her model ... [Her] achievement is [to have] written a full-scale textbook on what is probably the most important post-war subject by making use of an efficient dynamic theory.
>
> (Barna (1957) in Kerr with Harcourt (eds.) (2002), vol. III, 30–1, 33)

In contrast, we have Abba Lerner's rather perplexed review (Lerner, 1957; Kerr with Harcourt (eds.), 2002, vol. III, 34–40). For him, the volume is 'a pearl whose most conspicuous product is irritation' (Kerr with Harcourt (eds.), 2002, vol. III, 34). His judgement is that 'the most useful parts of the book are the errors and the ingenious confusions the search for which can give such first-class exercise in economics to graduate students (and to professors) who could do with a tough work out and who can stand the tough cuteness of Mrs. Robinson's style' [Ouch] (Lerner, 1957, in Kerr with Harcourt (eds.), 2002, vol. III, 40). He covers himself by a rueful reference to his own chastening experience with Joan Robinson (and friends) concerning *The General Theory* whereby he had come to scoff but remained to pray, his 'disturbing memory of ... feeling similarly supercilious about queer things going on in Cambridge ... before Mrs Robinson and her friends so patiently educated [him] on the incipient Keynesian revolution' (Lerner, 1957, in Kerr with Harcourt (eds.), 2002, vol. III, 34–5; see Chapter 2).

Be that as it may, her most enthusiastic and sympathetic readers regard the *Essays* as the best place to go in order to understand and build on her contributions as far as positive economic analysis of the dynamic processes at work in modern capitalist economies are concerned. This comes out clearly in Athanasios (Tom) Asimakopulos (1969; 1970) reprinted in Kerr with Harcourt (eds.), (2002), vol. III, 119–43, and in his last assessment after her death and sadly, just before his own, Asimakopulos (1991) reprinted in Kerr with Harcourt (eds.), (2002), vol. III, 144–63. He concluded that her 'extension of Keynes's General Theory to the long period is faithful to the essential features of that theory' (Asimakopulos, 1991, in Kerr with Harcourt (eds.), 2002, vol. III, 160).

Again, if we examine Harvey Gram's and Vivian Walsh's superb evaluation in the 1983 *Journal of Economic Literature*, Gram and Walsh (1983) reprinted in Kerr with Harcourt (eds.), (2002), vol. V, 365–406, of her economics in retrospect, an evaluation based principally on their reading of her five volumes of *Collected Economic Papers*, we find that most of their evidence for the masterly account they give of her approaches and achievements comes from sources other than *The Accumulation of Capital* itself (though it is clearly one, often the most important, starting point for the issues discussed and interconnections brought out).[5]

6.2

As we saw, see pp. 77–78 above, in the Preface to *The Accumulation of Capital*, Joan Robinson looked at the broad sweep of development in our discipline, from Adam Smith to the Keynesian revolution and after. Having outlined the preoccupation of the classical economists and Marx with distribution, accumulation and growth, underwritten by the need for a theory of value, she mentions the 100 years or so of neoclassical dominance where the principal propositions related to explanations of prices and the allocation of scarce resources between competing ends, usually in a static setting, so ignoring growth and technical progress but not the welfare implications. The trade cycle and other issues were often banished to an underworld until historical events and the Keynesian revolution brought them into focus again, with Keynes ultimately as interested in explaining sustained unemployment in capitalist economies as in explaining cyclical processes.

Now Joan Robinson's object was to move neoclassical preoccupations off stage and return to classical issues in the light of the advances associated with Keynes and Kalecki. (In her case, it was actually more Kalecki than Keynes because of Kalecki's direct link to Marx and Marx's schemes of reproduction.) In a preface to a later edition of her book, probably written in or after 1959 but never published, she explained very clearly the four main issues and questions with which she was concerned.

She considers a model of an unregulated free enterprise economy in which firms 'within the limits set by their command of finance' determine the rate of accumulation, while the members of the public, constrained 'by their command of purchasing power, are free to make the rate of expenditure what they please ... [a] model ... not unrealistic in essential respects'.

The model may be used 'to analyse the chances and changes of an economy as time goes by' by considering 'four distinct groups of questions':

(1) We make comparisons of situations, each with its own past, developing into its own future, which are different in some respect (for instance, the rate of accumulation going on in each) to see what the postulated difference entails.
(2) We trace the path which a single economy follows when the technical conditions (including their rate of change) and the propensities to consume and to invest are constant through time.
(3) We trace the consequences of a change in any one of these conditions for the future development of the economy.
(4) We examine the short-period reaction of the economy to unexpected events.

The first group of questions is more naturally handled in terms of comparisons of steady states (including stationary states). The conditions for steady states to be achieved are set out with no implication that the unregulated behaviour of decision-makers will ever bring them about.

The second set of questions concerns what happens when one of the conditions for steady growth is not satisfied. The third set relates to the path which the economy will follow when, having been in a steady state, a basic change occurs, for example, 'an increase in monopoly which causes profit margins to increase'.

The fourth set concerns the reactions of the inducement to invest to current events in an uncertain world and relates to the possibility of oscillation in the transition from one state of affairs to another, or even to the generation of a trade cycle by 'mere uncertainty' without any change in basic conditions. In principle, the author claims, 'this type of analysis enables us to deal with all the possible vicissitudes of a developing economy and prepare the way for discussions of public policy'.

What tended to obscure these objectives set out so starkly was the simultaneous development of a concentration on the conditions for steady growth, especially with technical progress going on, which preoccupied both Joan Robinson and mainstream writers on these issues. Though she and Kahn clearly thought of Golden Age analysis as a preliminary to the real business of exploring dynamic processes in historical time, the way she presented the analysis in *The Accumulation of Capital*, with 'reality' often breaking through, tended to blur the analytical boundaries between the two. It is not until we get to the *Essays* and the developments built on them that we see that analysis of the medium term with short-period situations growing out of those that preceded them becomes centre stage. Even then, it was Goodwin and Kalecki more than Joan Robinson who were to make the most substantial advances on this front. Asimakopulos was not that far behind these other two; he used her approach but differed starkly from her in one respect. Increasingly, Joan Robinson was inclined to see the short period as a point in time, as an adjective not a noun, not a defined period. This was Asimakopulos's most serious criticism of her contributions and, in his own work, he always used the short period in the sense of a definite stretch of time which he believed to be faithful to Keynes's legacy and also to be the proper setting in which to develop Joan Robinson's insights and conjectures.

Nevertheless, if we use the unpublished Preface as our map, we may see more clearly the nature and purpose of the structure of her book and of the other papers that preceded and followed it.

Kahn was probably even more clear in his own mind than Joan Robinson about the distinction between necessary but preliminary analysis and descriptive analysis of processes. Thus, in his 1959 article in *Oxford Economic Papers*, he provided extremely clear statements of the principles involved. The article explains succinctly and clearly all that can be said and done within the confines of Golden Age analysis in which use is made of heroic assumptions because 'for [his] own part, [he desired] to learn to walk before he tried to run' (Kahn, 1959; 1972, 195). Kahn is especially clear on the use and abuse of identities – in this case, saving equals investment – and on the definitions of different classes of income which are implied by them. He also brings out beautifully the two-sided relationship between the rate of profits and accumulation which is a (Kaleckian) feature of the analysis; the correct definition of the rate of profits as an expected variable; the nature of technical progress and how it may be tackled within this framework; and the distinction between a bastard Golden Age, in which unemployment may exist and worsen over 'time', and a 'true' Golden Age, truly mythical, in which the labour force and the stock of capital goods are fully employed over 'time'. (In Harrod's terms, the first case implies that g_w is less than g_n; the second, that they are equal.) Kahn stresses that the analysis is *entirely* confined to differences (comparisons), that it does not relate to changes (processes). Thus

> [w]hen one speaks of a Golden Age being preferred [to another one], it means it would be preferable to be in it. But to be in it involves *having* been in it for a long time past, and enjoying the legacy of the past in terms of the accumulated stock of capital and the degree of mechanisation. The desirability of a movement from one ... to the other, and the manner in which it might be smoothly negotiated, is ... [an] important and difficult [problem]. ... This paper is ... no more than prolegomena to the solution of real problems.
>
> Kahn (1959; 1972; 206–7, emphasis in original)

6.3

Joan Robinson herself was searching for fundamental and simple principles which underlie the process of growth. In particular, she investigated the creation of the surplus in the consumption goods sector for use in the investment goods sector as wages of labour, concentrating on what determined how much *potential* accumulation could be obtained from a given potential surplus. The surplus itself depended on the available labour force, employment and the productivity of labour in the consumption goods sector and the real wage. Between them, they determined the potential buying power over labour in the investment goods sector. How much accumulation this potentially made possible was determined by the techniques of production in force there. In her first run through, she assumed there to be only one method of production known at any moment of time and technical progress was handled by asking how the one dominant method could be changed from period to period. This was a shorthand way of overcoming the problem of the choice of technique at a moment of time. (This was analysed in great detail later on in the book.)

By using this approach, the links between real saving and real investment could be made crystal clear while their interconnections in a capitalist economy could come in later on by using the Keynes/Kalecki analysis of the determination of planned investment expenditure, planned saving and the distribution of income and their effects on the overall level of output and employment. This served to provide the link between potential surplus creation and its realisation, now set in an analysis of distribution, accumulation and growth, rather than in a one-period analysis of employment and unemployment.[6]

By page 84, she has completed her analysis of the story of accumulation with one technique of production and, as yet, no technical progress.[7] Reading the chapters leading up to this over 50 years later, it is easier to see both the influence of Kalecki on her approach and her impatience to get to the second strand of the overall project, analysis of accumulation in historical time. This leads at times to her being inconsistent with her views about the nature of equilibrium in growth models and the incoherence of a story of getting into equilibrium (though she covers herself to some extent by discussing the nature of tranquil conditions which create an atmosphere and environment akin to those of a true Golden Age equilibrium state where expectations are assumed always to be realised so that the stock of capital goods currently in existence is always in accord with what was expected to happen when each part of it was first installed). We do not think though that, at this time, she had faced up fully to the question of fossils from the past being inappropriate for today's conditions and how they could be scrapped over time from the capital stock without bursting even surrogate Golden Age conditions.

With these provisos, she concisely states on pp 83–4 her previous arguments in four propositions. She concludes that though many of her 'conclusions will have to be extensively modified as the assumptions of one technique and no rentier consumption are relaxed ... the argument [nevertheless] holds good in all essential respects, and provides a picture of the basic characteristics of accumulation under the capitalist rules of the game' (84). The propositions are:

> In an economy with only one technique, and no consumption out of profits, when the supply of labour adapts itself to demand, starting from any given situation (produced by past history), the future rate of accumulation is limited:
>
> (1) By the technical surplus available above the subsistence wages for the workers employed.
> (2) Within that limit, ... by the surplus above the level of real wages that the workers are willing to accept and able to enforce (by creating an inflation barrier against a fall in real wages).
> (3) Within that limit, ... by the energy with which entrepreneurs carry it out.
> (4) When the size of the labour force is independent of the ... demand for workers, a maximum is set to the ... rate of accumulation by the rate of increase of the labour force. When accumulation fails to reach this rate there is growth of long-period unemployment.

Joan Robinson was an admirer of Wilfred Salter's work (1960, 1965) in which he sharpened up the vagueness of Marshall's analysis by showing how, by accumulation, technical progress could be embodied in the stock of capital goods without the need to scrap all previous vintages. The latter could be used for current production provided only that they could be expected to cover their variable costs; the latest vintages would only be embodied if they were expected to cover their expected *total* costs, including the normal rate of profits, by their expected proceeds. A temporary equilibrium (in a competitive situation) could be attained when, for each, separated in time, burst of technical advances, capacity had so increased that the prices of products produced only allowed the normal rate of profits to be received on the latest vintage. Salter also included an analysis of the choice of technique alongside the analysis of the determination of total investment expenditure in the firm, in the industry and, ultimately, in the economy as a whole.

Salter's influence is implicitly present in Joan Robinson's discussion of the diffusion of techniques in Chapter 9 ('Technical progress'), though, unlike Salter, she discusses first the case in which there is only one possible method of production for each commodity which is 'superior to all older ones at every level of wages' (85). The analysis of 'a spectrum of technical possibilities [with] different ratios of labour to capital in a given phase of knowledge' (85) is left to the next chapter (see Ch. 7).

She discusses the diffusion of techniques, referring, again implicitly, to Schumpeterian innovators taking the lead and to laggards being driven out by competitive (in a Marxian sense) forces. This allows her to discuss a leap frog effect which depends partly on the physical durability of new capital goods and partly on the strength of competition, which, in turn, often leads to scrapping, or, at least, retirement, long before the physical lives of machines have come to an end. She refers to the paradox of patents:

> [A] patent is a device to prevent the diffusion of new methods before the original investor has received profits adequate to induce the requisite investment'. [The justification of the system] is that by slowing down the diffusion of new techniques it ensures that there will be more progress to diffuse [, clearly] a system rooted in a contradiction.
>
> (87)

Joan Robinson sets out the conditions for stability, movements in accumulation and wages over time to ensure a matching of overall demand and supply (and their compositions) in the economy as a whole. She reproduces in words much the same conditions as those Marx set out in more formal terms in the schemes of reproduction. As with Marx, she points out that '[it] is only necessary to set out the conditions required for stability [steady advance] to see how precarious [its] preservation is under the capitalist rules of the game'.[8] She lists the conditions for the 'smooth development of a progressive economy'.

First, the stock of machines (in terms of productive capacity) must grow at the rate appropriate to the increase in output per worker that is taking place, while competition must ensure that prices so move relatively to money-wage rates as to keep equipment working at normal capacity, that is to say, real wages rise with output per worker so that sufficient demand occurs to absorb the ever-growing output of the ever-growing stock of equipment.[9]

Secondly, any chance discrepancy between available labour and equipment must be quickly eliminated. If there is surplus labour, the real wage must rise less fast than output per head but outlay in the investment goods sector must be such as to speed up accumulation in terms of productive capacity. If labour is scarce, real wages must rise more than output per head and the rate of accumulation must slow down. 'When this mechanism is operating the supply of capital goods is continuously adjusted to the supply of labour ... any tendency to surplus or scarcity ... is promptly corrected' (89).

She proceeds by narratives concerning two economies, Alaph and Beth, that momentarily are alike as far as their labour forces and phases of technical development are concerned, but which have reached this position by different histories with regard to past development, giving their decision-makers different expectations. Rates of accumulation have differed and therefore the distribution of their work forces and levels of real wages are also different. She then looks for the conditions which should prevail if the conditions in one economy change to those of the other so as to allow the first economy to follow a path of smooth development, one akin to that followed in the other economy. Such gradual transitions technically could take place 'but there is no mechanism provided by the capitalist rules of the game that can be relied upon to steer the economy on to the appropriate course' (92).

This analysis is followed by sections on under-consumption, weak and strong accumulation, and biased technical progress, culminating in her definition of the existence of a Golden Age: 'When technical progress is neutral,[10] and proceeding steadily, without any change in the time pattern of production, population growing ... at a steady rate and accumulation going on fast enough to supply productive capacity for all available labour, the rate of profit[s] tends to be constant and the level of real wages to rise with output per man [*sic*] ... no internal contradictions in the system ... [if] entrepreneurs have faith in the future and desire to accumulate at the same proportional rate as they have been doing in the past, there is no impediment to prevent them [and] the system develops smoothly [with output and the stock of capital (valued in terms of commodities) growing at a rate compounded of the rate of increase in the labour force and the rate of increase in output per worker]' (99). Joan Robinson adds:

> We may describe those conditions as a *golden age* (thus indicating that it represents a mythical state of affairs not likely to obtain in any actual economy).
>
> (99, emphasis in original)

Moreover, if the rate of technical progress and of population increase are given by nature, the Golden Age is a state of bliss since consumption increases at the maximum feasible rate compatible with maintaining such a rate. In Joan Robinson's view, this is the equivalent to $g_n = g_w = g_a$ in Harrod's (1939) analysis. But it is far away from reality because '[t]he limit to the rate of growth of wealth, over the long term, is set not by technical boundaries but by the lethargy which develops when the goad of competition and rising wage rates is blunted' (100).

6.4

In section II of Book II entitled 'The technical frontier', we start on the analysis which would have been most familiar to readers because of Joan Robinson's 1953–4 article, 'The production function and the theory of capital', which, as we noted (see p. 79 above), brought into the public domain what subsequently came to be known as the Cambridge–Cambridge debates in the theory of capital. We discuss this in greater detail in Chapter 7. Chapter 10 of her book is titled 'The spectrum of techniques' and at the end of the final paragraph, the author has a footnote which reads: '[t]he reader is warned that the argument ... is difficult out of proportion to its importance [, that] we shall return to conclusions substantially the same as those of the last chapter' (n1, 101). She tells us that the diagrams illustrating the argument are to be found below at p. 416 (actually p. 411 when we get there). In the third edition, published in 1969, as well as reproducing the sections from the previous editions, she added a postscript containing '[an] alternative form of the foregoing diagrams, which may be easier to follow [and which] had been developed from the analysis of Piero Sraffa's *Production of Commodities by Means of Commodities*' (426).

Then off we go, analysing the choice of technique in the economy as a whole, inspired by Knut Wicksell and using what became known as a book of blueprints containing different known ways of producing consumption goods. Joan Robinson discusses how and why one technique over a range of possible values of either the wage rate (w) or the rate of profits (r) will be dominant, and how, because of discreteness in techniques, there are unique w, r values at which adjacent techniques are equi-profitable (or, for a given value of the rate of interest equal to the value of the economy-wide r, allow the same w to be paid). On pp. 109–10, the Ruth Cohen curiosum (capital-reversing) is explained. In a footnote, Joan Robinson writes that what she has called 'a perverse relationship' was pointed out to her 'by Miss Ruth Cohen ... a somewhat intricate piece of analysis which is not of great importance' (n1, 109)!

These matters are discussed in the next chapter. Suffice it to say here that Joan Robinson was basically explaining *differences* – what technique(s) would dominate in possible Golden Ages according to the values postulated for one of the factor prices – rather than *changes*, processes occurring in historical time, though she sometimes writes as if the latter is being considered as well. As we noted, in later years she rejected this way of looking at the choice of technique in the investment decision when she brought the analysis of technical progress into the picture. That is to say, she subsequently rejected the traditional neoclassical distinction between moving *along* the production function in response to different values of the relative factor prices, on the one hand, and movements *of* the production function itself – new books of blue prints – as a result of technical change occurring, on the other (see Robinson, 1971, 103–4). In this she was joined by Kaldor who from 1957 to 1962 produced a number of versions of his technical progress function (see Kaldor, 1957; 1959a; 1959b; 1961) and Kaldor and Mirrlees (1962)). Kaldor was explicitly dealing with processes in (he hoped) historical time whereby new advances in knowledge and known alternative input ratios were simultaneously embodied in the stock of capital goods in the processes of accumulation and growth, with their accompanying effects on the distribution of income and the immediate levels of activity and income (see Harcourt, 2006b, 114–19) for a critical evaluation of Kaldor's approach.

Joan Robinson's description of business people's behaviour is a strange mixture of real world practice and pure theory, dare we say it, neoclassical theory at that? At one point, she is near suggesting the use of the pay-off or pay-back criterion in order to determine in which technique to invest (as well as to stave off the effects of inescapable uncertainty). At another point, she writes as if she were a bright graduate of a leading business school, describing in words what is happening in the DCF procedures taught there.

The chapter closes with some sensible remarks about some special cases which could 'deflect [entrepreneurs] from using the technique that (at the ruling wage rate) yields the highest obtainable rate of profit on capital' (110). The constraints/cases include finance, management, monopoly and monopsony. Always, she contrasts the behaviour most appropriate for a world of tranquility with that in the more real world of uncertainty and attendant risks. In the latter, flexibility is at a premium and this explains, amongst other things, 'the success of many small businesses using simple techniques in competition with highly mechanised giants' (113).

6.5

The next major issue Joan Robinson tackled was the analysis of technical progress (Chapters 16–18). She examined in isolation, as is were, from what went before what types of technical advance could, at least in principle, be consistent with Golden Age conditions being achieved and sustained. At the same time, she warned readers that the analysis and results were far from what actually would be observed in growing economies. She wrote before Salter had published his 1960 book and 1965 IEA chapter (the latter was a simultaneous analysis of choice of technique and technical advance, taking in both movements along the *ex ante* production function induced by factor prices *and* movements of the *ex ante* production function itself due to technical advances, for the economy as a whole). As we noted, Joan Robinson was familiar with his earlier analysis at the level of the firm and industry of the same processes.[11]

It is fair to say that Joan Robinson did not succeed in her 1956 book in integrating the analyses of these separate issues as well as she could have wished when she gathered her main findings together in Chapter 18, 'Synopsis of the theory of accumulation in the long run' (173–6). She did feel, as we have noted, that while these added details, they did not lead materially to a departure from the main thrust of her findings in the first major section of the volume. There are 20 major findings gathered together. The author indicates in which chapters the analysis that led to the propositions stated may be found. Reading with hindsight through her synopsis it is relatively easy to see the major influences on her procedures in the preceding pages.

First are Marx's schemes of production and reproduction, together with conditions that have to be satisfied for each period's potential output in all sectors (departments) and their compositions to be absorbed; that is to say, for aggregate demand to equal aggregate supply and for their compositions to match up. It was Marx's contention, of course, that it would only be a fluke if the acts of individual decision-makers when taken together resulted in these systemic conditions being met; and that the failure to meet them would cause instability and possibly crisis in the behaviour of competitive economies. As Claudio Sardoni (1981) has made clear, Marx's schemes were not forerunners of modern steady-state constant growth models, for in Marx's analysis, the rates of growth could vary from period to period provided that in each period, aggregate demand and supply and their compositions matched. Joan Robinson does not mention this explicitly, probably because she was intent on establishing the conditions which Golden Ages have to meet and sustain, though she was well aware of the consequences of this not occurring. Especially was this so because she had a clear understanding of the possible volatility of accumulation plans in capitalist societies so that the distinction between the potential surplus which techniques and the conditions of the class war made possible, on the one hand, and the possibility of its realisation in the sphere of distribution and exchange, on the other, was very much an explicit part of her thinking.

Also underlying her analysis is her attempt to solve the two problems thrown up by Harrod's seminal work: first, the stability or otherwise of the warranted rate of growth (g_w) – the rate of growth which if attained would persuade business people that they had made the correct decisions concerning accumulation and production so that they should continue the same rate of increase of accumulation in the future. As we know, if their decisions taken together do *not* put the economy on g_w, the economy is most likely to give out misleading signals which lead to decisions that take the economy further and further away from attaining g_w (see Harcourt, 2006b, 102–9).

Secondly, Harrod distinguishes between the potential rate of growth of the economy, its natural rate defined by growth in the labour force together with the rate at which the representative worker's productivity improves over time, and the expected, warranted and actual rates of growth (g_a). Works by Harrod himself, and subsequently by Solow, Swan and Meade as neoclassicals, on the one hand, and Kaldor, Kahn and Joan Robinson as post-Keynesians, on the other, have examined whether there are forces potentially available in the economy which would take g_w (and g_a) towards g_n. In the neoclassical case, this is achieved (in simple models) by changes induced in the capital–output ratio (v); in the post-Keynesian case, especially in Kaldor's 1955–6 article, it is achieved by induced changes in the saving ratio, s ($g_w = s/v$).

A weakness in all these analyses, up to which Joan Robinson faces but does not, we think, solve satisfactorily, is Harrods's assumption that g_n be regarded as independent of the values of g_w and g_a. This assumption cannot be sustained once it is recognised that improvements in labour productivity are the direct outcome of the rate at which technical advances are embodied in the stock of capital goods by actual rates of accumulation, and that the growth of the labour force is endogenous, not exogenous (see Harcourt, 2006b, 109–13).

She also takes from the classicals and Marx, usually through Sraffa's revival of their approach, the concept of the rate of profits, where it comes from and what determines its size. When she wrote *The Accumulation of Capital*, she had already said that she was inspired by Sraffa's introduction to volume one of the Ricardo volumes, as we noted above, pp. 76–77.

Finally, the influence of Kalecki (and Keynes) is clear when Joan Robinson considers how aggregate supply and aggregate demand match up to one another in the growth process and in a Golden Age, especially when account is taken of the rates of accumulation over time and the effects of macroeconomic processes on the distribution of income between profits and wages, when the marginal propensities to save from these two categories of income differ. Joan Robinson's analysis is thus an overarching, original synthesis of all these strands set within the context of Golden Age conditions and the effects of lapses from them.

6.6

We now move to the remaining six books (Chapters 19–37) with Book III, 'The short period'. She deals more sketchily with nevertheless relevant topics. The chapters contain, as would be expected, shrewd insights and contributions, but are more in the nature of minor additions to her main task, tidying up, as it were. When she wrote her sequel volume (1962), she more successfully integrated the various strands she had analysed in her 'big book'. Nevertheless, as we noted, for sympathetic readers with eyes to see and ears to hear, it was possible to see what she was attempting and to applaud how well she had done it.

Chapter 19 is concerned with 'Prices and profits'. The author discusses non–Golden Age conditions. She starts with a section on long and short periods. For her, the short period, in an analytical sense, is not any definite period of time but a convenient abstraction meaning a period in which changes in the stock of capital goods can be neglected (179). In this sense, we do not think Asimakopulos would have disagreed with this – indeed he does not (see Asimakopulos, 1984, reprinted in Kerr with Harcourt (eds.), (2002), vol. V, 448). 'Although she does not attach a definite length to the short period here, it clearly encompasses some interval of time ... long enough to enable decisions to be made and carried out to change the degree of utilization of the relatively unchanged productive capacity' (448). It was only when she changed Marshall's short period to meaning a point in time, 'a moment in a stream of time ... a state of affairs', an 'adjective not a substantive' (Robinson, 1971, 17–18), thereby doing away with period analysis, that he and Joan Robinson parted company. There was now 'no time available to permit variations in the utilisation of productive capacity in response to changing short-term expectations' (448).

Joan Robinson makes utterly clear that 'everything that happens in an economy happens in a short-period situation, for an event occurs or a decision is taken at a particular time [when] the physical stock of capital is what it is' (180). But there are long-period as well as short-period aspects of all happenings, for example, the short-period aspect of accumulation is to be a major determinant of aggregate demand, while the long-period aspects concern the rate of growth of productive capacity – the rate of accumulation – and the technique of production. Moreover, long-period effects bring about the transformation of one short period into another.

Golden Ages and quasi–Golden Ages are 'imaginary situations ... an analytic device, not a description of reality. In reality to-day is a break in time. Yesterday lies in the past, ... has ceased to be relevant to what happens today, except in so far as experience of it colours expectations about what will happen next. Tomorrow lies in the future and cannot be known. The short-period situation ... is like a geological fault; past and future developments are out of alignment. Only in ... a golden age do the strata run horizontally from yesterday to to-morrow without a break at to-day' (181).

Having given concise descriptions of what may happen, she adds that 'when we descend from the clear air of a golden age, where normal prices always rule, into the fogs of historical time, our analysis cannot but be blurred and imprecise' (190).

'The rate of profit on capital, in a short period situation, is an even more foggy notion than the level of profits earned by given equipment, for to express profits at a rate we must know the value of capital. ... In reality, to find the expected return which governs investment decisions is like ... looking in a dark room for a black cat ... not there, and to give a true account of realized returns is like the ... chameleon on a plaid rug. [Nevertheless] the long-period influences ... are working themselves out through the fog of uncertainty in which short-period situations develop [but] ... cannot be seen with any great precision' (190–2).

In Chapter 20, 'Wages and prices', Joan Robinson considers the interaction between a number of possible short-period situations and the underlying long-period situation of, in effect, tranquility approximating to Golden Age conditions. She discusses different market structures – competitive, monopolistic and oligopolistic ones – and examines the impact of buyers and sellers markets on the likely course of prices *vis à vis* wages, effective demand in the short term and planned accumulation in the short term. In some situations, the initial starting point supposes there to be near-full to over-full capacity working; in others, there is surplus capacity. Also, there may be a long-term tendency to an over-supply of labour on which may be imposed either additional unemployment due to short-term fluctuations or a temporary rise in employment relative to the long-term tendency. Within this framework, she considers buyers and sellers markets for both consumption and investment goods, paying special attention to the setting of prices in the short term relative to expectations about long-period subjective normal prices.[12] In this way, her analysis may be seen as an update of Adam Smith's discussion of market prices and their movements around (or converging on) underlying natural prices.

She analyses the overall effects on effective demand of changes in prices and wages in different situations, taking into account the feedback on planned accumulation and the relative strengths of labour and capital in the particular class wars of the given situations. Always, she is on the look out for asymmetries in responses. For example, in the section on the adjustment of capacity to available labour, she writes at the end of three paragraphs of analysis: 'This strongly reinforces the conclusion that a deficiency of demand for labour relatively to supply is much less likely to be self-correcting than a deficiency of supply relatively to demand' (197).

The opening paragraphs of Chapter 21, 'Fluctuations in the rate of investment' is pure Kalecki. 'The accumulation of capital over the long run takes place as a result of decisions to invest made in a succession of short-period situations ... every day the sun rises upon an economy which has ... a particular who's who of capital goods ... and a particular state of expectations based upon past experience and the diagnosis of current trends. In ... a seller's market current experience indicates that more productive capacity could be profitably used and this is likely to cause decisions to invest. ... A high level of employment in the investment sector means high quasi-rents in the consumption sector ... high profits cause profits to be high ... in a buyer's market there is excess capacity ... investment is discouraged. Low profits cause profits to be low.

This double interaction between investment and profits is the most troublesome feature of the capitalist rules of the game, both from the point of view of entrepreneurs who have to play it and of economists who have to describe it' (198).

She tells a story of an investment boom due, say, to an innovation, concluding that 'The essential character of a boom (as opposed to golden-age accumulation) is that it is based on a contradiction. Investment is going on under the influence of the seller's market which investment ... creates ... there is some extra investment due only to the high level of demand (relative to capacity) induced by the investment. The seller's market [could] continue only if the rate of investment (and ... demand for commodities) continued to expand ... in proportion to the increase in capacity ..., and since the rate of increase in investment cannot continue indefinitely while the rise in capacity goes on continuously ..., the seller's market cannot continue. Investment due to a seller's market is sawing off the bough that it is sitting on by bringing the seller's market to an end' (201).

The author then sketches a typical trade cycle and closes by comparing two views of why cycles repeat themselves: one is entirely endogenous leading to the four phases of the cycle, the other needs an exogenous event to overcome the argument that 'the internal power of recovery ... is too weak to overcome the shock of the slump ... the apparent regularity of the cycle is accidental ... something always has turned up to cause a revival' (212). Many years later, this came to be called the real business cycle view.

The last chapter in this book is entitled 'Cycles and trends'. She argues that the 'trend which emerges *ex post* from the operation of the trade cycle is not the same thing as the growth ratio of a golden age, but is an imperfect reflection of it' (213). Here, we are reminded that Kalecki's initial analysis of the cycle was of a trend-less cycle, that is, the trend was due to another, independent set of factors so justifying the statistical procedure of de-trending time series. However, by the end of his life, he had scrapped this view and developed a theory of cyclical growth (as did Goodwin independently) in which the trend and cycle are indissolubly mixed. Kalecki's classic statement of this was that 'The long-term trend [is] but a slowly changing component of a chain of short-period situations ... [not an] independent entity' (Kalecki, 1968; 1971, 165). This later view is consistent with Joan Robinson's 1962 statement: 'The short period is here and now ... incompatibilities in the situation will determine what will happen next. Long-period equilibrium is not at some date in the future; it is an imaginary state of affairs in which there are incompatibilities in the existing situation here and now' (Robinson, 1962a, 690). However, she had not yet reached this view in *The Accumulation of Capital* where the Golden Age is a reference point for various possible scenarios, depending in part on the level of competition in market structures, on the nature of technical progress going on and on what is happening to the labour supply, the rate of increase of which is, for the most part, treated as exogenous.

Her concept of the inflation barrier, the situation in which wage-earners will no longer accept the implied level of consumption of wage goods associated with the existing level of production of investment goods by creating a wage-price spiral, plays a role as does the structure of vintages in the stocks of capital goods of both sectors. Much of her analysis in this chapter has been influenced, as she acknowledges, by a now little known article by Kaldor, 'The relation of economic growth and cyclical fluctuations' (1954).

One of her more fanciful scenarios is entitled 'The approach to bliss' (the state, not the economist). It involves what she called elsewhere moving down a well-behaved production function with decreasing rates of investment and of profits until a given total level of employment is attained in the consumption goods sector, except that which is needed to allow replacements for the constant stock of capital goods employed in the sector. With fluctuating investment, there is less investment boom by subsequent boom and consumption in subsequent depressions gets greater and greater. Total employment is constant over the long run, that is to say, on average – all this is 'a logical possibility ... most unlikely to be realised under the capitalist rules of the game' (219). A tendency for the rate of profits to fall, 'combined with cyclical fluctuations ... undermine[s] the urge to accumulate and promote[s] defensive monopolies. An economy heading towards bliss is never likely to be able unaided to pass through the slough of stagnation to arrive there' (219).

6.7

Five more books complete the main part of the volume. There is a prescient conclusion:

> The reader must draw his conclusions for himself. On parting I only beg him to glance back to Chapter 2 and recall that ... the outputs of saleable goods [are] ... not co-extensive with economic wealth, let alone with the basis of human welfare.
>
> (386)

The spirits of Marshall and Pigou shine through.

Book IV on 'Finance' is written at a high level of abstraction. There is a well-behaved banking system but no central bank. There are notes (issued by respectable banks) for transaction purposes, both to buy consumption goods and pay wage bills, there are short-term bills and long-term bonds. At any moment of time, entrepreneurs fall into two groups: those keen to accumulate beyond their available receipts associated with their activities, those who are saving because their current accumulation plans do not absorb all their current receipts. Through the banks and the bond market, finance is redistributed from the second group to the first group, not always without hitches.

Generally speaking, in this abstract world, provision of finance tends more to be a drag on accumulation than a boost, partly because of liquidity preference conditions, partly because of swings between euphoria and pessimism in the banking system which tend to amplify fluctuations in the 'animal spirits' of entrepreneurs. (There is a foreshadowing of Hyman Minsky's later work here.)

The conclusion of her detailed and careful analysis is rather disappointing: 'over the long run, the rate of accumulation is likely to be whatever it is likely to be' (244).

Introducing a rentier class complicates matters but leaves the analysis of accumulation basically unchanged. The most important result is that the rate of profits no longer equals the rate of growth but exceeds it. There are some nice paradoxes arising from the Kaleckian proposition that profits now equal net investment *plus* rentier expenditure, for example, 'the double-sided relation between entrepreneurs and rentiers'. 'Just as each entrepreneur individually gains by paying his workers less, but suffers through a loss of markets from others paying their workers less, so each entrepreneur would like his wife and his shareholders to be content with little, so that he can use the bulk of his profits for investment (or for reserves to finance future investment) while he gains from the expenditure of other wives and other shareholders, which makes the market for commodities buoyant' (256).

Rentiers also complicate the narrative of the trade cycle without affecting the main lines of former arguments. In particular, rentier expenditure may be an important buffer in the slump because of inertia in both the change in the money rate of interest and in rentier consumption itself. Joan Robinson refers to Robin Matthews's 1954–5 article on the saving function and the problem of trend and cycle in which Matthews related the ratchet effect in Duesenberry's (1949) model to unemployment levels rather than to output and income per head levels, that is, Matthews took into account the effects of productivity rising over time. Joan Robinson points out that '[c]onsumption out of profits plays an important part in the mechanism by which a long-run trend of accumulation emerges from the trade cycle. Each boom leaves behind it an increase in rentier wealth and consuming power due to ... savings ... while the boom was going on ... the drop in each slump is checked at a higher level of demand for consumption goods, and provided ... additional rentier wealth [is not wiped out by bankruptcies], each revival starts from a higher level of output than the last' (269).

Rentiers affect the nature of finance because a large part of wealth is now 'outside the direct control of entrepreneurs [and this influences] accumulation through its effect upon the control over finance' (274).

6.8

Book VI is entitled 'Land'. Historically, the author argues, land should be discussed before capital because it 'is of the greatest importance as a factor of production, and the development of a technical surplus of food is the first prerequisite for accumulation' (283). Moreover, the 'rules of the game' with respect to land tenure and inheritance, and the habits and traditions of landowners affect the subsequent behaviour in the industrial sector and society at large.

Following a rather stylised discussion of the reasons for historical diminishing returns in terms of the marginal products of labour and land, and modifications due to the actions of improving landlords, Joan Robinson discusses the vital role of the agricultural surplus in the process of accumulation.

Chapter 30 is concerned with factor ratios and techniques, and therefore is more related to the discussion in the next chapter on the choice of technique. In this, and the succeeding, chapters Joan Robinson discusses separately the relationships between possible factor prices and techniques chosen, and then varieties of technical progress with factor prices held constant, before attempting to bring the two analyses together to provide an overall picture. She is carefully explicit about the simplifying assumptions she invokes in order to make the analysis tractable (for her, if not always for the reader!) and is painfully honest about how far away even her most detailed narratives are from real world happenings. In order to make precise what is meant by marginal products in the analysis of labour and land, she uses a tranquil static state, finding 'a separate picture for each degree of mechanisation and for each overall ratio of land to labour when total output consists of commodities. There is a corresponding three-dimensional jigsaw puzzle for each ratio of investment to consumption.

And the whole complex alters through time as technical knowledge changes' (306).

'In principle', she adds, 'the whole of [the] formal analysis [could be repeated] in terms of this scheme' "a most formidable task" [upon which would have to be superimposed] all the short-period complications [smudged] over with the uncertainties of an untranquil world' (306). She does not embark on such an undertaking, preferring to take a couple of problems to illustrate how the analysis might be tackled.

Needless to say, by the time the reader gets to the end of the book, a tremendous amount has had to be digested, and many evidently were not up to the task. Joan Robinson followed up first with a symposium published in *Oxford Economic Papers* in 1959 in which David Worswick presented his stockade dictator model of her volume (a reading with which she was not that pleased) and Kahn (1959) contributed, as we noted, his extremely clear and helpful 'Exercises'. Solow, for one, found Worswick's construction of value when he gave his 1963 de Vries lectures on *Capital Theory and the Rate of Return*. GCH unknowingly[13] reproduced some of Worswick's analysis when he wrote a comment on Harry Johnson's 1962 article, 'A simple Joan Robinson model of accumulation with one technique' (see Harcourt, 1963; Harcourt, 2006b, 16–20). These papers illustrate her claim that the model of the second book in her 1956 volume allows the major, most fundamental propositions of her analysis to be established. Nevertheless, as we noted, Joan Robinson felt it necessary to provide a (very adult) 'told-to-the-children' guide to her volume, resulting in the publication in 1962 of *Essays in the Theory of Economic Growth*. This is the principal topic of Chapter 8. In Chapter 7, we discuss the choice of technique and the Cambridge–Cambridge capital theory controversies.

7

The Choice of Technique in the Economy as a Whole and the Cambridge–Cambridge Debates in the Theory of Capital: Joan Robinson's Role

7.1

On 27 October 1936, Piero Sraffa wrote to Joan Robinson:

King's College,
Cambridge,
27.10.36

Dear Joan,

Many thanks for your letter [alas, not to be found in either of their surviving papers] ... a valuable addition to my museum ... I shall hang it next to an extract from Sidgwick where, after lecturing Ricardo on how meaningless it is to talk of a quantity of labour, goes on cheerfully ... to talk of quantities of utility.

If one measures labour and land by heads or acres the result has a definite meaning, subject to a margin of error ... if you measure capital in tons the result is purely and simply nonsense. How many tons is, e.g., a railway tunnel?

If you are not convinced, try it on someone ... not debauched by economics. Tell your gardener that a farmer employs 10 men – will he not have a pretty accurate idea of the quantities of land and labour? Now tell him that he employs 500 tons of capital, and he will think you are dotty – (no more so, however, than Sidgwick or Marshall).

Yours,
P.S.

Kerr with Harcourt (eds.)
(2002, vol. III, 292)

In August 1968, GCH wrote to Joan Robinson to tell her that he had been commissioned by Mark Perlman (the founding editor of the newly created *Journal of Economic Literature*) to write the survey article on the theory of capital for the second issue (Harcourt, 1969). He asked her to jot down what she considered to be the central, crucial points at issue between herself and Cambridge, MA. (GCH had decided that this would be the principal organising structure of the survey.) She replied on 13 August 1968 and also sent GCH a copy of Amit Bhaduri's splendid paper, 'On the significance of recent controversies on capital theory: A Marxian view' (It was published in the *Economic Journal* in 1969; it is one of the most insightful interpretations of the central puzzles in the debates.)

Joan Robinson wrote:

> [T]he main point can be put this way. ... capital has two aspects, as means of production which raise the productivity of labour and as funds which enable capitalists to make profits. Capital in the first sense exists in a co-operative or socialist economy but in those societies income from work ... and from property are boiled into one ... the distinction between wages and profits does not arise ... Capital and the rate of profit[s] exist in a capitalist economy. In ... neoclassical theory the two aspects of capital are reduced to one ... capital in the physical sense is treated as though it were a homogeneous substance. The neoclassicals reacted to [her] challenge by various devices ... Swann's [*sic*] Meccano sets and Meade's Steel ... [do] not solve the problem because if there are even two commodities the price ratio between them affects the value of capital ... changes with every change in the rate of profit[s] ... a model in which capital as a physical substance and capital as a sum of value can be treated as a single quantity requires a strictly one commodity world. There is a flow of output of butter, part ... is consumed, ... part put aside as means of production; this is then congealed into physical capital which is perfectly durable [malleable?]. If we then add ... a continuing [continuous?] production function in labour and congealed butter we could ... define the marginal production [product?] of capital ... attempts have been made to move from the one-commodity world to a multi-commodity world ... these have been finally discredited in the double-switching controversy.
>
> the logic of the argument is now completely established ... very hard indeed for the neoclassicals ... to admit it.
>
> ...

> Since the marginal productivity theory cannot explain the rate of profit[s], we have to look for a new theory. [Her] most recent thoughts ... are [in] ... Volume III [of her *C.E.P.*] ... "A Reconsideration of the Theory of Value" ... [she] would now simplify it by leaving out Sraffa's [S]tandard commodity, which ... we can get on perfectly well without.

She suggested that GCH ask Luigi Pasinetti for a copy of a paper he was working on (probably Pasinetti (1969)) and Pierangelo Garegnani 'for a copy of his paper on Samuelson's jelly' (Garegnani, 1970; Samuelson, 1962).

In the early 1970s, she wrote a 'cryptic injunction' to Lowell Galloway and Vishwa Shukla when they were preparing their, soon to be refuted,[1] defence of the neoclassical production function against the criticisms of it implied by the capital-reversing and reswitching results (see Galloway and Shukla, 1974). Joan Robinson wrote to them: 'Do not bother. Neoclassical theory is no better off even when there is no reswitching' (see Galloway and Shukla, 1974; Kerr with Harcourt (eds.), 2002, vol. IV, 328). By this time, she insisted on emphasising her methodological critique concerning the error of using comparisons of positions of equilibrium to analyse processes.

In 1975, Joan Robinson published one of her last major incursions in the debate in the *Quarterly Journal of Economics*. The article was entitled 'The unimportance of reswitching' (Robinson, 1975c). It drew comments from Samuelson (1975) and Solow (1975).

This was followed by her contribution (in French) to the 1977 symposium on the controversies in the *Revue d'Economie Politique*, edited by Arnold Heertje (Robinson, 1977e). The English version of her article, 'The meaning of capital', is published in her *Contributions to Modern Economics* (1978d) and *C.E.P.*, vol. V (1979). In the 'Reminiscences' that open the 1978d volume, she tells again the history of the debate, as she saw it, as she candidly admits (xix). She concludes: 'Though the "Cambridge critics" were never answered, mainstream teaching ... seems to go on in the same old way. [She] was delighted to find in a dictionary the word mumpsimus, which means stubborn persistence in error after it has been exposed' (xix).[2]

In *C.E.P.* (vol. V, 1979), she reprinted her 1975 article together with part of Samuelson's reply to which she in turn replied. In the article she gave a brief history of how she came to find reswitching, evidently at the suggestion of Kaldor. He persuaded her that she 'ought to bring in the conception ... of deepening the stock of capital in a given state of technical knowledge' (78). She argues that the 'reswitching debate arose from confronting the conclusions of an attempt to develop a post-Keynesian analysis of long-run accumulation with arguments drawn from pre-Keynesian assumptions' (76). She argues that '[n]othing could be more idle than to get up an argument about whether reswitching is "likely" to be found in practice'. Not only does a pseudo production function not exist 'in reality' but also it would not be possible to move along it to pass over switch points.

> [For] there is no such phenomenon in real life as accumulation taking place in a given state of knowledge. The idea was introduced into economic theory ... to give a meaning to the concept of marginal productivity ... the pseudo production function was constructed in order to show that it has no meaning.
>
> (82–3)

A radical shift in her emphases and arguments may be discerned in the above narrative. It forms the background to an examination of the issues involved in which we concentrate on her interpretation of them.

7.2

Clearly then, Joan Robinson had been mulling over these issues from the 1930s onwards, though it was her 1953–4 article that brought them, from her point of view, into the public domain.[3] Avi Cohen and G. C. Harcourt in their 2003 retrospective article in the *Journal of Economic Perspectives* on the capital theory debates singled out 'three deep issues' which were 'still unresolved' and which were predicted to 'inevitably erupt in future controversy' (200). The first issue

> is the meaning and, as a corollary, the measurement of the concept of capital in the analysis of industrial capitalist societies. The second is Joan Robinson's complaint that equilibrium was not the outcome of an economic process and therefore an inadequate tool for analysing processes of capital accumulation and growth. The third issue is the role of ideology and vision in fuelling controversy when the results of simple models are not robust.
>
> (200)

Joan Robinson was explicit about the first two issues in her 1953–4 article. (Her views on the third issue are scattered through her writings over many decades; for a typical example, see Joan Robinson (1973a;

C.E.P., vol. V, 1979, 254–61) where she concludes that 'Analysis that is put at the service of ideology is not interesting, because we know in advance what the answer is going to be' (*C.E.P.*, vol. V, 1979, 261) (see also Chapter 11).

Her paragraphs about the units in which capital is measured in the aggregate production function are well known:

> [T]he production function has been a powerful instrument of miseducation. The student of economic theory is taught to write $O=f(L, C)$ where L is a quantity of labour, C a quantity of capital and O a rate of output of commodities. He is instructed to assume all workers alike and to measure L in man-hours of labour; he is told something about the index-number problem in choosing a unit of output; and he is hurried on to the next question, in the hope that he will forget to ask in what units C is measured. Before he ever does ask, he has become a professor, and so sloppy habits of thought are handed on from one generation to another.
>
> The question is certainly not an easy one to answer.
>
> (81), (*C.E.P.*, vol. II, 1960, 114)

It is also clear that she understood fully why such a unit was necessary. If the quantity of capital was to be an important determinant of the return to capital in the national product (and the return on capital itself), it had to be measurable before the analysis started in a unit akin to hours of labour and acres of land. It is no good saying that the return and the quantity may be simultaneously determined when the analysis is finished. Sraffa commented on this in several places, especially clearly in his 1962 comment on Harrod's review of Sraffa's 1960 book: 'What is the good of a quantity of capital ... which, since it depends on the rate of interest, cannot be used for its traditional purpose ... to determine the rate of interest [?]', (479). Yet such a unit had to exist before the analysis started if the relative scarcity of capital in relation to labour were to be regarded as an exogenous reason why rates of profits were what they were (even in ideal, highly abstract conditions).

Joan Robinson proposed a measure of capital, real capital, capital measured in terms of labour time, which though not independent of distribution and prices, made some sense of capital viewed as a factor of production in a neoclassical setting. It does not come up with typical neoclassical results (in the aggregate production function framework) of equality between marginal products and equilibrium factor prices in a competitive situation. David Champernowne (1953–4) attempted to provide such equalities by using a chain-index measure of capital. However, it was not a measure independent of distribution and prices; moreover, it required a subtle change in the concept of marginal product, one not to be found in the traditional account, for the results to go through. (The traditional concept relates to the (incremental) change in output relative to the (incremental) change in capital induced by an (incremental) change in the rate of profits. Champernowne's measure related to the increment in output relative to the increment in capital associated with an incremental change in the proportion in which two equi-profitable methods of production are combined (see Pasinetti, 1969, 529–31; Harcourt, 1972, 33–4, 44–5).

The 'profound' methodological error she attributes to the opposition is also stated explicitly if not, according to Dennis Robertson, clearly or coherently. Joan Robinson wrote:

> The neo-classical economist thinks of a position of equilibrium as a position towards which an economy is tending to move as time goes by. But it is impossible for a system to *get into* a position of equilibrium ... the very nature of equilibrium is that the system is already in it, and has been ... for a certain length of past time.[4]
>
> (Robinson, 1953–4, 85; *C.E.P.*, vol. II, 1960, 120, emphasis in original)

Robertson (1957, 95–6) regarded Joan Robinson's second sentence

> with respect, after taking the best philosophical advice, [to be] great nonsense ... anybody who rejects these two ideas, that a system can move towards equilibrium but that it may never actually get into it [did not understand Marshall and made it] extremely difficult ... to interpret the course of events in the real world.

Joan Robinson (*C.E.P.*, vol. II, 1960, 130–1), conceded that her remarks were not 'well worded'. Her point was that in a state of equilibrium there are no individuals who feel they could do better for themselves by changing their behaviour. When applied to the stock of durable capital goods, it means that the stock in existence today is what it would have been

> if those concerned had known, at relevant dates in the past, what expectations about the future they would be holding today ... periods affected by different positions overlap ... the relevant past stretches back indefinitely. Thus, an economy can be following an equilibrium path only if it has been following it for some time already.

It was not though until the *Quarterly Journal of Economics* symposium on capital-reversing and reswitching in 1966 that she began to emphasise this criticism as the fundamental one and to play down the significance of the capital-reversing and reswitching results (though not the demonstration that it was not possible to find a unit in which to measure capital which was independent of distribution and prices).

In her 1953–4 article and 1956 book, she discussed various possible measures of capital within the neoclassical framework, both in the short and the long period, in equilibrium and out of equilibrium. She was simultaneously searching for measures and meanings that fitted within the framework she developed in her book. She concentrated, as we have noted, on the measure she dubbed real capital, capital measured in terms of labour time,[5] as the most appropriate one to give content to capital as a factor of production, a productive agent in capitalist society, within the neoclassical framework. Sets of equipment with known productive capacities when combined with appropriate amounts of labour were to be valued in terms of the labour time required to produce them, compounded over their gestation periods at various given rates of interest (themselves equal in riskless equilibrium to corresponding rates of profits). Which set(s) of equipment would actually be in use in *given equilibrium* situations is(are) found by supposing the wage rate to be given and finding the set(s) which allow(s) the highest rate of profits to be received at this wage rate. Competitive forces ensure that this(these) set(s) will have been chosen. Such a measure has an intuitive appeal:

> [W]hen we consider what addition to productive resources a given amount of accumulation makes, ... the addition ... depends on how much work is done in [and time is spent on] constructing it, not upon the cost, in terms of final product, of an hour's labour.
>
> (Robinson, 1953–4, 82; *C.E.P.*, vol. II, 1960, 116)

Real capital could only be a rigorous measure within a situation of overall economy equilibrium. For then, because all expectations have been and always will be realised, whether we look at capital as inputs in the gestation period accumulated forward at the ruling rate of profits or as gross profit flows yet to come discounted back to the present at the ruling rate of profits, we must get the same answer. From this basically Wicksellian result, we deduce our measure of real capital and Joan Robinson's version of the production function. We consider a series of possible stationary states producing a consumption good in purely competitive environments exhibiting constant returns to scale, complete divisibility, where machines last forever.

From the definition of equilibrium, we may write:

$$K = wL_g(1+r)^t = \frac{Q - wL_c}{r}, \tag{1}$$

where K is the capital measured in terms of the consumption commodity; w the wage rate in terms of the consumption commodity; r the rate of profits (rate of interest); L_g the input, t periods ago, of labour required to produce a unit of equipment, where t is the gestation period of investment; and Q is the output of consumption good when L_L people work with a unit of equipment.

Capital in terms of labour time (K_L) is therefore as follows:

$$K_L = \frac{K}{w} = L_g(1+r)^t. \tag{2}$$

We then list all known techniques according to their outputs per head of the consumption good. Corresponding to each technique will be the following relationship:

$$Q = wL_c + rwL_g(1+r)^t \tag{3}$$

so that

$$w = \frac{Q}{L_c + rL_g(1+r)^t}. \qquad (4)^6$$

If we 'cost up' all the known techniques for all possible values of r and their corresponding values of w, and then relate output per head to real capital per head, we get Joan Robinson's version of the aggregate production function, that which came to be called the pseudo production function (see Figure 7.1). It is the then familiar (probably not now) zigzag construction; the zags reflect different combinations of equiprofitable techniques for given values of w; the (horizontal) zigs show the dominance of a given technique for a range of w and r values. The slopes of the zags do not measure in any simple way the equilibrium returns to capital associated with them. Points on the zigs and zags are all possible equilibrium positions and comparisons of one with another are just that, not accounts of processes induced by different values of w or r whereby one technique may be induced to replace another in a process of accumulation.

Moreover, though Joan Robinson called it 'a perverse relationship', a curiosum (a Ruth Cohen one at that; see Robinson (1956a, n1, 109) and

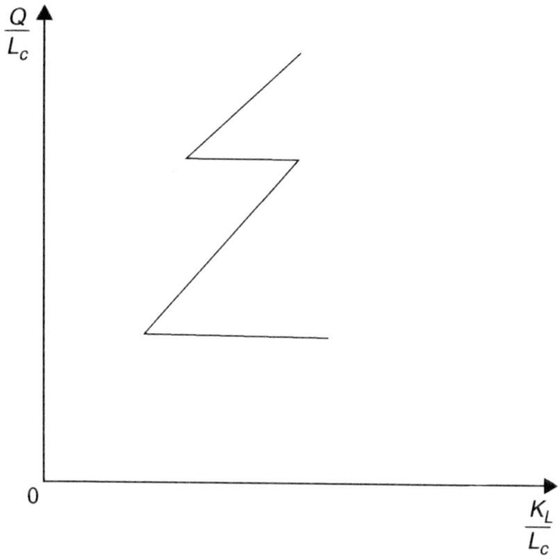

Figure 7.1 Joan Robinson's pseudo production function

Chapter 6), she did note that a lower rate of profits could be associated with less value of capital per person and a lower output per person. This, in turn, could mean that the same technique which was most profitable at one rate of profits, but not over the range of values that followed, could then become the most profitable again at another rate. These are, of course, the phenomena of capital reversing and reswitching, respectively.

She related these phenomena to a discussion of Wicksell effects and of Wicksell on capital (Robinson, 1956a, 396–7). Wicksell pointed out that the length of the period of production (which stands for what Joan Robinson called the degree of mechanisation) could not by itself determine the ratio of capital to labour because the value of capital required for a given method of production depends on the real wage rate. This is a price Wicksell effect, for Swan, '*nothing but an inventory revaluation*' (Swan, 1956, 355, emphasis in original). For Joan Robinson, it was a fundamental criticism of Böhm Bawerk's theory and

> the key to the whole theory of accumulation and of the determination of wages and profits. ... The main difficulty presented by Wicksell's analysis [is] that he [discussed] in the same breath a comparison between static states ... and a process of accumulation going on through time ... his fundamental proposition is equally

> important in both branches of the argument, but it cannot be well understood unless they are kept separate.
>
> (Robinson, 1956a, 397)

A real Wicksell effect relates to the adoption of a different method because of the values of *r* or *w* considered so that there are physical as well as value changes involved (see Harcourt, 1972, 39–45).

Champernowne and Solow responded to her article, and Swan wrote a sort of review of aspects of her article and book in the appendix to his 1956 article, 'Notes on capital'. Champernowne's 'comment' (which is nearly as long as her article) appears in the same issue of the *Review of Economic Studies*. His object was to preserve the traditional results whereby marginal products and factor prices were equal and also to allow the analysis of a 'slow' process of accumulation. To this end, he developed a chain-index measure of capital. The purpose was to measure changes in the 'quantity' of capital after the effects on value due to differing values of *r* and *w* had been precipitated out. He used the *w*, *r* relationships associated with each known method of production to form an outer frontier characterised by points where methods were equiprofitable. As they shared the same valuation procedures, differences in their values reflected differences in quantities. The relatives constructed from these allowed a chain-index measure of quantities to be formed. In constructing his examples of this procedure, Champernowne ruled out by assumption both capital-reversing and reswitching.[7]

In Swan's model of economic growth, capital–labour and capital–output ratios need to change considerably as accumulation occurs over time and a new equilibrium position is reached, following a change in the value of a key parameter, for example, the saving ratio. So Swan used in the text of the article an analysis which 'takes a neoclassical form' and enjoyed 'the neoclassical as well as the Ricardian vice'.

In the appendix he spelt out, in 'a back foremost' procedure, assumptions that allowed the approach, the scarecrow that would keep off both 'the index number birds and Joan Robinson herself' (343–4). A key assumption is that capital consists of Meccano sets which can be costlessly and timelessly transformed into any desired form as given by the latest book of instructions (Joan Robinson's book of blueprints but allowing for technical progress). This, together with other more familiar assumptions about the form of the production function (Cobb–Douglas), expectations and market structures, allows the traditional marginal productivity results to be maintained but 'in a form which deceived nobody' (344). Nor do they allow for the analysis of accumulation in historical time or, rather, applications of the findings to historical time processes. Swan is very clear about both these points (see Swan, 1956, 350–1).[8]

Solow (1956a) investigated the conditions under which it would be legitimate to treat social capital as a scalar. He seems to have had more in mind his subsequent econometric investigations than Joan Robinson's complaints. For him 'Capital as a number is *not* an issue of principle ... Rigorously valid results [only come] from *n* capital-good models ... no justification ever for supposing that output can be made a function of labour and the VALUE of capital whose partial derivatives do the right thing.' In empirical work, 'you want to get away with the smallest dimensionality possible' (see Harcourt, 1972, 46, emphasis in original).

6.3

In the 1960s, the debates intensified, starting with the publication of Sraffa's classic in 1960. In several places, Sraffa presents results which implicitly are critical of the neoclassical intuition that price as an index of scarcity is the organising principle behind price formation and within the theory of distribution. Allied with this is the argument that capital cannot be measured independently of distribution and prices. In the chapter on 'Reduction to dated quantities of labour', he states explicitly: '[t]he reversals in the direction of the movements of relative prices, in the face of unchanged methods of production, cannot be reconciled with *any* notion of capital as a measurable quantity independent of distribution and prices' (38, emphasis in original) (see also the chapter on 'Fixed capital', especially pp. 70–2, in which Sraffa analyses the 'remarkable effect' of different values of the rate of profits on the value of a balanced stock of capital goods). In Part III, he analyses the choice of technique and illustrates capital-reversing and reswitching possibilities.

> In view of this ... we cannot (contrary to what one might have expected) say in general that, of two alternative methods of production, the one that corresponds to a Standard system with a higher ratio of product to means of production ... will be the most profitable when the rate of profits is comparatively high, and the least profitable when it is comparatively low.
>
> (84)

In 1962, in a symposium in the *Review of Economic Studies*, Samuelson published his surrogate production function article. This was meant to rationalise Solow's growth model of 1956 (Solow, 1956b), and his econometric work in 1957 on the relative contributions of deepening and technical progress to the growth of productivity over time, by attempting to establish the robustness of the results obtained from J. B. Clark's jelly model when applied to the more complex, *n* commodity MIT highbrow model. In footnote 7 of the article, he acknowledges the results of Garegnani's paper (but it was not to be published until 1970), which much reduced the robustness of his results. Then David Levhari (1965) purported to show that Sraffa's results in Part III, while possible for an industry, were not deducible for a model of the whole economy. This was the article which most immediately brought about the 1966 *Quarterly Journal of Economics* symposium. Pasinetti (1966) was the first to show that Levhari was wrong. Many other contributors chimed in and Samuelson wrote his handsome 'Summing up' article (as well as acknowledging with Levhari, the latter's mistake) in which he concluded:

> If all this causes headaches for those nostalgic for the old time parables of neoclassical writing, we must remind ourselves that scholars are not born to live an easy existence. We must respect, and appraise, the facts of life.
>
> (583)

Joan Robinson and K. A. Naqvi's paper in 1967 also contributed to the themes of the 1966 symposium.

In the meantime, Solow in his 1963 de Vries Lectures had gone to Irving Fisher's concept of the social rate of return on investment as more relevant for analysing capital theory issues and also free of the criticisms of 'capital' and 'its' marginal product. He was not completely successful in avoiding capital and marginal products in his theoretical arguments and econometric specifications, and was criticised by Joan Robinson (1964a) for this. Pasinetti (1969) took the new results to see how they bore on Fisher's analysis and so on Solow's contributions.

Joan Robinson wrote a review article of Solow (1963). Central to it was her argument that using production functions in econometric specifications to estimate the values of key parameters from available time series data involved the illegitimate procedure of collapsing the long period into the short period. She illustrated this with her example of a butter economy. Butter was both input and output, related to each other through a well-behaved production function in which the butter to labour ratio and butter input to butter output ratio could take on any proportions required by the relevant economic incentives prevailing. Thus, whether the economy was moving up or down the production function in the short term (what she called the utilisation function) as a consequence of greater or less utilisation of a given stock of butter input, or was experiencing a long-term rise in the stock of butter input relative to the labour supply as a result of accumulation (deepening), the same values of key parameters would apply. In this way, estimates of the impact of deepening could be obtained by using time series data which came, of necessity, from observations on short-term values of output and capital. Of course, taking account of technical progress complicates the argument, as the extensions in Solow's book and subsequent work showed (see Harcourt, 1972, Ch. 3; 2006b, Appendix 2) but the underlying specifications and assumptions still held.

Pasinetti, too, was concerned with the argument that there was a negative relationship between capital per head and the return to capital. In the case of Fisher (or, rather, what Solow built on Fisher's base[9]), when heterogeneous capital goods were considered, the relationship was only robust when an 'unobtrusive postulate' – no capital-reversing allowed by assumption – was included. Solow (1970) strenuously denied this, carefully distinguishing between what was needed for rigorous theory, on the one hand, and econometric specification – 'cheap vehicles for interpreting data (which seem to behave that way)' (424) – on the other.[10]

7.4

Joan Robinson's paper with Naqvi in 1967 was her last intervention in the reswitching and capital-reversing debates as an analyst of the technical issues themselves. From then on, she increasingly stressed the other strand of the critical arguments (in which she was joined by economists within the neoclassical camp, especially Christopher Bliss and Franklin Fisher) about using differences to analyse changes. A particularly forceful statement of this view is in her 1974 paper, 'History versus equilibrium', which has been reprinted in volume V of her *C.E.P.*

We quote from the Preface to volume V. The first essay reprinted in it is 'What are the questions?' (Robinson, 1977c), first published in the *Journal of Economic Literature* in 1977. It is her 'response to a request for a survey of the state of contemporary economic theory as [she] saw it'. She tells us that the theoretical papers in section I which elaborate various points in this essay 'operate on two planes, an attempt to get the logic clear in a tightly specified model and an attempt to loosen it up in the form of approximations to make it useful for discussion of actual problems'.[11]

> On the logical plane, [she] frequently had occasion to complain of the inability of neo-neoclassical writers to distinguish between a *difference* in the parameters of an equilibrium model and the effects of a *change* taking place at a moment of time. [She] supposed it was difficult for readers to believe that such an error can be made by respected leaders of the profession.
>
> (vii, emphasis in original)

She thought 'apposite' in this context, the exchange between herself and Samuelson over 'the unimportance of reswitching'. She mentions that in her first publication (Robinson, 1932a), she 'was already aware of the pitfalls of theoretical controversies' (vii).

In 'History versus equilibrium', she quotes Maynard Keynes's description of equilibrium theory (Keynes called it 'the classical economic theory') as a 'pretty, polite [technique] which tries to deal with the present by abstracting from the fact that we know very little about the future' (Keynes, 1937; *C.W.*, vol. XIV, 1973b, 115). She builds on this insight.

> As soon as the uncertainty of the expectations that guide economic behaviour is admitted, equilibrium drops out of the argument and history takes its place ... post-Keynesian theory reaches back to clasp the hands of Ricardo and Marx, skipping over the sixty years of dominance of neoclassical doctrines from 1870 to the great slump. This accounts for the paradox that post-Keynesian analysis derives equally from two such apparently incomparable sources as Piero Sraffa's interpretation of Ricardo and Michal Kalecki's interpretation of the theory of employment.
>
> (Robinson, 1974; *C.E.P.*, vol. V, 1979, 48)

She concludes that, especially 'for a developing country, the choice of technique is an important problem'. But it does not concern 'the ratio of "capital" to labour or to output' but, rather, 'the allocation of investible resources'. The rise in productivity due to embodied investment might be called the return to such investment, but it has no connection with the rate of profits (or interest) 'on the pre-existing total stock of capital goods, or of wealth inherited from the past'.

Measuring capital is 'a minor element' of her criticism. 'The major point is that what [neo-neoclassical doctrines] ... offer as an alternative ... to the post-Keynesian theory of accumulation ... is an error in methodology – a confusion between comparisons of imagined equilibrium positions and a process of accumulation going on through history.'

With no 'comprehensible treatment of historical time' and specification of 'the rules of the game in the economy under discussion' their 'theoretical apparatus' is 'useless for the analysis of contemporary problems ... in the micro and macro spheres' (Robinson, 1974; *C.E.P.*, vol. V, 1979, 58).

On the way to reaching this devastating indictment, she also points out their failure (as she sees it) to distinguish between interest as a return on financial assets and profit as a (received, not earned) return on the accumulation of physical capital goods, and to a fudge in the justification of interest by failing to distinguish between what is received for ownership and what is required for future savings to occur.

7.5

As we have often noted, Joan Robinson always thought it most important to make explicit what sort of society/economy was implied in theoretical models: who were the decision-makers, what were the rules of the game, what institutions were implied, if any? A feature of her discussion in both 'History versus equilibrium' and her contribution to the 1977 symposium on the capital theory debates edited by Arnold Heertje in the *Revue d'Economie Politique*[12] is her analysis of just these features in different theories and the writings of different authors, and of their relevance for the disputes and results. Especially are these considerations relevant for the crossover, as it were, between the capital theory debates and their link to the theory of accumulation, that is, analysis of the processes of distribution and growth in historical time.

She puts this clearly in her 1974 article:

> Before we can discuss accumulation, we must ... deal with the questions Walras and Pigou left unanswered. In what kind of economy is accumulation taking place? ... [is it] Frank Ramsey's classless co-operative, a collection of peasants and artisans, or a modern capitalist nation? ... a property-owning democracy in which ... saving depends on the decisions of households. If so [how] is saving converted into [investment]? Or if investment depends on the decisions of industrial firms, how do they get ... finance, ... what expectations of profits [guide] their plans? Is there a mechanism in the system to ensure growth with continuous full employment? [Will] firms ... meekly crawl down a pre-existing production function [even though

> they expect a fall in the rate of profits to ensue] or [will] they introduce new techniques that raise output per unit of investment as well as output per [person]?
>
> Robinson (1974; *C.E.P.*, vol. V, 1979, 57)

The same theme in her critique comes out in an exchange of letters with Paul Samuelson in 1973 (in which there is an undercurrent of exasperation with the other in both correspondents), and, even more so, in a letter she wrote to Robert Dorfman in 1978.[13] Evidently, Joan Robinson gave a lecture at Harvard in March 1978 and Dorfman commented on it. She found their discussion 'rather unsatisfactory' and so wished 'very much ... to get the point cleared up'.

For her, Dorfman's

> contention was that, in a Walrasian model with an arbitrary endowment of inputs, including reproducible "machines" of various types, there is a position of equilibrium in which the cost of production of each machine is equal to the value of the rental ... There is a uniform rate of return over cost for all types of machines.

She wanted him to explain 'the basis for this argument'. She then set out how she looked at the problem.

> Today, in an equilibrium position, there is a certain pattern of prices for outputs and of flows of rentals for inputs ... if the latter were correctly foreseen when the machines in existence today were being produced, there must be a uniform rate of return over cost for every type of machine, because no saving would have been devoted to purchasing machines ... that promised a lower return than some other. ... When the flows of rentals of machines in existence today [the time-patterns of which are the same] are discounted at the rate of return, the value of each machine [equals] its cost of production.
>
> Taking the general conditions of the model ... there is one specific stock of machines in existence today that is compatible with equilibrium. With any arbitrary stock ..., the rate of return ... is not uniform.
>
> The trouble is that Walras tried to introduce the future into the argument – investment of savings today being guided by expectations of future returns – without considering the past. In his model, the machines in existence today are dropped from heaven without any regard to expectations about what conditions today would be like.

In her 1977 article on the meaning of capital, she argues that '"mainstream teaching" [is] based on three different types of model, often mixed up together'.

The first is a grand co-operative without private property where society saves and enjoys the increased income which accumulation provides. Frank Ramsey's 1928 'elegant formula' is cited, together with the assumption of an all-purpose homogeneous commodity, the production of which, like the utility derived from it, is subject to diminishing returns.

The second model is based on the general equilibrium of Walras in which the main emphasis is on exchange.

The third type of model derives from Marshall, 'vulgarised by J.B. Clark'. 'Capital', land and labour are factors of production, the returns to which are governed by their marginal productivities. In the case of 'machines' their marginal productivity governs the interest received by rentiers and profits, a separate item, is 'the return to "enterprise"', that is, the management of business, see Robinson (1977e; *C.E.P.*, vol. V, 1979e, 60–61)

Thus, her critique embracing the role of expectations and the requirements for being in equilibrium became more and more clear over the years. Gram (2005) has shown that she made the deepest and most central critique of the conditions required for equilibrium even in the most sophisticated of neoclassical general equilibrium models of growth. The deficiencies of these models could not be overcome, as has often been claimed (see, for example, Ferguson (1972, 175)), by assuming intelligent speculators agree to take advantage of any arbitrage possibilities. Essentially, it would only be a fluke if the initial starting point, the composition of the stock of capital goods, corresponds to what would be needed for a growth model eventually to attain an equilibrium path. Otherwise, all else would result in chaos.

8
After *The Accumulation of Capital*: Defence and Development

The publication of *The Accumulation of Capital* in 1956 was followed by three other books which explained, elaborated on and developed its themes. In 1960, Joan Robinson published *Exercises in Economic Analysis*, 'a textbook of a somewhat unusual kind' (1960a, v), an ingenious and innovative attempt to get readers, especially students, to learn economic analysis by doing it themselves, guided by her blueprints and instructions. Not only were they instructed in elaborate analysis, much of it covering themes in the 1956 volume, they were also encouraged to think conceptually and avoid the pitfalls that Joan Robinson already thought their orthodox teachers had not been able to. She drew 'attention to a few methodological rules [she] had tried to observe': time had to be taken seriously. Comparing two situations, each with its own future and past, is not the equivalent of tracing a movement from one to the other (not least because, as she came more and more to think, you are unlikely ever to get there). Quantities only have meaning if 'we can specify the units in which [they are] measured'. 'Technical and physical relations, between man and nature, must be distinguished from social relations, between man and man' (v).

Then came *Essays in the Theory of Economic Growth* (1962e), the specific objective of which was to overcome the incoherence and difficulties she now felt readers had faced in her 'big book'. The book was much narrower in scope, a concentration on pure theory and a refusal to indulge in 'real world' speculations of the sort which had often confused readers of the 1956 volume; she aimed in the book to set out her core findings and the arguments by which they were reached were in a straightforward and essentials-only manner.

Then in 1971 came *Economic Heresies: Some Old-fashioned Questions in Economic Theory*, a short book full of distilled wisdom and illuminating a further change in her style of writing.[1] More and more of what she presented to readers were but the tips of icebergs, with the submerged portions of which she was only too familiar but which were increasingly to baffle others, especially new readers. Nevertheless, the book is a treasure trove of insights and wisdom – a decade of Tripos essay questions could be extracted as quotes from its pages, followed by the instruction 'Discuss'[2] – as even her most stringent reviewer, Frank Hahn (1972), was willing to admit. Twice in his review, he, after quoting from the book, adds that he is 'willing to forgive and forget' the blemishes and howlers he feels he has exposed (Kerr with Harcourt (eds.), 2002, vol. V, 19).

Those whom she criticises may often have felt hard pressed to recognise themselves in her descriptions of what they had done and were doing. Yet she was, in effect, following Keynes's often used method of writing of the authors he was criticising that, to be logical and consistent, to have reached the conclusions that they have, these *must* be the structures and aims of their constructions.[3] Her one-time doctoral student, Stanley Wong, did the same thing to Samuelson and his theory of revealed preference, explicitly using the method of rational reconstruction (see Wong, 2006). It is not, of course, necessarily a good way of making friends and influencing people.

8.1

As we noted, these three books were principally designed as follow-ups to *The Accumulation of Capital* because it was difficult to read. This was partly because, as Kelvin Lancaster complained in his review article, Lancaster (1960, 66), there were very few 'pictures' in it even though he named Mrs Robinson as a leading member of the 'words and pictures' school of economic analysis. He is slightly unfair – there are diagrams for the sections on the choice of technique, including one thoughtfully designed as a bookmark. In any event, the defect is remedied in *Exercises* in an ingenious way by asking readers to draw the 'pictures' themselves, using her instructions. Students reading the book were thus able to establish for themselves important propositions in the following branches of economic theory: production and accumulation, accumulation and distribution, elementary demand theory, international trade theory, the theory of the firm, and resource allocation in a socialist economy.

The level of difficulty varies widely from part to part. Parts 3 and 4 ('An exchange economy' and 'Capitalist industry') could be the basis of first year courses in value theory and the theory of the firm, respectively. Parts 1 and 2 ('Production and accumulation' and 'Accumulation and distribution') contain, as is to be expected, the most difficult and original sections of the book, more appropriate for final year undergraduate and first year graduate courses. Part 5, 'Rational price system', is in effect a simplified and easy-to-read version of Lerner's *The Economics of Control* (1944). It is an excellent introduction to an advanced course on welfare economics.

Familiar Robinsonian traits and emphases are that three types of economy are considered in the book, to wit, a peasant economy, a socialist economy and a competitive capitalist economy. The first two are used 'mainly in order to throw light upon [the third] by way of contrast'. The capitalist economy has a consumption goods sector and an investment goods sector, and three classes: rentiers, entrepreneurs and wage-earners. The level of activity and the distribution of income in both the short and the long term depend upon the energy and desire to accumulate of the entrepreneurs and the saving propensities of the three classes. At each stage of the argument, an attempt is made to show what patterns of behaviour by individual economic units will be consistent with the macroeconomic relationships of the particular economy concerned. Three general methods of analysis are used: the comparison of different economies at the same point in time, the comparison of the same economy at different points in time and analysis of change over time in an economy. This ensures that time is 'taken seriously'.

There are a number of passages which provided additional clues for those readers of her then recent writings who found it hard to understand *exactly* why she thought 'that the marginal productivity theory of distribution is all bosh' (Robinson, 1961, 58).

> A great deal of confusion has been caused in economic theory ... by asserting that wages tend to equal the marginal product of labour from the point of view of the economy as a whole. ... It is true that the marginal *net* return on employing labour must be equal to the wage in equilibrium ... merely a restatement of the meaning of equilibrium as a position where no employer wants to employ any more or less labour than he is actually doing. It does not assert that wages are equal to the value of the marginal physical product of labour [but] draws attention to the fact that wages must be less than this to allow a margin for interest and profit.
>
> (69, emphasis in original)

Both Robert Clower (1961) in the *American Economic Review* and David Worswick (1962) in the *Economic Journal* were favourably impressed by *Exercises*. Clower pointed out that it was not simply a 'collection of exercises', it covered the whole range of economic theory, 'the end result ... a charming and provocative introduction ... original in outlook, full of pithy comments ..., delightfully dogmatic about ... scope and method, essentially accurate from a technical point of view but not so rigorous as to stifle independent thought' (Kerr with Harcourt (eds.), 2002, vol. III, 164).

Clower credits its author with magnificent economic intuition, a clear view of which is to be found in *Exercises*. He criticises her for finding it difficult to take seriously the works of continental and American scholars so that her handling of monetary and capital theory, 'to which English economists other than Keynes have contributed virtually nothing, is woefully inadequate'. (Clower has overlooked her knowledge of and respect for Wicksell (and Marx!) and surely has forgotten his Oxford mentor, Hicks?) He also saw a tendency 'to confuse theory with applications; to proceed as if "the nature of Reality" dictated the use of particular theoretical models to describe particular concrete situations' (Kerr with Harcourt (eds.), 2002, vol. III, 165). If we substitute 'illuminate' for 'describe', it could be argued that Clower's is a misplaced criticism, reflecting more one of his own characteristic idiosyncrasies than a deficiency of Joan Robinson's approach. In any event, he felt that the stimulation of critical faculties, which, in his view, such shortcomings would provide, was a plus.

Worswick worried about the lack of real world case studies in *Exercises*. He thought the exposition was 'beautifully logical and taut [with not a] word in the wrong place'. Yet he wondered whether a beginner would have the same reaction as he had with his many years of teaching and reading theory and his knowledge of economic institutions and developing situations behind him. He further felt that a knowledge of mathematics was a necessary complement for drawing the diagrams so that as the models emerged they could become playthings, rather than realised ends in themselves.

In the King's College Archives there are some unpublished comments, written in 1958, by Meade on the manuscript of Joan Robinson's book. (Hicks, Harry Johnson, Meade and Amartya Sen are explicitly thanked by the author in the preface.) Meade was especially worried about the practice of not including a government sector in models of modern capitalism (this was more characteristic of growth models than of short-period models of overall activity.) Their omission, he argued, in some important ways transformed the nature of the system. Government surpluses or deficits had orders of magnitude of much the same size as private saving; government fiscal policy and taxation systems provided automatic stabilisers, and welfare state provisions meant a divorce between the distribution of personal incomes and the distribution of income between the factors of production. (It is surprising that he did not add the need to include the overseas sector with which so much of his own work had been concerned.) Joan Robinson's views on the nature of the process of inflation, in particular, how money wages responded to changes in prices, and aggregate expenditures, for example, on capital accumulation, responded to inflationary processes, were too special and limited.

8.2

Prior to the publication of *Essays*, there was a flurry of articles stimulated by the publication of *The Accumulation of Capital*. The most insightful and sympathetic was Kahn's 'Exercises in the analysis of growth' published in *Oxford Economic Papers* in 1959. Kahn concentrated on the nature, use and limitations of Joan Robinson's concept of a Golden Age. He discussed the nature of causation – he refers to a comparison of Golden Ages between 'which there exists a stated difference but which in other respects are subject to the same conditions. It is one thing to *correlate* two characteristics involved in such a comparison ... but it would be quite another thing ... to regard one as causatively determining the other. (Kerr with Harcourt (eds.), 2002, vol. III, 46, emphasis in original) He examines how to include technical progress in the narrative, concentrating on neutral technical progress. Kahn not only had in mind Joan Robinson's book but also had Harrod's concepts of g_w and g_n, especially the possibility of them reaching equality, and Kaldor's 1957 *Economic Journal* model of growth and 1959 *Economica* articles on growth and inflation. Kahn was much more cautious in his claims for the application of the analysis than Kaldor who always wished immediately to do descriptive analysis of the processes of distribution and growth. Such processes were explicitly excluded from the objectives of Kahn's analysis: 'what I have said ... is intended as no more than prolegomena to the solution of real problems' (Kerr with Harcourt (eds.), 2002, vol. III, 51).

Kahn always attached utmost importance to the identical equality of saving and investment in Keynes's analysis and he carried this over into his incursions into growth theory:

> [A] glorified version ... a useful instrument for detecting error against those detractors who contemptuously dismiss it as a "truism" or,

> more contemptible still, a "tautology". [His] glorified version of the Keynesian identity would be as consistent ... with a system of ideas under which the rate of growth of capital was derived from the rate of profit as with a system under which the rate of profit is derived from the rate of growth.
>
> (Kerr with Harcourt (eds.), 2002, vol. III, 42)

The opening pages of the article are concerned with consistent definitions of income, profits (both share and rate of), wages and capital. In particular, he insists that to get correct and consistent relationships, we must always deal with the rate of change in the value of capital, 'not in any sense [with] the value of change in the amount of capital'. (Here, he surely had in mind Swan's criticism of Joan Robinson's treatment of the meaning and significance of Wicksell effects.) Even though Kahn is concerned with Golden Ages, he is careful to distinguish between actual profits as capitalist's income and expected profits as the relevant concept when discussing the investment decision. He also discusses the role of the rate of interest which he takes to be a general proxy for the overall 'state of finance' that is potentially or actually available to allow investment expenditure.

He also discusses the concept of a Bastard Golden Age, 'a state of equilibrium growth which has all the attributes of a Golden Age other than that of full employment' (Kerr with Harcourt (eds.), 2002, vol. III, 47). Whether it is maintained depends on whether the state of finance may be progressively eased by falling money wages (due to the pressure of the unemployed), or the quantity of money increasing faster than money wages, or credit becoming progressively easier.

In the same issue of *Oxford Economic Papers* is Worswick's 'comment with algebra'. Worswick's principal object was to reproduce in algebra (with an accompanying economic explanation and intuition) the propositions of Joan Robinson's model with one technique which, as we saw, is the central core of her book. Worswick uses the device of a (benevolent) dictator within a stockade to direct production and plan accumulation. Within the stockade there are advanced production techniques and the stockade is surrounded by a hinterland from which unlimited supplies of labour may be obtained. (Unlike Solow (1963) who adopted Worswick's model, the labourers in the hinterland play little part in determining the level of real wages.) For most of the analysis, production is concentrated upon, and assumptions are set up, so as to be able to have physical units in which to measure the outputs of consumption goods and machines.

Worswick works out the conditions which decide the distribution of employment between the production of consumption goods and machines, given the initial inherited stock of machines, and with a constraint of full employment sometimes imposed. Towards the end of the article, Worswick introduces something akin to profits and asks how they are created (realised) by expenditure, being potentially there as a surplus of consumption goods in the consumption goods sector.

Worswick concludes that the discussion might appear to be a sustained attack on Joan Robinson's model of accumulation with one technique. It was certainly not his intention, adding that the main difference in presentation was his introduction of the planning dictator. This may be why Joan Robinson was *not* that pleased with the article. Worswick claims that their respective conclusions mostly overlap but that his exposition brings out 'certain points more clearly ... not remarkable. We all know that the best approach to Ricardo or Keynes is not to read their original work' (Kerr with Harcourt (eds.), 2002, vol. III, 67).

This leads Worswick to question whether using the dictator to arrange the economy may be more than a mere trick of presentation. It is: '[t] he system [will] only "break down" if the dictator goes mad' (Kerr with Harcourt (eds.), 2002, vol. III, 68) whereas the conditions for a Golden Age (a mythical state as Joan Robinson pointed out) will only be met in an unregulated capitalist economy by the uncoordinated actions of individual business people in a competitive situation by a fluke (shades, as we have seen, of Marx's analysis of schemes of production and reproduction).

Ronald Findlay (1963) drew on Kelvin Lancaster's model of *The Accumulation of Capital* (Lancaster, 1960) to go over in algebra (and geometry) the same ground on Golden Ages as that which Joan Robinson covered in her book. His is a comprehensive and helpful article, reaching many of the same conclusions as Joan Robinson had and explicitly relating the findings to the other principal contributors at the time – Harrod and Domar, Solow and Swan, Kaldor – and at the end of the article to antecedents – Keynes (Harrod/Domar), Wicksell (Solow/Swan) and Marx (Joan Robinson), with Kaldor possibly drawing on all five. He gives Keynes a relatively low input at what was then the present state of play but suggests that when money and finance are introduced, as they must be, Keynes will play a much larger role – 'it is almost certain that liquidity preference, and perhaps even the ideas of the "mysterious" Chapter 17 ..., will play a central role' (Kerr with Harcourt (eds.), 2002, vol. III, 84).

Before discussing Joan Robinson's response to Worswick and Findlay, we note Lancaster's stringent critique in his review article. He tries to soften the blow by writing that 'any work of Mrs Robinson must command respect'. Moreover, when it is a book which is meant to do for growth what *The Economics of Imperfect Competition* did for price theory, her book must be judged only by the highest standards; 'judged as a whole in terms of its fabric, method and its general sweep: in terms of these, it does not succeed' (Lancaster, 1960, 63). Lancaster thought that the chief fault was 'failure of communication' and he quotes her reply to Worswick that she was 'very sorry that my book should be so difficult. What I meant is quite simple, but I evidently failed to make it clear' (Robinson, 1959, 141).

The chief reason is that the comparative statics method that is so appropriate for *The Economics of Imperfect Competition* (not that Joan Robinson subsequently thought so) is 'not at all well suited to handling dynamic problems of capital' (64) because the 'words and pictures' tradition is 'inadequate to the task of dynamic analysis in economics'. He adds that 'The "arts" tradition of jumping straight from a simplified abstract analysis to a Grand Conclusion about the real world proves too strong for the more austere scientific caution' (64). (Lancaster should have known for his first degree was in English Literature.)

He concentrates on Joan Robinson's basic model and shows the model is fine when the provision of equilibrium conditions is the task set it (as Joan Robinson made explicit anyway). But she was after process analysis and the materials have not been provided, as it becomes absolutely clear to Lancaster when attempts to set up any dynamic equations for the model are attempted. He is explicitly harsh about this.

> In the section of her book in which she has a more or less clearly defined equilibrium model, that of long-run accumulation, her discussion of processes consists either of a reiteration of the equilibrium conditions, or the arbitrary selection of one possible process from an infinity of possibilities, with no particular attempt to justify the selection.
>
> At best one can *describe* verbally a process which has been traced out by other methods, just as we can describe the course of the planets and the sun without being able to show verbally why the course is as it is.
>
> (69, emphasis in original)

He concludes that 'what is little more than a two-by-two linear equilibrium model (and well deserving of discussion as such) can be dressed in a woolly cloak of words to appear to be a full-blooded economy' (70).

As we noted in Chapter 6, Joan Robinson did lay herself open to such a critique through some of her asides. But what is also clear from Kahn's paper, her aims were in general much more modest, at that stage, than Lancaster implies. Moreover, when she gets to grips with Worswick's and Findlay's versions of her model, she more than holds her own because of her superb intuition concerning the driving forces at work in capitalism. (Findlay anticipates her response by making explicit his MIT credentials so suggesting that he does not find her ideas very plausible 'because [he] went to the Massachusetts Institute of Technology' (Findlay, 1963, 412).)

In her comment on Worswick's article (Robinson, 1959), she takes up two points, one minor, one major. She wonders why he makes such heavy weather about what happens when there are no machines in the capital goods sector. If there is literally no capital there, employers have no hold over workers and a different economic system would be relevant. If we use Worswick's own algebraic expression, as capital becomes vanishingly smaller, the cost of machines tends to their wage costs and the quantity of profit in the sector tends to zero (in competitive conditions) but the *rate* of profit remains at the overall rate, a typical example of Joan Robinson's analytical mind at work.

The major point concerns the limitations imposed by setting the wages in terms of 'treacle', the homogeneous consumption good. Joan Robinson prefers to set the wage in money terms, sell treacle to workers and allow the market to set the price, responding to the expenditure of the wages bill from the capital goods sector. Then, the larger the labour force in that sector, the higher will be the price set and the lower will be the treacle wage (a variant of Kalecki's model, of course).

If too many people are called to make machines, the real wage will fall below the level tolerated outside the stockade, wage demands will rise inside it, the inflation barrier will bite (though Joan Robinson does not claim this to be the *only* cause of inflation). If the wage is too low to attract workers, a shortage of labour will appear. If the dictator's equivalent of animal spirits is sluggish, few are called to make machines, the price of treacle will be lower and treacle wages in the stockade will be higher.

From this starting point, the analysis can be extended to analyse a basket of consumption commodities, and the dictator as a planning authority adjudicating between the interests of those inside and outside the stockade. Worswick's analysis gives only limited illumination 'so long as he leaves the dictator stuck in the treacle' (142).

Joan Robinson (1963) was worried about being 'ungracious' by complaining about 'a reader [Findlay] who [had] taken so much trouble on her behalf'. Her main complaint was that Findlay had set up her model in such a way that by standing it on its head, he had emptied causality out of the model. In particular, she objected to the real wage determining accumulation in his accumulation function. This is all right in a Ricardian corn model but not in one – her's – where the wage bargain is in terms of money so that the real wage depends upon price. In her model, the rate of accumulation and the marginal propensity to save out of profits determine the rate of profits and it, in conjunction with technical conditions, determines the real wage. The prime mover in the whole affair is the overall rate of accumulation emerging from the struggles of individual firms to increase productive capacity.

It is here that Findlay parts company with her, arguing that it is unfortunate that Joan Robinson like Keynes adopts a uni-linear conception of causation whereas his model, a feedback mechanism used to relate the rate of accumulation, the rate of population growth and real wages, is one of mutual determination. He illustrates this by an analogy. If the temperature of a room is regulated by a thermostat, it makes little sense to ask whether the supply of heat governs temperature or the other way around – the values of the variables are mutually determined. He adds that his Figure 1 illustrating this bears the same relation to *The Accumulation of Capital* as the *IS/LM* diagrams do to *The General Theory* (ouch).

Findlay has tried to reconcile propositions common to the neo-neoclassical model and his version of Joan Robinson's model. A rate of accumulation in excess of population growth drives up real wages and reduces the rate of accumulation. (Both authors pitch their discussion in terms of reconciling discrepancies between the values of g_n and g_w.) Joan Robinson wants animal spirits to dominate and so uses feedback from rising real wages onto the nature of technical progress as the mechanism, just as Marx did. Findlay hoped that after thesis and antithesis, his synthesis finally had Joan Robinson's ideas right even though as an MIT person he did not find them very plausible (412).

8.3

The scene is now set for the discussion of *Essays*. Its objectives have been signalled in some of the papers discussed above and are set out explicitly in the Preface. There she apologises for the 1956 book being 'found excessively difficult'. She attributes this to 'too terse an exposition of the main ideas' and to not making explicit enough the departure required from old (neoclassical) ideas, 'the confused but weighty corpus of traditional teaching', when 'a Keynesian approach to long-period problems' is adopted.

Much of the trouble comes, she felt from her own experience, from conflating Walrasian supply and demand prices with Marxian and Marshallian prices containing the conception of normal profits. This is the subject of Chapter I, 'Normal prices'. Chapter II, 'A model of accumulation' was her latest and, she hoped, was her more persuasive attempt to 'generalise' *The General Theory* to the long period.

In *Essays*, she had steadfastly refrained from jumping from very abstract theory to conclusions applicable to reality – 'actual problems'. This has the implication that Chapter III, 'A model of technical progress', is 'even more formalistic' but does, she hopes, clear up some points. Chapter IV, 'A neoclassical theorem', 'distils the essence of the analysis of the technical frontier' with less heavy weather than her first attempt (v). Her 'main concern is to get economic analysis off the mud of static equilibrium theory' (v).

The heart of the book is undoubtedly Chapter II and its heart in turn is on page 48, her famous banana diagram of the determination of the rate of accumulation of the capital stock and the distribution of income, exploiting the two-sided relationship between profitability and accumulation that she took principally from Kalecki (and also Keynes), behind whom, in turn, lay the classicals and Marx. It contains her version of Harrod's g_w.

She does not explicitly in the diagram itself introduce Marx's sphere of production but concentrates instead on his sphere of distribution and exchange with Kaleckian/Keynesian additions. But the analysis is easily extended to bring in Marx's analysis in terms of the role of the class war in affecting levels of the real wage and the potential surplus available to be realised by the coming together of the factors responsible for accumulation and distribution in the other sphere. It was Donald Harris (1975, 1978) who has most exploited the putting together of Marx on the left (of the diagram) and Joan Robinson and friends on the right (see Figure 8.2 below). He also brought out the possibilities of establishing an actual rate of growth (g_a) with full employment, a Bastard Golden Age with sustained or rising levels of unemployment and a Harrodian situation of inflationary pressure when g_n is so far in excess of g_w as to create such pressures.

What the banana diagram does is to take propositions concerning accumulation and distribution, presented as determining levels and shares of levels, and relate them as rates, for example, of growth and of profits. There are a number of grey areas involved because establishing actual rates (of both growth and profits) rather than their Golden Age counterparts runs into the problems of valuing capital in order to make precise what is meant by both the rate of growth of the stock of capital (accumulation) and the rate of profits. These are problems which Joan Robinson never completely solved in this context. As Asimakopulos (1984; Kerr with Harcourt (eds.), 2002, vol. V, 454) points out, 'the diagram ... she presents to illustrate the double-sided relationship between the rate of profit and the rate of accumulation is inappropriate according to her own methodological position, since outside of long-period equilibrium the rate of profit[s] does not have any clear meaning'. Furthermore, while the effects of technical progress may be taken into account when examining possible movements over time in the relationships concerned, it is not done by Joan Robinson herself though, as we noted, she has a separate chapter on the formal analysis of types of technical progress within, usually, Golden Age settings.

We move now to the banana diagram itself (see Figure 8.1). Prior to it, in Chapter II is an explicit discussion of the distinction between logical and historical time, with which is associated

> two kinds of economic arguments each of which is useful in analysis provided that it is not stultified by being compared with the other.
>
> [The first] proceeds by specifying a sufficient number of equations to determine its unknowns, and so finding values for them that are compatible with each other.
>
> ... The other ... specifies a particular set of values obtaining at a moment in time, which are not ... in equilibrium with each other, and shows how their interactions may be expected to play themselves out.
>
> ...
>
> At any moment in logical time, the past is determined just as much as the future [, there is no causation]. ... In an historical model, causal relations have to be specified. Today is a break in time between an unknown future and an irrevocable past. ... Movement can only be forward.
>
> Robinson (1962e, 23–6)

Not only is 'time ... a device to prevent everything happening at once' (Joan Robinson includes this quote from Bergson on the title page), it also differs from space by being irreversible.

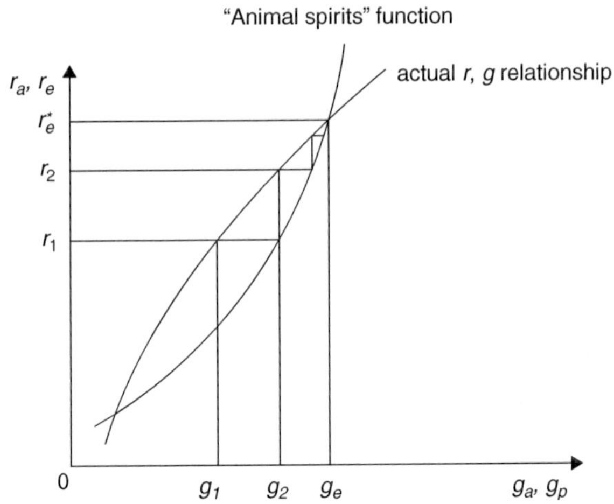

Figure 8.1 The banana diagram

Coming now to the diagram itself: on the vertical axis we measure actual (r_a) and expected rates of profits (r_e) for the economy as a whole (presumably aggregates of individual decision-makers' expectations and actual experiences); on the horizontal axis, we measure actual (g_a) and planned rates of accumulation (g_p) (similarly aggregated). She uses the Keynes–Kaldor–Kalecki version of distribution to show the relationship between actual accumulation and realised profitability where the position and slope of the relationship reflects thriftiness and financial conditions which determine how much profitability a given rate of accumulation may establish. She draws on Keynes to establish a link between actual profitability and expected profitability; Keynes argued that as we cannot know the future in an uncertain environment, we must draw on the present and its continuance as a convention:

> [T]he facts of the "*existing* situation enter, *in a sense disproportionately*, into the formation of our long-term expectations; our usual practice being to take the existing situation and project it into the future, modified only to the extent that we have more or less definite reasons for expecting a change.
>
> (Keynes, 1936, 148, emphasis added)

With a given state of 'animal spirits', expected profitability so determined (we make it one for one for simplicity, that is, what is achieved is expected to be continued) will call forth given rates of planned accumulation.

This relationship is dubbed the 'animal spirits' function (see Figure 8.1). Where the two relationships intersect (at the top of the banana), we get consistency in the sense that implementing accumulation, which had been planned in expectation of a certain rate of profitability, creates profitability of the same amount and justifies continuation of the same rate of accumulation, other things remaining equal. This is her version of Harrod's g_w.

Suppose we are not at the intersection point. Then an iteration procedure will take the economy towards it (see Figure 8.1). If actual accumulation were g_1, this would create actual profitability of r_1. This in turn leads to a higher rate of accumulation, g_2, and of profitability, r_2; and so on until the economy reaches g_e, r_e^*.

In an historical time analysis, not only may g_e^*, r_e not be reached, if the economy is not initially there, but even if it is, there is no guarantee that it will stay there. First, the 'animal spirits' function is defined for a given state of long-term expectations and finance conditions. Were either of these to change, either through endogenous feedbacks or external shocks, the function would change its position and shape too. Secondly, as actual accumulation occurs, national productivity changes and this will affect levels of employment and unemployment which in turn may feedback into the 'animal spirits' function. As for the distribution relationship, the very composition of national output over time may affect the corresponding distribution of income and therefore the thriftiness conditions which would in turn alter its position and shape. All these eventualities (and no doubt more) are referred to by Joan Robinson in her chapter. She also tries to tackle the problems raised by Asimakopulos about the measurement of profitability and accumulation away from the intersection but, as we noted, her discussions did not meet the strict criteria she herself had laid down. All this analysis may be regarded as an application to the theory of growth of Keynes's theory of shifting equilibrium (Keynes, 1936, 293–4, see also Kregel, 1976).

Now we examine a number of possible equilibrium scenarios. Suppose we know the level of the real wage in the existing conditions when the inflation barrier would be met. (This is the equivalent of Kaldor's upper band to the share of profits in full employment national income in his 1955–6 paper, beyond which an inflationary spiral sets in, except that the share of investment in full employment national income in his model is assumed to be such that the economy grows at its Harrodian natural rate.) Add a wage rate, rate of profits relationship defined by existing technical conditions on the left hand side of the diagram (see Figure 8.2) and let Ow^* be the real wage rate defined by the 'inflation barrier'. Then Or^* is the highest rate of profits it is possible for the economy to realise in the existing conditions, and Og^*, the highest rate of accumulation. Now let g_e, r_e be associated with the corner of the rectangle defined by Or^*, Og^*. This is a Golden Age with full employment.

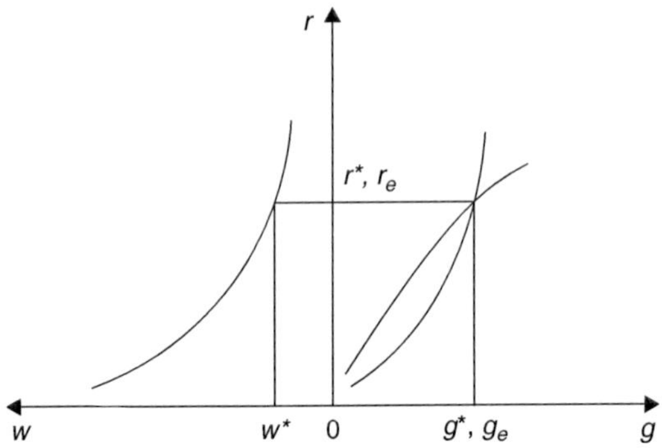

Figure 8.2 The 'inflation barrier', distribution and growth.

If the 'animal spirits' function were to intersect the distribution function below and to the left of this point, we have a potential Bastard Golden Age with sustained, possibly even rising unemployment over time. If it does not cut the distribution function before the upper limit defined by the 'inflation barrier', we have an inflationary impasse. And if the 'animal spirits' function is above the distribution function, the only possible resting place is a stationary state with a zero rate of accumulation.

If now we allow feedback onto the left-hand side of the diagram, actual accumulation which embodies technical progress will, period by period, shift the *w*, *r* relationship outwards, enlarging the potential surplus and rate of profits period by period. Since actual events will also be affecting the relationships on the right-hand side of the diagram as well, as we have seen, Joan Robinson's analysis allows us to show in a geometric manner, the processes of cyclical growth, in which trend and cycle are indissolubly mixed, of both late Kalecki (1968) and Goodwin for many years before (and after) his famous 1967 growth cycle model in the Maurice Dobb *Festschrift* (Feinstein, 1967).

Following a review of the then existing growth models – classical, neoclassical, Keynesian, Kaldorian – Joan Robinson provides a very succinct conclusion. She warns us again that all are

> too much simplified ... for it to be possible to confront them with evidence from reality ... they must be judged on the a priori plausibility of their assumptions.

> There is an important difference in emphasis ... according as they exhibit some kind of inbuilt propensity to maintain full employment over the long run or as they follow Keynes in regarding it as dependent upon enterprise that cannot be relied upon, unassisted, either to achieve stability in the short run or to maintain an adequate rate of growth in the long run.
>
> (87)

It is clear that at this stage in her thinking, the factors responsible for the cycle were independent of those responsible for the trend. Indeed, it is not clear that she ever explicitly went the whole way with Kalecki and Goodwin even though their insights and developments in this regard were even then implicit in her approach.

8.4

We move to the analysis of technical progress which 'cannot be both neat and life like ... nothing in reality which remains constant through time to provide us with neat units in which to calculate' (88). Her object therefore 'is to set up a ... simplified model in ... which analysis can be conducted in a definite clear-cut manner [hoping] that it may yield insights which retain some validity when applied to the vaguer and more complicated processes of actual development' (88). Having set it up, she proceeds logically with sections on classification, a Golden Age, biased progress, unsteady progress, surplus with scarcity of labour, a conclusion, followed by an appendix containing three sections: criterion of neutrality, Cobb–Douglas and Kaldor's technical progress function.

The general simplifying assumptions are a closed system of competitive private enterprise, two classes of households, workers and rentiers, and two classes of income, wages and net profits. There are no land (scarce resources) and no economies of scale beyond the efficient size of an individual plant.

All technical progress is associated with the design of equipment used to produce the consumption good. Equipment in the investment goods sector is used to make itself and the consumption good equipment, and it never changes once made. The real cost of consumption good equipment is its price when measured in terms of labour time at the ruling rate of profits (see Harcourt, 1972, 23–4). The money wage is constant as is the number of (large) firms.

Joan Robinson argues that her model provides simple criteria for classifying types of improvements according to their neutral, or capital-saving, or capital-using bias. The real cost of plant is reflected in its money cost. If we compare a new plant with the last vintage in use and their money costs are the same but the output of the first is higher, we have a neutral improvement; if the cost is less, it is capital-saving, if it is more, it is capital-using. Neutral improvements always produce superior designs but this is not necessarily so for the other two if the biases are extremely strong. Then we have *partial* improvements, lowering one cost element only by raising another.

Biases in the course of technical progress are, of course, not the same as differences in the capital–labour ratios available at any moment of time from the *ex ante* production function, 'from which a choice is made for new investment' (92). 'Great confusion', our author tells us, 'arises from confusing the *ex ante* production function with the succession of techniques chosen in the course of development through time' (n2, 92–3).

Joan Robinson sets out the conditions for a Golden Age with technical progress in Harrodian terms of $g_a = g_w = g_n$ in order to distinguish 'various types of disharmony which are liable to arise in an uncontrolled economy' (99) when a Golden Age cannot be realised. She considers biased technical progress, changes in the rate of technical progress, and disharmony between the rate of accumulation and the rate of growth of output which technical progress makes possible. She applies a constraint of full employment in the first scenario and then examines what conditions have to be fulfilled in order to be consistent with the constraint. When considering unsteady rates of technical progress, the possibility of cumulative causation processes emerging are much enhanced (107).

While stressing that the 'austere assumptions' made her analysis 'unlifelike', she nevertheless felt that relationships so uncovered seemed 'to correspond to those that can be vaguely perceived through the fog of index-number ambiguities that hangs over real problems' (111). There was still a long way to go though because the effects of technical progress on the types of commodities produced and on workers' and consumers' characteristics had not been considered.

In the appendix on the criteria of neutrality, she considers how her approach compares with those of Pigou, Hicks and Meade. In the section on Cobb–Douglas, she sees its traditional use as not always keeping clear the distinction between choice of technique at a moment of time and changes in the opportunities available on the *ex ante* production function over time. The final section is on Kaldor's technical progress function of 1957. She thought it a rather *ad hoc* construction as far as discussing differing types of possible technical progress were concerned.

The last chapter is on 'A neo-neoclassical theorem'. Here she sees the Golden Rule of accumulation as emerging from combining a rate of profits determined by accumulation, thriftiness and the choice of technique from a given spectrum of possibilities, so that the highest rate of output of consumption goods is achieved when the rate of profits is equal to the rate of accumulation. As Joan Robinson would have been the first to admit, this is all very much economics for the economists.

8.5

In the Foreword to *Economic Heresies*, dated December 1970, Joan Robinson especially thanks Tom Asimakopulos, John Eatwell, Donald Harris, Jan Kregel and Amit Bhaduri for 'arguments and discussions'. All had made or were to make significant contributions to our understanding of her contributions and approaches, sometimes in collaboration with Joan Robinson herself, for example, the Robinson and Eatwell textbook (1973), which was intended to capture the hearts and minds of coming generations of students (see Chapter 10), and Bhaduri and Robinson (1980), her last statement on the roles of Kalecki, Marx and Sraffa in her proposed theoretical framework and approach.

She is even more than characteristically forthright in the opening paragraph of the introduction. She refers to the 'clear message' of the orthodox doctrines which were dominant in the last quarter of the nineteenth century: support for *laissez faire*, free trade, the gold standard and the 'universally advantageous effects' of the pursuit of profit in a competitive environment. They were at one with the objectives of the authorities in an expanding and flourishing capitalist world.

But the arguments on which the doctrines were based had 'little relevance to the problems on which they pronounced'. The structure of economic theory was 'a deductive system based on *a priori* premises'. It was constructed in terms of arguments of either the effects of displacement from an already established equilibrium or in terms of comparisons of equilibrium positions without discussions of the process of changing from one to another – an omission of which Keynes was aware and wished to remedy in his *Treatise on Money* (1930).

> My object [in Books III and IV] has been to find a method which is useful in describing, not merely the characteristics of static equilibrium, but also those of disequilibrium, and to discover the dynamical laws governing the passage of a monetary system from one position of equilibrium to another.
>
> (Keynes, 1930, vol. 1, xvii)

'The lack of correspondence between the assumptions of the theory and the facts in reality did not matter because the doctrines were acceptable' (Robinson, 1971, viii). Moreover, as policy was overwhelmingly *laissez faire*, actual situations to which policy could be applied could be ignored. The whole situation was especially agreeable to the English (but not necessarily British) authorities.

In the 1920s, the US enjoyed a long boom while Great Britain experienced low profitability and heavy unemployment, facts which were inconsistent with Say's Law, an axiom of the orthodox scheme. Hence, we had the use of the Treasury view in 1929 to argue against public works expenditure: there was at any moment a given fund of saving to finance investment. If the government borrowed part of it to finance public works, there would be an exactly equal reduction in foreign investment [why *foreign* investment – she does not say], so that increased unemployment due to reduction of the balance of trade would offset increased employment due to public works.

When the world slump set in, the 'total bankruptcy' of the prevailing theory was obvious to all except 'professional devotees' – enter Keynes of *The General Theory*. Keynes broke out of the theological system of orthodox axioms by looking at the actual economy's behaviour, bringing the argument down from stationary states into the present, here and now, when the past cannot be changed and the future cannot be known.

The seeming revolution though did not last for long as the Keynesian innovations became orthodox in their turn. In particular, by assuming Keynesian policy would keep investment at the level which absorbed (created) full employment saving, the remaining doctrines of the neoclassicals were revived (x) – partly with Keynes's own blessing, it must be said (see Keynes, 1936, 378–9).

Joan Robinson argues that there are serious inconsistencies in the old scheme which make the new synthesis unsatisfactory. First, there is an inconsistency between assuming a perfectly competitive market and that every trader is maximising gain.This is especially applicable through a flaw in the case for free trade and the extension of stationary state analysis to that of a continuously growing economy.

The most serious problem concerns concepts of factors of production. One view comes from Wicksteed in which there are *n* factors, each measured in its own technical unit; this view underlies the point of view of the Walrasian system. The other point of view is that factors of production are in the broad categories of Ricardo: labour, land and capital. She adds an understatement: 'The nature of capital was always a source of anxiety and trouble' (xii).

She discusses Marshall's attempt to use the concept of waiting with both the stock of capital and the new flow associated with saving. Joan Robinson identifies three dimensions of capital at any moment of time: a who's who of equipment and commodities but also a sum of wealth. Mediating between the two is a third dimension of capital as finance (xii). She then discusses profits, interest and real productivity, how these worried Marshall. He put up a smoke screen of ambiguity, while modern neo-neoclassicals, for example, the late Charles Ferguson, had 'faith in the theory and [were] not afraid to make it clear and definite' (xiii). Some of the propositions in Ferguson (1969) follow Walras but at the level of the economy as a whole, capital as a whole is treated in the same way as the input of services of a specific machine with the wage measured by the marginal product of labour and profit by the marginal product of capital. 'Apart from logical incoherence, the flaw in the new orthodoxy destroys the validity of its message' (xiii).

She refers to their conception of society as harmonious especially with saving (as a present sacrifice) leading to investment in order to increase future consumption. This Keynes destroyed by having investment determined by private profit opportunities and creating saving in the process and not guaranteeing full employment. But if we follow Keynes and do guarantee it, what sort of employment do we want? The orthodox, by having the rate of return on investment to the individual firm derived from the marginal product of capital to society, resurrected *laisser faire* and dodged the question.

The new doctrine was now coming to a crisis because their *laisser-faire* view is discredited by the awakening of public opinion (this is 1970) to poverty in even wealthy nations, pollution, manipulation of demand by salesmanship, the arms race and, of course, the problems of developing nations. Her object is 'to find the roots of modern orthodoxy in the neoclassical tradition ... [Her re-examination of] old-fashioned questions [is meant] to clear the way for a more penetrating discussion of the problems of today' (xv).

Joan Robinson's discussion of orthodoxy brought a response, rather more in sorrow than in anger, from Frank Hahn (1972) – her

> view of the "orthodox" [was] like that of a medieval citizen of Lincoln of the Jews ... she attributes quite absurd beliefs and takes it for granted that these reflect wickedness. [It being] a free country, and if she does not engage in pogroms ... there is no reason why she should not enjoy herself.
>
> (Hahn, 1972, 205; Kerr with Harcourt (eds.), 2002, vol. V, 18)

Patronisingly, he adds that 'it is a pity. For when Professor Robinson is not engaged in either fantasies about orthodoxy or in expounding once again the "formula" of thrift and animal spirits or the "pseudo-production function" she can be very stimulating' (ibid., p. 18–19). Even more patronisingly, he concludes by admitting that there is 'a kind of crisis in economic theory at present, [that] the gap between theory and fact is far too large'. People like Hahn are aware of this but do not discuss it 'endlessly' because they have 'not yet found an alternative precise route which points to salvation' (Kerr with Harcourt (eds.), 2002, vol. V, 20).

What a contrast to Stephen Marglin (1973) who agreed to review the book for the *Economic Journal* because she was one of two members of her generation who helped him 'to see orthodox micro-economics ... for what it principally is, an ideological defence of capitalism' (Marglin, 1973; Kerr with Harcourt (eds.), 2002, vol. V, 21). Its practitioners fail to recognise this because the way the orthodox paradigm is developed 'ensures that embarrassing questions don't get asked' (21). He identifies the three questions she responds to and writes that his 'generation of heretics owes her a profound debt of gratitude ... for keeping the critical spirit alive and keeping the vision of an alternative before [them]' (ibid., p. 23).

8.6

There are eight chapters and a Conclusion in what is a short book of 150 pages. Chapter 1 is titled 'Stationary states'. It takes in her reading of the contributions and influences of Walras, Marshall and Wicksell. Chapter 2 is on the short period; Chapter 3, on interest and profits. In the latter, Keynes and the neoclassicals enter the story as do Ricardo and von Neumann. Chapter 4 is on increasing and decreasing returns, setting the scene for, first, non-monetary models and, then, money and prices in which she puts forward her very stringent views on Chicago and the Monetarists. Chapters 7 and 8 cover areas where she has made her own original contributions – the theory of the firm and growth models. Though a short book it may be seen that she encompasses a major part of the structures on which modern economic theory, at least at that time, was built.

Much of what she writes is a gathering together of themes she has analysed in detail in earlier articles and books. The newest parts are especially concerned with her critique of Chicago and Monetarism. Hahn gives her full marks for her deep understanding of the nature and role of money in modern economies and modern economic theory.

He especially singles out for praise her argument that 'Money ... gets the blame for the fact that the future is uncertain' (Kerr with Harcourt (eds.), 2002, vol. V, 19). This occurs in her discussion of market prices and how equilibrium is more likely to come about in situations in which dealers have a good idea what the equilibrium price is, based on past experience. When such knowledgeable market-makers are not present, either because of the nature of the markets or the commodities concerned, cumulative causation processes rather than equilibrating ones are much more likely to prevail.

When we examine the economy as a whole, she sees the difference between Chicago and Keynes as relating to how they read the quantity theory of money equation (in the form $MV=PT$). Chicago reads it from left to right while Keynes and Keynesians (in so far as they use the quantity theory) read it from right to left, the essence of the endogenous money approach. She wished Keynes had set out his theory with the rate of interest as a given rather than the quantity of money, for this would have prevented the subsequent takeover of his ideas within the neoclassical synthesis.

As Hahn points out, she makes a hash of presenting *IS* and *LM* (see Robinson, 1971, 82–5). But she is surely right to argue that Keynes would never have argued that even a substantial cut in the rate of interest would result in a *permanent* rise in investment expenditure. Just as he would never have argued for a sustainable long-term relationship between unemployment levels and rates of inflation (neither did Phillips). He, rightly, would have insisted that in any given short-period situation (and with his assumptions about short-period pricing behaviour), higher levels of employment would be associated with higher levels (not necessarily rates of change) of prices.

Joan Robinson never considered Salter a neoclassical economist even though Salter explicitly built on a Marshallian base; perhaps she did not consider Marshall a compleat neoclassical either! In her discussion of the choice of technique in her chapter on the theory of the firm, she deplores any use of a pseudo production function, surely an economy-wide concept, to discuss the choice of techniques in the investment decision. Of course, she is right to do this but it is a criticism beside the point as far as Salter's work is concerned. For he uses an *ex ante* production function to describe the choices of the investment–labour and investment–output ratios available at the moment at which the investment decision is made. The firm then has to be supposed to devise investment-decision rules to aid its decisions on how much and what sort of investment may be done. Salter's *ex ante* production function can be associated with many different investment-decision rules being used, a procedure which is not at odds with Joan Robinson's own discussion of the choice of technique in this chapter.[4] There, she brings in Kaldor–Mirrlees's case of the pay-off period criterion (1962) and Mario Nuti's extension of the analysis to imperfectly competitive market situations (1969).

Finally, one of Joan Robinson's principal objections to modern mainstream analysis is the establishment of what she considers to be an unfortunate and misleading dichotomy between microeconomic and macroeconomic theory. In her view, the two aspects are indissoluble and she illustrates this well in the sections of her book on investment behaviour. She points out that regardless of the objectives of the firm, its chances of achieving them depends upon systemic behaviour. This is because, ultimately, profit creation, and therefore the establishment of expectations of profitability relevant to the investment decision, depend upon the overall rate of accumulation, regardless of the market structures and decision rules ruling in various firms and industries.

9

Joan Robinson's Views on Development Economics as Political Economy

9.1 Economic development as an extension of the theory of economic growth

Joan Robinson's writing on issues of underdevelopment and development is often divided into categories. There is her writing on the underdeveloped economies struggling against poverty and towards capitalist industrialisation; there is her writing on those with the same aims but within the context of socialist industrialisation; and there is her writing on China, which too, can be divided into various stages of her critical awareness of the information she was given and the various stages in China's political and economic development. Her writing could also be divided between that which emphasised information gathering, her selection and documentation of the relevant 'facts' of the situation and, informed by these, her theoretical interpretation and policies. For example, she claimed that her China visits were to learn rather than to advise or teach, and much of her writing on China is descriptive; but it is also necessarily interpretative.

Her ideas about development and the structure of her thought increasingly came from Marx's schema of reproduction through Kalecki to her own interpretation of it. As we have seen, the latter was set out most perceptively in her tribute to Kalecki in the memorial issue for Kalecki of the *Bulletin of the Oxford Institute of Economics and Statistics* (Robinson, 1977c). There, she divided the economy into two sectors: the wage goods sector and the investment goods sector. She showed how activity, employment and distribution in the short term were determined by the rate of accumulation, the differing saving behaviour of the wage-earners and profit-receivers and the pricing policies of the wage goods (more generally, consumption goods) sector. Employment would tend to settle at a level where there were sufficient consumption goods produced to provide the wages of wage-earners in the investment goods sector as well as those of wage-earners in the consumption goods sector itself. Given the rate of investment and the employment required for the production of capital goods to meet it, the prices of consumption goods, the money wage rate, and the productivity of the wage earners in the consumption good sector between them would determine the surplus per person in the consumption goods sector available for wages in the investment goods sector, and so the required level of employment overall. For a given level of investment, real wages are lower and profits higher, the less thrifty is the community. Similarly, given the level of real wages, the less thrifty is the community, the lower is the rate of accumulation it can undertake. Her early approach to the analysis of underdevelopment was firmly based in *The Accumulation of Capital* (Robinson, 1956a).

This framework led naturally, in the context of development, to a discussion of the sorts of land reform that would best serve to raise productivity and therefore the potential surplus in the agricultural sector. In the late 1970s, Joan Robinson was still uncritical of the Chinese experience. Having pointed out that the drawback of small holdings was that each family had to produce a range of products so that land would not be specialised to its best use, she argued that the then Chinese system of large communes divided into small teams combined the advantage of intensive use of labour with control over the use of land in large units. She felt that this provided a strong incentive for teams to put in extra work to improve their land in schemes organised on an appropriate scale because they collectively shared any improved income that resulted (Robinson, 1978c, 52–3). She comments wryly on land reform in parts of Latin America which was intended to save the peasants from exploitation 'but had been turned into a more efficient, because less brutal, method of exploiting them' by making them wage-labourers on commercial farms (ibid., p. 54). She also describes India, where real wages are at subsistence so that all savings must come from the wealthy classes. This again involves forms of land reform. So she saw the transition from feudalism to capitalism in agriculture as providing the opportunity for accumulation as the surplus was shifted from rent to profits. But this capturing of surplus could be achieved far more effectively by creating a socialist organisation in agriculture. Socialist agriculture could both increase productivity by allocating land, machinery and labour more efficiently, and could extract and redirect the surplus, on the basis of some plan for national development. It 'could enjoy all the advantages of a monopoly without the political drawbacks' (Robinson, 1957b, 108). In fact, 'as far as the underdeveloped economies are concerned, it seems that socialism is going to beat capitalism at its own game, and the reason that it will do so is that it is a far more powerful instrument than capitalism for extracting the investible surplus from an economy' (Robinson, 1957c, 98).

Similarly, a scheme for distributing both agricultural and manufactured consumer goods had to be devised. While disagreeing with the claim of *laisser-faire* economists that because the market depersonalises production and exchange, it is inherently 'fair', she recognised that a market-based scheme of distribution was the most efficient way to distribute consumer goods. And the relative prices of each group would establish the terms of trade between sectors and the relative real wages.

For capitalist systems, it was easy to show in this framework that full employment was unlikely to occur. But neither was full employment inevitable in the context of planned development, which would also have to take into account foreign exchange constraints associated with trade and lending and borrowing, and the Kaleckian view that the workers must have some extra jam today rather than wait for a tomorrow which in reality often never came. It was within such a framework that Joan Robinson commented on different institutional forms, actual and ideal, the roles and limitations of government, and what behaviour could and would be expected of citizens at work and in their own community.

9.2 China[1]

Joan Robinson always admitted to a leaven of advocacy in her writings on China because she felt it could do something to offset what she perceived to be the hostility of most other scholars and commentators writing on China. It is true that some of her writings and assessments were far too partial and uncritical, especially during the period of the 'Cultural Revolution' when Mao's influence was at its greatest and the spirit of the (radical) age was a yearning for cult figures and the immediate establishment of Utopias. But if we look at the whole body of her writings on China from the early 1950s to the early 1980s, we get a more balanced view. We are able to see that her changing views may usefully be classified into three distinct phases, with the last one overlapping considerably with the first, and that, typically, she was willing to admit she had been wrong *once* she was convinced of it; a hard task, of course

Moreover, it is possible to show that when her writings are stripped of advocacy and the rather euphoric and starry-eyed traits of the middle phase, she had relevant, sensible, down-to-earth views on what should, could and was being achieved. Her views were similar to those Kalecki articulated when he returned to Poland in the 1950s and tried to have them implemented, alas, with little success.[2] In particular, there are in Joan Robinson's papers in the Archives of King's College, Cambridge, a set of unpublished lecture notes which encompass in broad outline most aspects of her views on sensible development in a country such as China. In them, she carefully identified the principal problems and set out the economic principles that could be used to provide *integrated* solutions to them. Aspects of the lectures are to be found in her published writings but as the lectures are set out so concisely in their unpublished form, it seemed sensible to examine them systematically. A major reason for doing so is that her views in turn are very much in accord with at least the economic aspects of what the Chinese authorities have, by and large, attempted to do since Mao's death.

On the economic front, the Chinese economy has performed far better than the economies of the former European socialist economies and than what was the USSR, both before and after 1989. So it is a sensible and relevant task to take a retrospective look at Joan Robinson's economic thinking on these issues.

Joan Robinson visited China eight times: in 1953, 1957, 1963, 1964, 1967, 1972, 1975 and 1978. She wrote an enormous amount on and about China, some of which is still unpublished. The published material may be found in periodicals (which vary from the well-known to the hardly known) and in pamphlets. A complete list may be found in the Appendix to this chapter.

As we noted, Joan Robinson's writings on China may be divided into three broad phases. The first contains her writings before her third visit in 1963. Though she showed tremendous enthusiasm for the Chinese experiment, she had definite views on how China should develop as a socialist economy. The initial visits allowed her to gather evidence in support of her views. The first phase came to an end with her third visit. What she saw (and had seen before) provided her with a laboratory with which to test intuitively her thinking about economic development in backward, overpopulated economies. In the first phase, her ideas were broadly similar to the views of the Right in China, to wit, a high rate of capital accumulation, the establishment of which nevertheless was to be achieved without an intolerable sacrifice of consumption, especially by the less well off; the use of profit-orientated industrial management in order to avoid the inefficiencies and drawbacks of a 'bureaucratic tendency'; the use of prices backed up by moral imperatives; control of population growth; reward for work done and the extraction of an agricultural surplus through gradual collectivisation. Inequality, Joan Robinson argued, was basically associated with the institution of private property. Eliminate it and justice will prevail in the non-agricultural sector though tax-free collective property differentials in agriculture would remain a source of inequality. On the whole, she found that the planning arrangements in China worked well in industry but she still felt uneasy about the suitability of socialism as a system for agriculture, mainly because of the difficulties of organising labour on a large scale.

In the second phase which began after her visit in 1963 and lasted until 1975, Joan Robinson took a sharp turn to the Left. From the 'Great Leap Forward' (1958–9) to the end of the decade of the 'Cultural Revolution' (1976), a period of statistical and informational blackout, she argued that the problem of socialist organisation lay in industry, not in agriculture. She thought that the communes had resolved the dilemma of organising labour in agriculture, whereas Soviet-type industrial management (even in its reformed decentralised form) was criticised for being motivated by profit and for its hierarchical structure which resulted from differentials associated with intellectual property. (She thought the latter was an unfortunate result of equal opportunity-education.) She saw the planning system as plagued not only by inherent bureaucracy, but also by the inequity of the property system. She argued that the 'Cultural Revolution' provided the possibility to create a cooperative system based on the ideology of serve-the-people. During this second phase, enthusiasm for the Chinese experiment became advocacy for the Maoist position on economic as well as political issues. She believed the information supplied to her at the time of statistical blackout. Her analysis inevitably was constrained by the quality of the information she could use. Her usual incisiveness returned when she was able to rid herself of its distorting influence.

After Mao's death in 1976, she discovered, to her horror, that the Chinese had not told the truth even to trusting analysts. This discovery marked the beginning of her third phase. As more information became available in post-Mao China, she looked back at her previous writings and put some of the record straight. It was a period of self-criticism; she admitted to having been starry-eyed about the decade of the 'Cultural Revolution' and she returned to supporting Rightist economic reform.[3] Her story was not always plausible, even when she was not misled by the Chinese, for sometimes she did not fully follow the logic of her own argument. Nevertheless it is possible to salvage from her thinking about and enthusiasm for economic development in China, a set of ideas that differ little from the views of those dubbed the Rightists in the so-called two-line struggle of Mao's China. As this set of ideas is now, on the whole, dominant in China itself, it is, as we said, relevant and timely to consider them in our discussion of Joan Robinson's approach and analysis.

We consider now the lectures she gave during her second visit in 1957. Joan Robinson had arrived at a set of conclusions about Chinese development before this visit. Capital accumulation was the key; to overcome 'backwardness', China needed a high rate of capital accumulation. As backwardness and overpopulation existed together, the relevant variable was the growth of capital per head. Capital accumulation had to accelerate, but population growth had to decelerate at the same time. (Richard Kahn told Pervez Tahir in December 1986 that the basic reason for Joan Robinson's early interest in socialism was the possibility of accumulation at a desired higher level than under capitalism.) In fact, in a review of Rowse, 'Mr Keynes and socialism' (Robinson, 1936c), she expressed this view.

But, in the process of raising capital per head, Joan Robinson expected China to learn from the Soviet mistakes so as to minimise human costs. This was to be ensured by putting in place a system of planning and management – a different set of the rules of the game – which would allow a smooth transition from private property in agriculture and industry, without ignoring consumer demand. These conclusions are reflected in the 1957 lectures (JVR/iii/5.1–5.3).

In the first lecture on 4 September 1957, 'The Relations between the Rate of Accumulation and the Price Level' (ibid.), she argued for the superiority of socialist rules over capitalist rules in ensuring rapid capital accumulation. The 'limits to [the] pace of development' were set by (i) the digestive capacity of the economy to absorb investment and education and (ii) the amount of surplus in agriculture and manufacturing sectors. If capital goods had to be imported, the availability of exportable funds, foreign exchange, would limit the ability of the economy to digest investment. Given this, the limit to the pace of investment was set by the surplus realised from agriculture and manufacturing. Under capitalism, the limit implied that prices rose, real wages fell, leading to a subsequent rise in money wages. There was also the problem of consumption out of profits received in the manufacturing sector. The situation under socialism would be different.[4]

'In a planned economy you haven't got the problem of inflation because money wages are controlled. But you have got the problem of squeezing the people to a certain point without giving way. Therefore this question of the pace of development involves a question of political judgement' (JVR/iii/5.1).

She considered an economy in which the digestive capacity could be stretched. If it is larger than the surplus which can be produced, then it is a question of how much surplus can be squeezed out and this is a question of political fact; therefore, she argues, it is doubtful whether pure economic theory is useful in a planned economy (JVR/iii/5.1).

She set up a simple numerical model to illustrate the limits on the pace of development, see Table 9.1.

Table 9.1 Limits on the rate of accumulation

	Agriculture (a)	Manufacture for sale (b)	Social outlay (c)	Investment (d)	
Income	45	25	10	20	=100
Tax and profit	5	25	—	P_i	
Value of output	50	100	—	$20+P_i$	$=170+P_i$

The model assumes that raw materials and consumer goods produced in agriculture are purchased by the official agencies for 45 reckoned in some unit. This constitutes income accruing to (a). The output of (a) is the input for (b), which is processed and sold to the public for 100. The income of sector (b) is 25. There is a gap of 30 between the total income of (a) and (b) and the sales value of the output of (b), on which the whole of national income is assumed to be spent in the absence of personal saving. The gap is realised as taxes and profits which are spent on social outlay, yielding no profit, and investment. Profits and taxes ensure that the national product of 100 is not consumed entirely by (a) and (b). Joan Robinson treats profits that might be generated in the investment sector as mere bookkeeping, so that P_i does not enter the discussion. Similarly, the gross value of output, $170+P_i$, has no bearing on her analysis.

Related to the political determination of the pace of development was the issue of allocating the burden between tax and profit from agriculture and income in the manufacturing sector – the terms of trade. Under capitalism, income in agriculture depends on prices, while the same in manufacturing depends on money incomes. A socialist economy had to exercise political judgement in this case as well. The criteria suggested included fairness and the provision of the right incentives. She stated the riddle as follows:

'Sometimes we can provide more incentive, but it is not fair, such as squeezing the workers. These two purposes are of course not separated because feelings of fair dealing also provide incentive. You must find a solution which is fair and also gives incentive (JVR/iii/5.1).

Within agriculture, the quality of soil would cause unfair income differentials. With income depending on prices, equal amounts of work yield different incomes on different soil. Her solution was to introduce money rent and to 'so arrange it that those working on better land will get the same income for an equal amount of work as those working on poorer land' (ibid.). What would in time have otherwise become a major source of inter-collective inequality was thus identified at the very beginning.

In the second lecture delivered on 6 September 1957 (JVR/iii/5.2.), 'The Problem of the Choice of Technique for a Planned Economy ... with Limited Industrial Resources', she dealt with the question of the choice of techniques and how a Poznan-type situation – that is, a situation in which the workers' consumption was so squeezed and its rate of improvement so low that eventually the situation became intolerable and unacceptable – may be avoided. She assumed surplus labour and scarce capital goods but rejected maximum employment as a criterion. Nor did she favour implementing the technique which yielded the highest output per head.

> You want a large income for the next Five-Year Plan, so you want to get out an additional flow of output, that is, more surplus. ... If you use capital in a form which employs a lot of labour, you have got to allow those people to consume. ... This is in a sense a brutal theory. (JVR/iii/5.2)

The image of China was that of a more humane economy. She was looking for an intermediate solution, '[T]he first distinction which has to be made is between those [techniques] which are superior and inferior and those which are less mechanised' (ibid.).

> The technique which will give the maximum profit is the same as that which ... makes the maximum contribution to your future surplus. Now some economists have argued for this maximum surplus as being the real object. I think they are overlooking the fact that

> additional wages are themselves a benefit. Potentially, a large output is that which leads to a large surplus. The larger the total output the larger the potential surplus it contains. Therefore to look for a technique which will give the maximum profit is oversimplifying the question. On the other hand, to look for a technique which will give the maximum output is unrealistic.
>
> (ibid.)

She illustrated the argument with a diagram (see Figure 9.1). *O/C* indicates output per unit of investment and *L/C* is employment per unit of investment. The angle represents a constant wage rate and the curve indicates known technical possibilities. Beta technique is stated to be the Chinese choice because there is a surplus of f-Beta and at the same time, employment is higher by *ab* than the 'Dobb method'.[5] The latter method is represented by D, which gives the highest surplus eD, and the least employment, O*a*. At the other extreme is the maximum-employment and zero surplus technique, E, a 'humanitarian' break-even point.

The coexistence of the old and new techniques, which she noticed on her first visit (Robinson, 1954, 33), was stated to be 'perfectly rational' as it involved 'using [a] superior technique in some enterprises because in other things ... [the Chinese had] to choose between a variety of techniques none of which are superior but some of which are more mechanised than others' (JVR/iii/5.2). (This was later to be called 'walking on both legs'

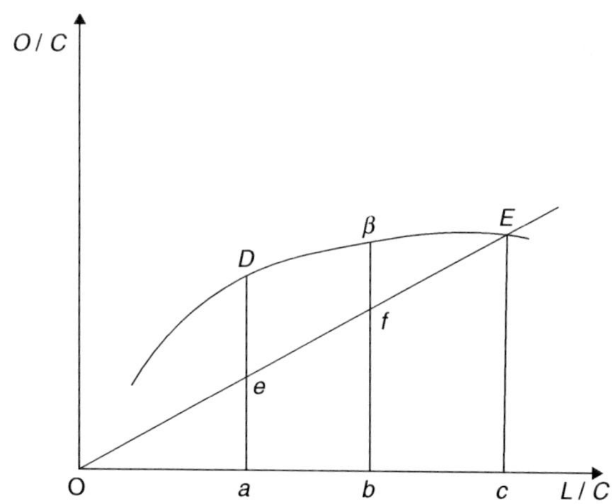

Figure 9.1 The choice of techniques in China

and is consistent with Salter's (1960) explanation of the coexistence of new and old vintages working side by side in capitalist economies.) Joan Robinson believed that this approach was consistent with rapid accumulation without imposing an intolerable sacrifice of consumption. In brief, the rate of accumulation and thus development would be higher under socialism than under capitalism because under socialism the surplus was a political decision. While she doubted the usefulness of economic theory in this present context, nevertheless, she did think

> at the same time ... that economic theory [was] very useful in the socialist world. For instance, on the population question you have a very special question because there are very few places on the earth's surface which [are] not over-populated. The Soviet Union is such a case and that gives a certain twist to their habits.
>
> (JVR/iii/5.3)

The third unpublished lecture, delivered on 9 September 1957, 'How Far and in What Way can the Price System be useful in a Planned Economy', addressed the all-important question of how to run the economy.

> It seems to me very strange that you find that you can use Marx's analytical apparatus in discussing problems of [a] planned economy because Marx's analytical apparatus was built up in order to analyse [a] capitalist economy in its early stage. It is appropriate to dealing with that particular kind of economy. It is very surprising if you can tailor-make that to fit to a totally different economic system.
>
> (JVR/iii/5.3)

In considering the question of how any economy would operate, 'what we have to look at is the means which [have] to be used to make it run' (ibid.). Three types of mechanisms were available: legal, market and moral. The legal mechanism specified a set of administrative laws and procedures. It 'has an advantage in that you can decide what is to be done and tell people to do it. But it has also very serious drawbacks, and when making complicated decisions it gets tied up in bureaucracy'. This was the problem in the Soviet Union. The market mechanism was based on self-interest with people following 'the line which is going to give them a better return in money terms'. She observed, profoundly:

> Now the market mechanism has very great merit in that it runs itself. Everybody is doing what he wants to do. This has really immense

> merits. ... In the West the price system is always glorified as a means for maximum satisfaction, and it is criticised by many people that it does not give maximum satisfaction.
>
> This is really beside the point, its merit is not in maximizing anything, but in the fact that it will operate itself. It does not need any policing and does not need any bureaucrats, and that is [an] enormous benefit. This one comes to realise only by contrasting it with other systems.
>
> (JVR/iii/5.3)

Among the defects of the market mechanism were mentioned monopoly and a badly skewed distribution of income. 'So many of the evils of capitalist society are associated with the market system. The basic objection to capitalist society is its distribution of property. That is not necessarily the same thing, although it is historically connected with the market system' (ibid.). As 'perfectly egotistical behaviour is not possible, a moral code ... is an essential ingredient of any system' (ibid.).[6] She mentioned here loyalty to the firm. The uniquely Chinese contribution consisted of a moral code – 'a sort of proper behaviour is being developed in everybody and being formalized'. She considered it to be 'another way of running the economy'. On a limited scale, its Western prototype was found in some professions, where a code of ethics was adopted for social rather than profit considerations. But the method had its problems. The difficulties of working out a moral code constituted one such problem. More seriously, 'people are not saints'. Therefore, the 'moral method can never operate alone, it has to be backed up by others', especially when the complexity of economic life increases. She put it to the Chinese:

> But as I see it, this development of the moral code I think is a unique contribution of China of another way of running the economy, and an extremely important contribution. What one would like to know is what will be the situation 20 or 30 years later when the main tasks are done and life is easier, then will be the difficult times. Your economy is still at an early stage, and the problem of administration gets more and more complicated as the level rises. When the question is to provide people with more food, more cotton, it is rather simple, and you know you need more steel, so providing a little more or a little less is not very important.
>
> (JVR/iii/5.3)[7]

The question of prices under socialism was discussed more formally in Joan Robinson (1958) and its rewrite, Joan Robinson (1960b). En route to China in 1957, Joan Robinson had also gone to the Soviet Union where the Khrushchev reforms were being debated. She had the chance to discuss the questions involved with Soviet economists, who invited her to write a paper for the Soviet journal *Voprosi Ekonomiki*. She had been reflecting on some of the issues raised in the lectures given in China for some time. Joan Robinson (1958) is the paper she wrote on the philosophy of prices, but the Soviet journal in question did not publish it (Robinson, 1975b, v). It contains all the important insights of her third lecture in China.

In a socialist system, she wrote, the objective was not 'maximum satisfaction' but 'a system of prices which will operate itself, without any need for rationing or any temptation to black marketeering'. The purpose was to lessen the resort to a bureaucratic system. Furthermore, as workers were paid according to work done, it was analytically convenient to call 'the earnings of workers *wages* and the excess of the receipts over costs in the operation of socialist enterprises' *profits*'. The requirements of the government to finance social outlays on non-saleable output determined what overall profits needed to be, and thus the relationship between price and wages. In other words, it followed the sectoral distribution of burdens decided in the overall plan. Broadly, the pattern of final prices of commodities should follow the rule of balancing demand with available supplies. There was no unique pattern of prices; however, 'A range of patterns of prices can all give an equally good fit with a given pattern of supplies. The pattern which happens to be ruling in any given situation must be largely a matter of historical accident'. Like the pattern of final prices, the ex-factory prices must also be established by the planners. Leaving their prices to the enterprises would require additional administrative measures 'to prevent them from behaving like capitalist monopolists'. Joan Robinson did not approve of the general practice of fixing final prices on a cost-plus basis, as it would be a disincentive to cost-minimisation, apart from the need to tell them 'in great detail ... what to produce instead of having a simple motive to select the assortment of commodities within their range that yields the highest selling value per unit of costs'. On the whole, 'any scheme which makes a rational use of prices takes the weight off direct administration' (Robinson, 1958, 130–2, 135).

Joan Robinson regarded 'a fair distribution of income between agricultural and industrial workers [as the] major problem of price policy in a planned economy'. To arrive at some desired distribution, she stressed the need to fix the farm prices below their demand prices so long as supply lagged behind demand. The problems were recognised frankly.[8] A black market emerges if private sales are disallowed. If private sales are allowed, the 'work-time and the use of land' shy away from producing for sales to government. Even in the case of crops with no permissible private use and therefore running no risk of a black market, labour and land may be deflected to alternatives more lucrative than black or free market prices.

As in the lectures discussed above, she favoured the principle of money rent, operating 'like Ricardian rent' and mopped up as 'land tax, assessed in terms of money instead of in terms of crops'. To the extent that the land-tax yield covers government expenditure, the need to mop up a surplus in the industrial sector would be reduced. It would thus be possible to ensure a desired inter-sectoral distribution of income. As the land tax was proposed to be levied according to the differential qualities of land, it would contribute to intra-sectoral equity in agriculture. According to her, these quality differentials were in the nature of property differentials; there was no justification for permitting the resulting income differentials (Robinson, 1960b, 33–6).

The lectures brought together several of the variables involved in the process of planned development. They did so at a most general or abstract level in order to illustrate the basic interactions involved in different policy choices. For example, a technique which maximised output per head would involve further decisions about taxing the industry's surplus, or pricing its products appropriately to provide subsistence to other workers. The general categories of the lectures were to be given the specificity of China's successive policies in order to pursue their implications. Perhaps the most problematical of her models is that of the social infrastructure, comprising legal, market and moral structures, all mutually reinforcing each other in the smooth running of the economy. Again, these categories gain meaning when given a specific form but it is not clear whether these systems are planned and imposed, or evolving out of their own interactions and their interactions with society at large.

To conclude, Joan Robinson considered China to be a socialist economy which would avoid the setting of detailed bureaucratic rules, use prices to take as much load off direct administration as possible and promote moral incentives in conjunction with other incentives. So to answer her own question (how far can the price system be used in a planned economy?) in lecture 3, she seemed to be saying that the price system could be used alongside a legal system and if propped up in its (distributional) implications by a moral system.

In her book *Aspects of Development and Underdevelopment* (1978c), Joan Robinson stated that her aim was to examine the validity of

Western doctrines on development and the manner in which they have been applied to the problems of the would-be developing world. She had, as early as 1960, criticised orthodox theory for its irrelevance to students from developing countries (Robinson, 1960b). Her Table of Contentsreveals the targets for and the structure of her argument as it moves through the issues of the conditions of production of a surplus, the terms of trade between the rural and the urban sectors, the attempt to gain a foreign trade surplus from primary products in a regulated world of international trade, the difficulties of aid and loans in planning development and the misuse of the surplus to build up an arms industry. 'Western teaching pretends to be scientific and objective by detaching the economic aspect of human life from its political and social setting; this distorts the problems that it has to discuss rather than illuminating them' (Robinson, 1978c, 3).[9] Joan Robinson, by this stage in her career, acknowledged and incorporated the political aspects to her economics, so that her examination of all these issues was not simply 'scientific'. This is not to say that she eschewed theory: '[t]he basic economic theory which seems to me to be useful is a reinterpretation in post-Keynesian terms of the Classical and Marxian theory of accumulation, distribution and trade' (ibid., Foreword). She has in mind the classical reproduction schema, Keynes's theory of effective demand and employment, both of which models underlie her own approaches to growth and distribution (Robinson, 1956a; 1962e), and Marx's circuits of capital. She devotes an appendix (to Chapter 2) to explaining the use of her theoretical concepts and arguments. She observes that the Marxian model is too oversimplified but it nevertheless provides a framework for understanding where the surplus is created and where it must be directed in order to achieve further growth in output in the next period.

She points out in Chapter 1 that many Third World countries are striving for not only a way out of poverty for the masses but also for a national identity which will be recognised and respected by the many international councils which make decisions which affect them. In particular, these are bodies influencing flows, and terms, of international finance. This dimension is outside the scope of orthodox theory.

In assessing the projects and strategies of development, economists typically turn to the measures of Gross Domestic Product (GDP) or GDP per head as indicators of progress from poverty. This, she argues, overlooks the fact that such an indicator will be misleading; it does not take into account that activities previously carried out within the family or community and outside the commercial sector may have now been displaced into the market. The composition of the total can only be known in broad aggregates. And nothing in the recorded figures reveals their new conditions of production or their distribution. She cautions against simplistic interpretation of the available data as a basis for assessing needs and policies.

Using the reproduction schema, she shows how it is fundamental to development to produce a surplus in the wage good sector, primarily in the agricultural sector, and traces through many examples of changes in land–labour relationships. The critical factors are the way by which the surplus is extracted from its producers and the uses to which it is put, including the forms in which it is redistributed.

She saw that, in effect, much land reform, intended to save the peasants from exploitation, has been turned into a more efficient, if less brutal, method of exploitation (Robinson, 1978c, 54–5). She also notes that where land is distributed more equally, it tends to be farmed more productively: 'some kind of cooperative or collective property in land and in means of production is necessary in order to provide a frame in which modernisation can go on without the polarisation between wealth and poverty which it is bringing about all over the Third World today' (ibid., p. 135). She observes that there is a cumulative effect of a growing surplus which has enabled growing investment into new and higher productivity methods in some Chinese communes which leads to widening divisions of income between communes; but there is also a bottom line below which incomes on all communes are not allowed to fall. With this guarantee, the cultivator has less to risk by innovating.

A turnover tax to collect the surplus is effectively the same as a profit margin but its allocation to investment rather than consumption is more reliable if collected by tax and allocated according to a plan, than if it is left to private decisions (see also Robinson (1949) where she proposes a strategy of fixing the level of prices including turnover tax such that total consumer demand just absorbs the total available stocks and flows of consumer goods: a socialist equivalent of full employment policy). Alternatively, the surplus product may be exported in which case its revenue can be used for importing capital equipment thus creating new capacity, employment and potentially higher outputs of wage goods through its effect on increasing productivity, or, the revenue may be used for luxury imports. The use of the surplus depended on the nature of the land–labour relationship and political balances.

Her understanding of the problems of development is based on a division of the economy between those who control the production of output and its distribution and those who directly produce it, in three sectors: agriculture, means of production or industry, and luxury goods.

In order to produce a surplus from a given investment, productivity must be increased and this is closely related to the relations of the cultivator to (generally) his land, and the decision of the owner to invest in new methods or crops rather than diverting the surplus to expenditure on luxury consumption. With an initial body of funds invested in new capacity, through the productive process, a surplus above the initial value of the investment is created, and this expanded reproduction must then be realised through the sale of the produce; and this expanded value must then be recirculated as finance capital – she discusses the various points at which the flow can be interrupted (see also Robinson and Eatwell, 1973): accumulation 'requires three ingredients: finance, ... saving, the restraint on consumption to allow resources to be used on investment; and imports to supplement resources at home' (Robinson and Eatwell, 1973, 332, see also Chapter 10).

The success of the agricultural sector rests as much on international, as it does on domestic, prices for its output. But one needs case studies for the many variants on the determination of primary product prices. Some general points can be made. Since the Third World countries take part in the world market system, they are entangled in the conditions it imposes and they have very little financial or commercial power unless, like the Organization of the Petroleum Exporting Countries (OPEC), they hold a monopoly over a scarce and essential resource. Secondly, the demand for most primary products from any one country is likely to be price inelastic downwards and elastic upwards, any one country may be a price-taker, so that price bargaining will not necessarily bring greater revenues. Thirdly, unfavourable terms of trade can emerge even in a more-or-less competitive world market. And fourthly, the individual producing country can do nothing against commodity speculators. Third World countries are more vulnerable to short-term fluctuations in prices, having neither the reserves to call upon if prices are low, nor the power to dictate selling prices. And there are also long-run and cyclical forces acting on demand and price. Furthermore, the divisions of interests between buyers and sellers are seen in terms of national boundaries rather than as internal class boundaries: the capitalist and wage-labour classes of the developed country have a common interest in holding down the prices of Third World commodities. These all interact and make planning based on export revenues difficult to carry out. They also disturb the internal terms of trade between agriculture and industry.

Finance may come in the form of aid and loans. She criticises orthodox theory for assuming that 'capital' as finance is automatically transformed into 'capital' as productive equipment. When capital comes as finance, it is frequently diverted into repaying interest on accumulated debt from the country's history of loans. Of the funding that does go to investment projects, much is tied to projects which give priority to the donor's interests and which involve payments back to the donor country for its inputs and even its personnel, so that not even new skills are learned from the imported technology. She also notes the cases of transnationals taking over a local business, its plant, its labour force and its market, and then remitting their profits back to the home country. She remarks that a country needs to have a carefully planned programme of projects which it wants to be funded and then to acquire loans which are based on its own terms of implementation and repayments; she also remarks that such a country would probably not get any funding from the West!

The path by which a country aims to undertake its development is generally industrialisation. Although some countries with a scarce and necessary primary resource may develop without initially building up an industrial base, for most countries it is the desired path. Technology can be copied or imported without the lags and costs of invention and trials which characterised the long process of industrialisation of the West. Aid or foreign investment is generally required to finance development in the industrial sector; redirecting the surplus away from luxury consumption provides insufficient funds for a programme of industrialisation. She observes that often foreign investment is not part of a development plan but is the decision of a producer to produce offshore where labour is cheap and there is the possibility of new markets. Typically, she observes, new investment is in import substitutes which are goods supplied to the luxury end of the market and so use up the scarce surplus which might have been coaxed into the production of wage goods and of more capacity. She notes that typically the output to capital ratio is lower in the branch plant than in the home plant; but the cost of capital equipment is lower to the transnational because its research and development costs are already paid for. Similarly, a developing economy may import plant from the origin which has become obsolete there but which can still create a surplus with the cheap labour available in the branch country. It tends to be more highly mechanised than other local businesses and its share of wages in value-added is lower than in local enterprises more generally, and the share of profits and managerial salaries higher, so that the distribution of income tends to become even more unequal and to be consolidated in the structure of production and the market for its non-basic products. Import substitution which follows the indications of the market typically takes the form of luxury imports as so much of 'the market' does not receive a surplus above subsistence to express its 'votes'. Thus, valuable and scarce foreign funds are diverted away from addressing the problem of poverty.

She shows the extent to which net outflows of finance and investment have tended to be substantially greater than net flows of private finance into developing countries. (Her observations were based on United Nations Conference on Trade and Development (UNCTAD) and International Labour Organization (ILO) data; cf. Helleiner (1980) who claims that she only 'refers to the writings of sympathetic friends'.)

By comparison, she draws on the Chinese example of allocating the surplus to areas where it will have the greatest net increase in productive capacity. This introduces the problem of choice of technique. 'In heavy industry and long-range transport, a high ratio of capital stock to men employed is necessary. There the increase in productivity due to mechanisation is indefinitely great, for almost nothing could be produced without it' (Robinson, 1978c, 116). She recalls the Chinese principle of 'walking on two legs' (see above). Mechanisation of the wage goods sector which tends to be characterised by small-scale production and which employs a large part of the population, should be delayed until there is full employment. That is, the aim should be for 'the maximum possible economy of investible resources to secure desired growth of output, and this entails the maximum possible increase in employment per unit of investment'; '"widening" is to be preferred to "deepening" the stock of means of production' (ibid.). In general, she argues, new technology should not be chosen on the basis of the amount of employment it creates. Rather, the objective should be to maximise output per unit of investment. This tends to favour techniques with lower ratios of investment per unit of labour. A higher degree of mechanisation might produce a greater surplus and so the potential for further investment and employment. But this depends on the level of wages. Where the saving on the wage bill of introducing a more mechanical technique is greater than the value of output foregone, the technique which favours the larger output per unit of investment may be replaced by the one which offers a higher surplus to investment ratio (see also Robinson and Eatwell, 1973, 328–30). In some circumstances the means, that is, the opportunities for higher employment, might themselves be as important as the end objective.

She distinguishes between disguised unemployment, Keynesian unemployment and underemployment (also called elsewhere surplus labour and non-employment).[10] Keynesian unemployment describes a situation in which a chance rise in effective demand leads some employers to find it profitable to take on more labour and produce more output. It is a short-period state in which the level of capacity is fixed and there is unutilised capacity and available labour to meet the new demand. Disguised unemployment describes the state of labour working with minute amounts of 'capital' generally in the urban sector; it is a form of Keynesian unemployment, insofar as the capital stock available is insufficient to employ the available labour, and meant to refer to urban economies. She also refers to Marx's concept of unemployment as the situation where the growth of surplus labour exceeds accumulation of capital (also in Robinson, 1951b, 141). Underemployment occurs where there is too much labour to work a given plot of land, typically where land is unevenly distributed. If there were to be an increase in expenditure in any of these situations except the Keynesian, where there is excess capacity, it would lead to inflation. The Keynesian solution might help in the short run but investment in new capacity is needed to absorb the labour in other situations over the long run. Tahir (1990a) interprets Joan Robinson's analysis of migration of rural labour to the city as indicating a response by the underemployed labour in the rural areas to the opening up of new job opportunities in the industrial, and urban, sector, rather than as a response to the expected differential wages (or indeed to wages per se). The rural worker costs less to support than the urban worker so that the total wage bill of the newly distributed labour puts pressure on the supply of wage goods (food), while the now growing urban unemployment keeps the real wage in that sector at a minimum.

Another source of interruption in the flow of surplus is its diversion into the production of arms. She argues that insofar as the arms trade influences the nature of regimes, it has an all-pervasive influence on economic development. This is directly, in terms of its usage of the scarce foreign exchange, and indirectly in the opportunities foregone, the effects on the production of capacity which alternative and productive use of the surplus and of skilled labour could have achieved. The effect of armaments expenditure can be inflationary as it yields no marketable product, and will incur an opportunity cost by a tightening of expenditure on more constructive areas such as health or education. 'The military establishment limits civilian development not only directly by limiting foreign exchange and scarce home resources and skills, but also indirectly, through finance. ... The amount of borrowing that can be undertaken without ruining the financial system is also limited.' (Robinson, 1978c, 125–6). Unfortunately, she observes, 'The market for arms, unlike all other markets, can never be saturated, for an increase in supply to one country in any region increases demand from its neighbours' (ibid., p. 127; see Robinson (1982) and Chapter 12).

From her classical post-Keynesian position, Robinson concludes her argument in this book by restating the fundamental role which the agricultural sector plays in the development of a country, referring to 'the basic problem of development – the need for re-organisation and technical improvement of the agricultural sector in the Third World' (ibid., p. 137). The agricultural sector must first produce a surplus and then allow part of the surplus to be allocated to the industrial sector to pay for wages and investment there. So the terms on which this surplus is supplied to the non-agricultural sector must be established and similarly the relative wage rates and the terms of trade between sectors. Where a rise in food prices causes urban wages to increase followed by increases in the prices of manufactured goods so that the relative real wages of rural and urban workers diverge, the process could turn into an inflationary spiral. The choice of investment that would most benefit the process of a developing economy such as India or some Latin American economies, should consider both the technology and the organisation of production itself. In general, 'technologies which promote a symbiotic and mutually reinforcing ... rather than ... dependence of metropolitan industry upon the rural population' are advocated (Robinson quoting Reddy (1973), ibid., p. 139). She argues that planning enables a more rational basis for achieving the goals of development than *laisser-faire*. The market will not provide social infrastructure or very large-scale capital works; it will produce where there are profits, viz., the luxury goods market or markets for the upper middle-classes.

> Inequality in provision of essential services has been cemented into the class structure of would-be developing nations as firmly as inequality in the consumption of luxury goods has been embedded in the structure of production. It would need an even greater wrench to redirect education to the benefit of society as a whole than to redirect industry to the requirements of mass consumption.
>
> (ibid., p. 141)

She observes that at that time (1978) the 'third stage' of the international division of labour had now been reached which is the use of cheap labour from the periphery to supply manufactured exports to the developed centre.[11] This has created a tendency in developed countries to protect their manufacturing industries with their relatively high wages. The *laisser-faire* argument is that the developed countries should sacrifice their high-cost industries and replace them with industries where they have an advantage (see also Robinson and Eatwell, *op. cit.*, 331). One outcome of protection of high technology import substitutes of middle-class commodities is that these industries typically work at less than optimal efficiency. Joan Robinson is not opposed to protection per se, but is against it being used to encourage and sustain industries which contribute nothing to the wage goods sector.

Her aim in writing this book had been to dispel some illusions about the role of the orthodox theory and the developed world in the process of development of Third World countries, and to advocate a more deliberated strategy of development. She noted that teaching in the West pretends to be scientific and objective by detaching the economic aspect of people's lives from its political and social setting. Joan Robinson instead takes into account the particularities of every situation and understands these through the framework of classical political economy and a post-Keynesian development to growth and distribution theory. One of the reviewers of Robinson (1978c) regarded her work as 'characterised by unsubstantiated generalisation, idiosyncratic emphases and references, and casual empiricism of the most amateur kind' (Helleiner, *op. cit.*). This comment interprets the apparent simplicity and directness of her writing as superficial when in fact she is demonstrating throughout the book, an awareness of the complexity and interdependence of the whole set of relationships which are responsible for maintaining the continued presence of Third World countries after 30 years of aid. She uses the study of particular cases to construct her analysis, and then to demonstrate for each case, its specific elements and powers: every paragraph is the outcome of a theoretical dialogue. The result is to dispel all illusions about the beneficence of First World countries in their aid-giving, their foreign investment and their technology transfers; and about the validity of their theoretical rationales. There is no set of neatly summarised principles, leading via deduction to reach a unique conclusion. Perhaps (as in Robinson and Eatwell; see also Chapter 10), because she refused to reduce her account of the Third World in such a pedagogically simplistic way, this book was never taken seriously. Yet here, she abandons her previous caution about separating the political from the economic, or the values from the science. Perhaps exhibiting what Said (2003) depicts as 'late style', she is at last openly letting go of this methodological constraint on her thinking. Ideas may superficially appear as 'irresolution, unsynthesised fragmentariness, [which] are constitutive ... not symbolic of something else'(ibid., 12). Robinson can now 'let go' of the preoccupation she had for so many years with scientific method, abandon the demands of the academy and enter a form of exile even from those who have supported her views, where her writing is 'unco-opted by a higher synthesis' (ibid.) and is unashamedly on political economy.

Appendix: Joan Robinson's writings on China (compiled by Pervez Tahir)

(1954), *Letters from a visitor to China*, Cambridge: Student's Bookshops.

'Unemployment and the Second Plan', *Capital*, 20 December 1956, Annual Supplement, 7–9; also in *C.E.P.*, vol. 3 (1965), 182–91.

'Employment and the Plan', *Economic Weekly*, 24 March 1956, 8 (12), 355–6.

'The Choice of Techniques', *Economic Weekly*, 23 June 1956, 8 (24–6), 715–18.

'Time and the Choice of Technique, Comment on Chakravarty', *Economic Weekly*, 17 November 1956, 8 (46), 1333.

'Choice of Technique', *Economic Weekly*, 27 April 1957, 9(17), 137 (letter).

'Birth Control in China', *New Statesman and Nation*, 18 January 1958, 55 (401), 66–7.

Review of *The Economic Development of Communist China*, by T. T. Hughes and D. E. T. Luard, *Economic Journal*, July 1960, 70 (278), 409–10.

(1962), Review of *Contemporary China*. Ed. E.S. Kirby, *Economic Journal*, September 72(287), 734.

'The Chinese View', *Seminar*, October 1963, 50, 44–6.

'Are we Exerting Ourselves Enough? Compete with Chinese', *Yojana*, March 1963, 7 (1), 7–8.

'Communes in China', *Listener*, 30 January 1964, 71 (1818), 177–89.

'Notes from China', *Economic Weekly*, February 1964, 16 (5–7), 195–203.

'A British Economist on Chinese Communes', *Eastern Horizon*, May 1964, 3 (5), 6–11.

'Chinese Agricultural Communes', *Coexistence*, May 1964, 1 (1), 1–6.

'The Chinese Communes', *Political Quarterly*, July–September 1964, 35 (3), 285–97.

'The Chinese Point of View', *International Affairs*, April 1964, 40 (2), 232–44.

'Prospects for China', *New Scientist*, 18 June 1964, 22 (396), 756.

Notes from China, Oxford: Basil Blackwell, (1964).

Review of *The Chinese Inflation, 1937–1949*, by S. H. Chou, *Economic Journal*, September 1964, 74 (295), 680–1.

'India, wake up!' *Economic Weekly*, 5 December 1964, 16 (49), 1917–20.

'China, 1963: The communes', *C.E.P.*, vol. 3 (1965), 192–206.

'What's New in China?', *Eastern Horizon*, January 1965, 4 (1), 11–15.

Review of *The economy of Chinese mainland: National income and economic development, 1933–1959*, by T.-C. Liu and K.-C. Yeh, *Economic Journal*, September 1965, 75 (299), 604.

'Economic Principles in China', Review of *Construction du socialisme en Chine*, by C. Bettelheim et al., *Broadsheet*, October 1965, 2 (10), 1–3.

'China Today: The Organisation of Agriculture', *Bulletin of the Atomic Scientists*, 1966, 22 28–32.

'Organisation of Agriculture', in *Contemporary China*, R. Adams (ed.), London: Peter Owen, 1969, 221–34, 1966.

Reviews of *La reforme agraire en Chine populaire* by Chen Chi-yi; *The steel industry in Communist China* by Yuan-Li Wu. *International Affairs*, 1966, 42 (3), 546–8.

Review of *La construction du socialisme en Chine*, by C. Bettelheim et al. *Coexistence*, 1966, 3 (4), 105–7.

'The Communes and the Great Leap Forward', Reviews of Crook and Crook, 1965; Dumont, 1966, *New Left Review*, May–June 1966, 37, 69–72.

Reviews of *The economy of Communist China*, by Y.-L. Wu; *Market control and planning in Communist China*, by D. H. Perkins; *Food and Agriculture in Communist China*, by J. L. Buck, L. Dawson and Y.-L. Wu. *International Affairs*, January 1967, 43 (1), 192–3.

Reviews of *China's wartime finance and inflation, 1937–1945*, by A. N. Young and *Foreign investment and economic development in China 1840–1937*, by C.-M. Hou. *International Affairs*, April 1967, 43 (2), 404–6.

Review of *Eyewitness in China*, by H. Portisch. *International Affairs*, 1967, 43 (3), 611–2.

Review of *The awakening of China 1793–1949*, by R. Pelissier, *International Affairs*, October 1967, 43 (4), 797.

'The Economic Reforms', *Monthly Review*, November 1967, 19 (6), 45–50.

'The Chinese Cultural Revolution', *Now*, 22 December 1967.

Review of *Report from a Chinese village*, by Jan Myrdal. *International Affairs*, 1968, 44 (1), 152–3.

'Intensive Look at China', *SACU News*, 1968, 3 (2), 1–5.

'The Cultural Revolution in China', *International Affairs*, 1968, 44 (2), 214–27.

'Reply to Sussex Internationalists' Attack', *SACU News*, 1968, 3(6–7), 5.

'China Today: Economic Organisation', *Journal of the Royal Society of Arts*, 1968, 116 (5144), 683–93.

'One Quarter of Mankind', *Canadian Forum*, 1968, 48, 150.

'The Decentralised Society', Review of *China's economic system*, by A. Donnithorne, *SACU News*, 1968, 3 (12), 5.

(1969) *The Cultural Revolution in China*, Harmondsworth, Middlesex: Penguin Books.

'Ten Years of Communes', *Broadsheet*, 1969, 6 (1), 3.

'India and China: A Comparison', *Listener*, 1969, 82 (2124), 816–18.

Preface to *China's economy*, by N. Brunner, London: Anglo-Chinese Educational Institute, 1969, 1–2.

Letter to *Tribune*, 24 January 1969.

'Reply to A. J. Watson', *China Now*, 1970, 2, 4.

Reviews of *The transformation of the Chinese earth*, by K. Buchanan and *Economic geography of China*, by T. R. Tregear, *Broadsheet*, 1970, 7 (7), last page.

'Society and Economics in China Today', in *China and the West: Mankind evolving*, by R. Jungk et al., London: Granstone Press, 1970, 35–47.

'Chinese Economic Policy', *Studium Generale*, 1970, 23 (12), 1267–74.

'Chinese Economic Policy: Prescription for Development', *China Now*, 1970, 4, 5–8.

Foreword to *The Chinese road to socialism* by E. L. Wheelright and B. McFarlane, New York: Monthly Review Press, 1970, 7–10.

'Chinese Economic Policy' in *Hand and brain in China and other essays*, by J. Needham et al., London: Anglo-Chinese Educational Institute, 1971, 19–27.
'Something to Live for', Review of *The revolution continued*, by J. Myrdal and G. Kessle, *New Statesman*, 1971, 81 (2094), 631–3.
'For Use, Not for Profit', *Eastern Horizon*, 1972, 11 (4), 6–15.
'Through Western Spectacles', Reviews of *China Today* by K. Mehnert; Terrill, 1972 and *Red guard*, by K. Ling, *Spectator*, 1972, 7522, 321.
'Chinese Agricultural Communes', in C. K. Wilber (ed.), *The Political Economy of Development and Underdevelopment*, New York: Random House, 1973 (2nd edn, 1979).
'Structure of Management', *China Now*, 1973, 29, 10–11.
'Planning and Management in China today', *Cambridge Review*, 1973, 94 (2212), 106–20.
'Achievements of a Generation', *China Now*, 1974, 45, 2–3.
'Two Revolutions', *Broadsheet*, 1974, 11 (10), 4.
Economic Management in China (2nd edn), London: Anglo-Chinese Educational Institute, 1975.
Foreword to *Education in China*, by R. Mauger et al., London: Anglo-Chinese Educational Institute, 1975, 1–2.
Review of *To phoenix seat: An introductory study of Maoism and the Chinese communist quest for a paradise on earth*, by L. R. Marchant, *History*, 1975, 60 (199), 272–3.
'National Minorities in Yunnan', *Eastern Horizon*, 1975, 14 (4), 32–43.
'In the Deep Southwest', *New China Magazine*, Fall 1975, 1 (3), 21–3.
'Hsishuang Panna', *China Now*, October 1975, 55, 10–11.
'The Fall of Lin Piao', Review of *Inside China*, by P. Worsley and *The second Chinese Revolution*, by K. S. Karol, *Spectator*, 1975, 7677, 217.
'An Eyewitness Account of the Cultural Revolution', Review of *China's Socialist Revolution*, by J. Collier and E. Collier, *Monthly Review*, 1976, 28 (5), 50–1.
'Walled in', Review of *Russian Studies of China*, by E. S. Kirby, *Spectator*, 1976, 7699, 17.
'Employment and the Choice of Technique', *Society and Change*, K. S. Krishnaswamy et al. (eds), Bombay: Oxford University Press, 1977, 165–9.
Reports from China 1953–76, London: Anglo-Chinese Educational Institute, (1977).
'China 1978: Comments on Bettelheim', *China Now*, 1978, 80, 4–7.
Review of Mao Tse-Tung 1977, *China Now*, 1978, 80, 26–7.
Review of Mao, 1977, *Monthly Review*, 1979, 30 (8), 52–3.
'China since Mao', *Monthly Review*, 1979, 31(1), 48–56.
'The Pros and Cons', *China Now*, 1979, 86, 25–6.
Review of *China's road to development*, N. Maxwell (ed.), *Broadsheet*, 1980, 17 (3), last page.
'Introduction', *China Now*, 1982, 100, 3.
and Adler, S. (1958) *China: An Economic Perspective*, London: Fabian International Bureau, Fabian Tract No. 314.
and Berger, R., 'Thinking about China: The Economic Impact of Communism', *Listener*, 1961, 65 (1962), 220–2.
and Needham, J., 'Too much for "The Times"', *SACU News*, January 1969, 4 (1), 1–2.

10
An Introduction to Modern Economics: A Light that Failed?

When Joan Robinson 'retired' in 1970, one of the first tasks she set herself was to write a first year introductory textbook. She asked John Eatwell, who was then a Fellow of Trinity, and who had been an undergraduate at Cambridge in the 1960s and then done a Ph.D. at Harvard, to be her co-author. The principal aim of the book was to introduce students to her Cambridge approach to economic theory and to contrast it with the principal tenets of the mainstream's theory and approach. Though she had continued to be in touch with students through informal means, she felt that having a co-author who was very much at the coal face, lecturing and supervising, was absolutely necessary for the tone and content of the proposed book. On most issues, she and Eatwell were then at one, though increasingly they were to part company on the application of the long-period method in economic theory championed by, especially, Garegnani's interpretation of Piero Sraffa.

While the book was being written in 1971–3, the authors circulated drafts of chapters to a number of people, most of whom were in Cambridge for at least some of the time during which the book was created. The authors met with this group once a week in Full Term to discuss their reaction to the drafts.[1] The group included one undergraduate, Martin Fetherston, a Part II student at Trinity, who subsequently obtained a very good First in Part II of the Tripos. So he was not exactly the counterpart of a Marshallian representative firm.

The aims of the volume were splendid. Students would be introduced to the distilled wisdom of a sage allied to the clarity and enthusiasm of a younger scholar. We have recently re-read *An Introduction*.[2] With hindsight and, overall, we continue to admire both its aims and execution. Yet it failed significantly to take off.

It did receive a most favourable review by John Gurley in the *Economic Journal* (Gurley, 1974; 2002). Gurley nevertheless sensed why the book might not be the success he wished it to be.

> As capitalism increasingly comes under attack by real movements in the world, its self-serving ideology will also be challenged as never before [we wish!]. This book contributes greatly to that end. It is too bad, then, that it is not likely to be widely used by beginners in economics ... the trouble is that it would be tough going for beginners. [The authors] do not use many words to explain difficult ideas ... the ideas and analyses are presented so concisely, without sufficient leisurely elaboration, that beginners are apt to stumble many times. ... While the book is strong on theory ..., on comparative economic systems, and on the development of economic thought, it is weak on contemporary institutions ... All [this] is too bad, because this type of economics can much better prepare the coming generation of students for understanding and solving the real problems of the world than neo-neoclassical economics ever can, and it could further serve to stimulate students' curiosity about Marx and ... lead them to an even more powerful framework for understanding current movements of history.
>
> (450; Kerr with Harcourt (eds.), vol. V, 2002, 307)[3]

In this chapter, we discuss the approach and contents and try to assess why it *may* be judged a light that failed.

As far as the pure mechanics of presentation are concerned, especially the level of presentation, it has to be conceded that both authors were only used to teaching very bright undergraduates so that they vastly overestimated the absorption capabilities of more average students. Had Joan Robinson collaborated with, say, either Tom Asimakopulos or Keith Frearson, both superb teachers of the less gifted as well as the gifted, mainly in Canada and Australia, this limitation may have been overcome, though both Tom and Keith were in the group that read the drafts. Whether that would have ensured the success of the book is still problematical. The political background to its reception calls to mind the scandalous treatment of Lorie Tarshis's 1940s textbook which contained the first textbook account in the US of Keynes's system (see Harcourt, 1982a; 1982b; 1995a; 2001a). Moreover, as we have noted, Joan Robinson's writings were becoming more and more 'tips of icebergs' which often troubled even experienced readers who were familiar with her work.

In the Preface (xvi–xvii), the authors write that the book 'is offered, in the first instance, to students who are beginners in economics' but suggest that others may also be interested. Three main topics are covered – Economic Doctrines, Analysis and Modern Problems.[4] They could be taught/read either as a cross-section or a time series. On their method of presentation, they write that while 'pure economic logic may be regarded as a branch of applied mathematics', they have not put much of their argument in this form. In their view, many economic relationships cannot be adequately represented by simple, smooth functions. 'To cut them down to fit into algebraic formulae may be seriously misleading.' The authors prefer arithmetic examples and diagrams, less 'fashionable but more enlightening'.

Finally, they warn that 'Book 3 touches upon problems that involve political judgments [that] cannot but be seen from some particular point of view. The authors intend their own prejudices to be sufficiently obvious for the reader to discount them as he feels right' (xvii).[5]

10.1

Though a very succinct account (48 pages) of the development of our subject, it nevertheless encapsulates the major themes of our trade. Starting before Adam Smith, especially with the Physiocrats, it rightly emphasises, in Chapters 1 and 2, the foundations laid by the classical political economists – class analysis, the central organising concept of the surplus, that theirs was a dynamic analysis, associated with the beginning and then with Ricardo, Malthus and Marx, the full flowering of manufacturing built on technical progress associated with the division of labour. For Ricardo, the stress is on value and distribution, Say's Law and the debates between Ricardo and Malthus on the possibility of general gluts. Marx is seen as both the fulfilment of classical political economy and a major jump in analysis of the capitalist epoch through his own original innovations in concepts and method. The third chapter concerns the neoclassical era. The discussion closes with Section 3.6, the Keynesian revolution, in which time, prices, saving and investment, and the rate of interest are emphasised. Their views are in general consistent with Sraffa's and Dobb's – that Marx and Keynes (they would give Keynes more brownie points than Sraffa and Dobb would, of course) are the true fulfillers of classical political economy, while neoclassicism, old and new, a misnomer if ever there was one, leads us all down a false trail. Marshall gets his rightful place but his attempt to present the old and the new as evolution rather than a split is of course rejected. (Nevertheless his innovative diagrams and analytical treatment of time, though modified, influence the presentation of the analysis in the later books of their volume.)

In the pre-Smith discussion, the authors refer to the overriding importance of natural law for the free thinkers of the eighteenth century – that the 'principles of harmony and justice' could be built on the same basis as Newton had set the regularity of the physical universe. This is modified, they argue, by the emergence of Bentham's Utilitarianism, whereby the results of actions are the criteria for judgement, not morals. They add that '[d]espite its humanitarian slogan, Utilitarianism quickly turned ... into a hard-headed devotion to expediency in which the conception of social class became more rigid than ever' (1), a worthy quote for another Tripos question if followed by the instruction 'Discuss'.

There follows a section on problems and functions of economic philosophy where within the space of just over a page, the authors draw out the main themes of Joan Robinson's influential 1962 volume, *Economic Philosophy* (Robinson, 1962b): where does profit come from and how capital as well as labour create wealth? What are the persistent forces that underlie the surface phenomenon of prices? What role for money? Why is modern society so seemingly associated with a lack of social justice; not even the Soviet Union had found a 'satisfactory answer' to that one! Next, the question of effective demand: 'where does demand come from, and why is there rarely enough to keep everyone fully occupied?' (2).

As we noted, they show that

> [e]conomics can never be a perfectly 'pure' science, unmixed with human values. Often, the moral and political viewpoints from which economic problems are seen have become so inextricably entwined with the questions asked, and ... with the methods of analysis used, that these ... elements ... are not ... easy to keep distinct.
>
> (2–3)

Finally, *metaphysical* is defined as 'a use of language that conveys no factual information, describes no logical relations nor gives precise instructions and yet is calculated to affect conduct' (3). The object of the definition is to distinguish fact and logic from elements which are metaphysical in this sense.

10.2

In Chapter 1, 'Before Adam Smith', the authors first discuss under the general heading of leading ideas, the Mercantilists and their insights concerning aggregate demand, that the Mercantilists were correct to argue that a surplus of exports made the home economy buoyant while a surplus of imports tended to depress it.[6] Prior to this, they point out that the first problem out of which political economy developed was international trade and they link the ideas of the Mercantilists to the growth in British overseas trade in the seventeenth and eighteenth centuries.

In the next section on money and wealth, they rescue David Hume from being regarded as a primitive monetarist.

> [Hume] was arguing that a general diffusion of small amounts of extra purchasing power would not 'gather into sums' that would be available to provide finance to promote trade and industry. He [put] the question in its social setting [but was not] supporting a mechanical theory of the relation of the stock of money to the level of prices.
>
> (7)

They have high praise for 'The last Mercantilist', Sir James Steuart, whose views on aggregate demand were clearer than those of any others until Keynes restated the case in *The General Theory* (1936).

Next, the Physiocrats are identified as 'the first to present the mechanism of an economy in terms of its system of social classes' (8). Their definition of metaphysical arguments is used to debunk the claim that since only land produces a surplus, only landlords had a right to enjoy it, a slogan favourable to the landlords. They conclude that

> the moral that Physiocrats drew from their metaphysic was acceptance of the social system in which they lived ... mere subservience to existing authority ... their economic analysis ... was penetrating and original [and] bears a different moral at the present time in those countries ... emerging from feudalism in a struggle for modernization. If ... the surplus from agriculture is the basic requirement for developing industry, ... it is by no means desirable to allow the landlords to consume it.
>
> (10)

This illustrates their view that the facts of the case may be regarded as independent of the morals drawn from it.

In Chapter 2, Ricardo is quickly brought onto the scene as deserving, far more than Quesnay, of the title 'father of modern economics' because he developed the method of analysis of setting up a *model* (they seem to have forgotten the *Tableau Economique*). Basic essentials are extracted, irrelevant details are cut out and the relations between them are examined. The secret of a great economist is not to leave out elements which are important. Ricardo gets high praise for this and for submitting his ideas to criticism and modifying his views when convinced they should be revised.

Malthus also is praised. He is most known for his perceptive *Essay on Population* (1798) and his exchanges with Ricardo 'were all written with wisdom and affection'.

Poor John Stuart Mill is damned with faint praise. He added little of analytical substance but did provide the basic textbook of political economy, *Principles of Political Economy, With Some of their Applications to Social Philosophy* (1848) until the rise of the neoclassicals. His book reflected the rising self-confidence of mid nineteenth-century Britain, often obscuring the clarity of Ricardian thought.

The conclusions of Marx and Mill drawn from classical analysis were dramatically opposed. Marx combined classical ideas with his philosophy of history, leading to a deep analysis of the dynamics of capitalism and its inherent contradictions. Surprisingly, Mills's and Mrs Taylor's views on the good society and socialism are not mentioned. Nevertheless fundamental ideas underlie all the writings of these authors and these are discussed in the next section.

The first is class analysis, especially the influence of the different functions, and spending and saving behaviour of different classes on the economy's development. They pay proper due to Smith's sceptical views on the motives and behaviour of the different classes, especially manufacturers and landlords, and of the effect of differential access to power in relations between classes. Nevertheless, they feel that the main force of the arguments of the classical political economists is 'a defence of the rising power of industrial capitalism, and an appeal to release the play of self-interest from hampering restrictions' (13). Coupled with this is the role of the use of surplus for reinvestment leading to an ever-expanding spiral; an early example of a later distinctive theme in post-Keynesianism of cumulative causation processes (see Harcourt, 2006b, Ch. 8). They see in the classical concept of capital as a wages fund with machines, the embodiment of past advances of the wages fund, the reason for regarding work as the fundamental agent of production.

The determination of the surplus receives much prominence, culminating in a discussion of Marx's view that historical episodes may be classified by how the surplus is created, extracted, distributed and used, especially in capitalism. The role of the Malthusian principle in determining the wage rate and so the potential surplus in Ricardo's model is discarded by Marx who looks for the interactions between the capitalists and the working classes in the sphere of production for the determination of the size of the potential surplus. All classical economists developed the concepts of dynamic development towards a long-way-off stationary state as its end product, a view revived later by Keynes and Hicks as a desirable state of society.

The authors also emphasise Smith's discussion of the division of labour, the beginning of a theory of endogenous technical progress. They perceptively conclude that

> [n]o other classical economist, apart from Marx, paid so much attention to problems of technical change. ... Instead, the technological effects of accumulation were taken for granted, and interest was focused on the main determinant of the rate of accumulation, the proportion of total product acquired by the capitalist class.
>
> (17)

Ricardo's theory of distribution and its role in the Corn Law debates are highlighted. The corn model is used to illustrate the main thrust of his argument, possibly attributing more confidently than the evidence allows the use of the corn model to Ricardo. They explain clearly why Ricardo sought an invariable measure of value: to allow him to discuss the size of the surplus at a moment of time and over time in a dynamic theory of accumulation and development, so as to generalise the findings of the corn model to those of a world of heterogeneous commodities.

The debates between Malthus and Ricardo are examined, not only over measures of value but also about the possibility of general gluts and the validity of Say's Law. They see in Malthus's rather confused arguments the embryo of the need for sources of autonomous demand outside the consumption goods sector to make possible profits and accumulation (as well as to offset overproduction), a pointer to a central part of their arguments in the second book, 'Analysis'.

Chapter 2 closes with several pages on Marx's contributions: social relations and the creation of surplus, the significance of the distinction between value and price for his purposes, a distinction about which Joan Robinson was always most sceptical, feeling it was unnecessary in an analysis of distribution, price formation and accumulation. She never could see why the labour theory of value was needed to explain why those who had access to finance and who owned the means of production could push round those who did not.[7]

Chapter 3 on the neoclassical era starts by naming the principal founders in the 1870s: Jevons, Menger, Walras (the earlier pioneers, Cournot and Gossen, are also noted). They point out that while

> Marshall ... dominated the teaching of economics in the English-speaking world [probably] until ... the outbreak of war in 1939, ... the neo-neoclassical revival of orthodoxy in the mid-twentieth century was based ... on conceptions derived from Walras. ... [W]hat became known as *Neoclassical* economics ... replaced the classical concept of accumulation with an analysis of the equilibrium of supply and demand in a stationary state.
>
> (34) (emphasis in original)

The victory of the new school is attributed, first, to the failure of classical economics to solve some 'purely' theoretical problems and, secondly, to changes in political and social conditions which made classical ideas not irrelevant but dangerous.

In the section on fundamental ideas, the authors stress the suppression of social classes in favour of analysis built in the main on individuals and individualism. This was accompanied by a shift of focus from production to exchange, and the relating of prices to utility. In discussing equilibrium, they in effect argue that Walras ruled out path dependence by arguing that equilibrium prices were known (found) before production and/or trade took place. His modern followers are content to find 'the conditions necessary to ensure that at least one position of equilibrium exists' (37). Marshall, they say, used supply and demand analysis much more robustly whereas the Walrasians can only say that everything depends upon everything else. In Walras, the 'scarcity of resources relative to demand is the essential determinant of prices' (39). They go over old ground for Joan Robinson in the discussion of Marshall's analysis of the reward for waiting to justify interest and profit.

They mention Marshall's essential conundrum that while his scheme emphasises scarcity, it is scarcity at a moment of history. 'To him, time and change were always present, and he was continually perplexed in trying to reconcile historical processes with a concept of equilibrium based on the mechanical analogy of a position of rest, established by a balance of the contrary forces of supply and demand' (40).

There is a critical section on 'marginal productivity' in which Wicksell comes out best for his honesty in admitting its limitations and lack of simplicity as far as the theory of profits was concerned. Marshall's well-known statement that marginal productivity is not a theory of wages as opposed to throwing a 'clear light' on the actions of one of the causes that govern wages is quoted. For our authors, this doctrine is 'purely circular. It states that, when a businessman maximises his profits ..., he is combining various factors of production in such a way that he could not make more profit by combining them differently' (41).

The concept of normal profits is discussed within the context of whether they could coexist with a growing economy. As the creator of a growing Golden Age, Joan Robinson had come to accept that they could coexist, which was not her initial position (see Araujo and Harcourt (1993), Harcourt (1995b)). There is a short section on the relative movements of decreasing and increasing return industries in a growing economy, with a footnote reference to Marshall's Appendix H. They conclude that 'Marshall himself knew that he was fudging when he tried to squeeze these conceptions into the frame of equilibrium in a stationary state' (43).

Section 4 discusses, first, the non-treatment of effective demand in the long-period competitive equilibrium of the neoclassicals and the acceptance of Say's Law. The trade cycle is included in the analysis of money. It is treated as the cause of short-term fluctuations around the long-period Say's Law position. Money itself was mainly concerned with clarifying the quantity theory by introducing the concept of the velocity of money.

The critics of the emerging and emerged neoclassical theory include Bukharin as a Marxist and Veblen as a populist. Joan Robinson, after the Cambridge–Cambridge debates had been going for several years, pointed out that the essence of the critique was to be found in Veblen's review of J. B. Clark's statement of marginal productivity theory. Three paragraphs are quoted from his review (Veblen, 1908). The crux of his argument is that

> [t]he continuum in which the 'abiding entity' of capital resides is a continuity of ownership, not a physical fact. The continuity ... is of an immaterial nature, a matter of legal rights, of contract, of purchase and sale. Just why this patent state of affairs is overlooked ... is not easily seen.
>
> (45–6)

Schumpeter, 'Marx upside down', was a critic who, though 'much enamoured of capitalist enterprise ... maintained that orthodox static analysis [did] not bring out its true character' (46). They end on a note not dissimilar in foresight to John Stuart Mill on demand theory: 'Like Veblen, [Schumpeter] has left little trace in modern teaching' (46).

The scene is now set for Keynes and the development of *The General Theory*. The story told has the usual features of the interrelationships between history and policy, and the search for a relevant theory to back up measures to tackle prolonged unemployment. On prices, it is argued that '[i]n some ways, the most important aspect of the Keynesian revolution was the recognition that ... the general level of prices at any phase of technical development depends mainly on the level of money-wage rates' (49) and that cutting money-wages because of this connection with prices will not cure unemployment. They conclude that 25 years of full employment has let neo-neoclassical theory come into its own, yet it too 'has now come to a crisis [so that it] is time to go back to the beginning and start again' (51).

10.3

Book Two starts with a concise and, to those who know Joan Robinson's approach, predictable section on method. 'Modern' is in the book's title because the authors wish 'to draw from traditional and contemporary teaching ... those elements which ... contribute to an understanding of modern problems' (53).

Models are used as one of their principal vehicles, selecting from 'the flux of history', past and present, key entities, specifying their environment and modelling their interactions 'by a kind of quasi-mathematical logic' (53). Because the subject matter of economics is not susceptible to controlled experiments and because too many things are happening at once, the correctness of models' predictions is likely to be problematic. This may lead to the making of models which are logical within their own narrow confines but whose connection to the reality they are intended to illuminate is non-existent. Such a procedure may be merely 'idle amusement' or a failure to investigate how far the special assumptions used in the making of the model vitiates applying its results to reality without further checking.[8] As we cannot avoid making simplified models – 'A map at the scale of 1:1 is of no use to a traveller' [Joan Robinson was an enthusiastic traveller and walker] – the art of model making is to cut out inessential complications 'without eliminating the features necessary for safe guidance' (54). The most essential feature of a model is 'the nature of the social system' which is being analysed.

There follows an explicit, honest account of the simplifications the authors would use for their 'first stage of analysis'. (As with *Exercises*, the aim is to help readers build up their own intellectual and analytical muscles and critical faculties.) Nevertheless, the simplifications are all meant to be of reality, 'not parables or fairy tales'. Their own models are clearly Kaleckian. The argument is explicitly post-Keynesian, 'economic life as a process going on through time, in which the future is not known in advance' (56). At the end of each chapter are summary accounts of 'the corresponding pre-Keynesian equilibrium theory'. They add: 'Some teachers ... will regard these sections as a caricature, and protest that it is not what they have ever believed. If so, so much the better' (56).[9]

The authors provide a convenient synopsis of what is to come. Again the development is predictable from a knowledge of *The Accumulation of Capital* and *Essays* (1962e). Chapter 1, 'Land and labour', concerns 'relationships that can be exhibited in terms of the simplest possible type of production' (56). Social relationships are displayed in terms of private property in land, taking readers through, in effect, Smith's 'early and rude state' to Ricardo's model of capitalist tenant farmers, via peasant producers and tenants of feudal landowners.

Chapter 4 is on technical change including accumulation and innovations. The so-called technological unemployment, the interaction between rising productivity and real wages, obsolescence and amortisation, and the relationship of inventions to accumulation are discussed. The last section on neutral and biased accumulation is described as 'somewhat formalistic' so may be skipped first time through. (Joan Robinson was a dab hand at 'somewhat formalistic' analyses all through her working life; such exercises served to keep her critics honest and on their toes.)

Chapter 5, 'Commodities and prices', covers what is usually called microeconomics, Shove's necessary 20 minutes that Maynard never took! Kalecki's two main market structures – prices determined by supply and demand, and prices determined by mark-ups on costs – are considered. As the book was written in the early 1970s, the problems of market structures and the pricing of services are not considered. It is pointed out that price fluctuations are much greater in the first type of market than in the second. The relationship between the two structures are analysed. In a section on dynamics, the use and misuse of Marshall's equilibrium analysis is illustrated. Students and readers generally should perhaps look at a Cambridge economist lecturing at Oxford for a more entertaining account of the same issues (Robinson, 1953; *C.E.P.*, vol. IV, 1973, 247–68).

Chapter 6 on rates of profit is difficult, both analytically and conceptually. Set in the long period, the authors discuss the impossibility, except under very abstract conditions, of defining a rate of profits because of the difference between expectations and realisation, and because of the process of transforming financial capital into hard objects. The authors claim that '[I]t is worthwhile to examine an abstract system in which the difficulties [in conceptualising and measuring profits] are eliminated, in order to understand the central problem of economic philosophy – the nature of profits' (183). The authors are very much influenced by Sraffa's analysis.

> Sraffa's argument show[ed] that the 'value of a stock of capital', in general, has no meaning independently of the distribution of the net product between wages and profits; so that there is no meaning in the idea that the rate of profit[s] is determined by the 'marginal product of capital.'
>
> (184)

'Sraffa's analysis of the distribution of the product of industry between wages and profits in given technical conditions provides the indispensable framework for an understanding of the problem of distribution in a private-enterprise economy' (187).

Chapter 7, 'incomes and demand', looks at prices and incomes from the point of view of the consumer. A rider is added: 'Unfortunately, the analysis of consumer demand has been so long trapped in a circular argument in terms of "utility" and "preferences" that economic theory has little to say about it' (58). They employ a point of view on public finance that brings it within the scope of post-Keynesian analysis, away from its more usual (in modern times) highly conventional analysis. They add an appendix defining the relationship of accounting identities to causal equations. The discussion is much influenced by Kahn's insistence on the crucial importance of understanding this distinction and Kalecki's powerful use of the distinction.

Joan Robinson had often developed the theme that neo-neoclassical principles were relevant for an explanation of the processes at work in a kibbutz but not for explaining those of even competitive capitalism (see Robinson, 1964a; *C.E.P.*, vol. III, 1965, 36–47).

10.4

Book Three starts with a paragraph which is even more prescient than the authors themselves may have realised when it was written at the start of the 1970s. With great confidence, up to the start of the 1930s, economic doctrines meant that the 'duty of a national government was to keep its budget balanced, maintain the gold standard, eschew protection, and observe the rule of *laissez-faire* in its dealings with industry' (293). Some economists now, they tell us, look for assumptions which would make the old doctrines correct but 'those who concern themselves with what goes on in the world' cannot be as serenely complacent as their predecessors. In the light of the Washington consensus, which only came into its own after Joan Robinson had died, we wonder!

The emphasis in Book Three is on problems and difficulties, and on conflicts of interests in attempts to solve them. Economic reasoning is not enough because all solutions involve political, social and human considerations as well. We should not so much propound solutions as suggest what must be taken into account when we try to make up our minds about issues in the situations in which we live.

Chapter 1 is concerned with the capitalist nations. It starts with the role of expenditure on armaments and its relationship to the Cold War, and subsequently in maintaining effective demand in the US, 'an easy and unobjectionable means for underpinning full employment policy' (296). (Joan Robinson was subsequently to give the Tanner Lectures on the arms race (Robinson, 1982), a major preoccupation and source of distress to her in the last years of her life (see Chapters 11 and 12)).

The authors list the drawbacks of such a full employment policy; first, that the same amounts could have been better spent on providing civilian amenities and/or helping to raise productivity. Secondly,

> [t]he conduct of research in conditions of secrecy, devoted to devising ever-new means of annihilation (quite apart from its effect on the morality of the intellectual elite) deprives industry and developments favourable to human life of the services of a great part of scientific manpower and the fruits of education.
>
> (296)

While conceding that there may be benefits from unexpected spin-offs from such research, these could be so much greater if the same amounts of expenditure were devoted to other ends.

Spending on armaments in France and the UK was not needed as part of their full employment policies but rather reflected nostalgia for past imperial splendours and the burdens associated with dissolving their empires.

West Germany and Japan escaped the need for armaments expenditure for much of the post-war years and so could concentrate, with the help mainly of the US, on reconstruction and modernisation. Moreover, both countries still had agricultural populations available to draw upon, giving them, in Arthur Lewis fashion, 'a somewhat tame and undemanding workforce' which kept inflation at bay much longer than it had been kept in the UK or the US. In the case of West Germany, it was also immigration, 'guest workers', that helped keep wages down in the 1950s and the 1960s. 'Energetic businessmen and compliant workers made it possible for the defeated nations to take full advantage of the bonus that the victors gave them' (298). The effects of these advantages came to a head for the US in the crisis of 1971.

The next section is on employment policy. In true Kaleckian fashion, the crux of the problem is identified. 'Discipline in industry is easier to maintain when the loss of his job is a serious threat to every worker. (Humane methods of management may be efficient in the long run but brutal methods are quick and easy)' (298). Against this is the role of confidence associated with a belief by the leaders of industry that the government will not allow a slump to occur. 'This promotes expectations of profitability so as to encourage large-scale investment and innovations that would be much too risky in fluctuating markets ... accumulation and technical development keep going because they are expected to keep going' (298).

In writing of fiscal policy and pump-priming, the authors point out the greater efficacy of cuts in commodity taxes for lower income groups with high marginal propensities to consume. They point out that this is nevertheless not usually done, so resulting in a less effective rise in demand and wasted 'increased saving' by higher income groups.

They see control over credit 'as much less powerful'. For risky projects, especially high rates of return have to be expected so that cuts in interest rates are of little importance for large companies (though they may be of more significance for small firms). House building is the item of expenditure most likely to be affected. Here, the experience of the 1930s in the UK is influencing their judgement and, of course, the levels that real interest rates were to take in the 1970s and the 1980s were not anticipated by anyone at the time our authors were writing. Despite the critical tone of much of their discussion, they do say that the actual outcome though not perfect still allows post-war capitalism to 'claim credit for a very remarkable change in its behaviour' (301).

Section 3 is on open economies because 'not even the United States is entirely free from external influences, and for all other capitalist countries, international problems are the main preoccupation of policy' (301). They first discuss fixed exchange rate regimes, writing that even then

> the most important influence on short-term flows arises from expectations of changes in exchange rates. ... Grieved politicians complain of speculation, but the phenomenon is produced by traders, financial institutions, and owners of wealth prudently trying to avoid losses and make profits, according to the proper rules of the private-enterprise system, which the very same politicians, in other contexts, often extol.
>
> (302)

The authors are 'disconcerted' that, since 1971, the US dollar, which supplies the greater part of international currency, has called *misére*. The US authorities have ceased to worry about an unfavourable balance of payments because either surplus countries have to buy dollars to prevent their currencies appreciating or the dollar will be devalued 'in practice if not in name', so boosting the US economy. They add: 'The traditional lore of central bankers gives no guidance in this situation and they are obliged to look for new ways of dealing with it' (303).

Then follow two sections on competitive success and competitive weakness. Under the first head, the cumulative causation process associated with export-led growth is appraised both for its strengths and its limitations. The worst of the latter is that 'all the labour, technical ingenuity, and salesmanship which goes into the surplus of exports is earning nothing for the home economy ... except unnecessary foreign exchange reserves. More imports or more socially beneficial home investments might be considered preferable' (304).

They sketch a post-war version of 'beggar-my-neighbour' policies whereby competitive strains are set up from unequal rates of growth of economies. The new Mercantilism, rather than 'fighting over trade (and loot) in what is now the third world' as had the old Mercantilism, is more concerned with trade among the industrialised nations themselves, with 'competitive struggles take[ing] more devious forms' (304). The authors single out the UK as an economy with a weak competitive position which leads to an unfavourable balance of payments that needs to be corrected. The means are protection, devaluation (either a single step or a downward float) and dampening effective demand to cause unemployment.

None of these is necessarily effective – protection may lead to retaliation, devaluation depends upon conditions in the rest of the world. A floating exchange rate may be a useful device against short-term speculative flows but otherwise is severely limited. First, devaluation may be accompanied by higher interest rates (to restrain home activity), the appreciating effects of which offset the devaluation. Devaluation does not have its effects quickly but only after a year or more (J-curve effect). Finally, by raising the prices of imported foodstuffs, it may precipitate an inflationary price-wage spiral. The consequent adverse effects on profits, reducing the availability of retained profits as finance for investment and planned investment itself, leads to a fall in accumulation and so to a slowdown in the rate of increase of productivity due to a decrease in the rate of embodied technical progress, the relative lack of which was the cause of trouble in the first place. A vicious downward cumulative causation process has been created.

Section 4 is on growth, starting with a sub-section on economic miracles, the 25 years after the end of World War II which 'for the capitalist economy as a whole ... was a period of a long boom, interrupted by only minor set-backs' (306–7). This very success resulted in side effects which unrolled in the 1970s: inflation, 'poverty in the midst of plenty', migration, pollution. On inflation, they write that

> [i]t was obvious from the first that continuous near-full employment, without other change in institutions and attitudes, would lead to a continuously rising price level. The only way to combine high employment with stable prices would be to control the growth of incomes in money terms, but there were too many difficulties in the way of doing so, and too many powerful interests opposed to the attempt.
>
> (307)

(Since 1936, Joan Robinson often said that 'Incomes policy' was her middle name.) They outline the social consequences of inflation, making the perceptive point that when all kinds of property become vehicles for speculation, 'finance is deflected from productive investment to buying pre-existing property for resale' (307). They claim that once an inflationary process has taken hold, inducing an 'artificial' recession will not check it. This is not a prediction that Mrs Thatcher took on board in the 1980s, but, then, our authors understandably never predicted the ruthlessness of the combination of monetary policy and anti-trade union legislation that was then implemented. On voluntary incomes policies, they show great perception in their comments that workers are enjoined to be patriotic but capitalists, bosses *and* managers, need not be (because of the temptation of relocation of capital and of a brain drain if profits, salaries and bonuses do not keep up with international levels).

They discuss the trickle-down argument, pointing to a contradiction: 'growth depends, for each country, on its position in international competition; each must be careful not to put too great a burden on its industry in the attempt to alleviate poverty, for fear of hampering the "growth" on which the elimination of poverty is believed to depend' (308). 'Poverty in the midst of plenty', 'a slogan of the great slump', therefore has 'a different meaning for a family today, goggling at television advertisements for ever-new commodities that they cannot afford to buy' (309).

On migration, they note the paradox that while immigrants do the low-paid unskilled jobs providing services cheaply for the rest of the population, if they were not there, reorganisation of the provision of services would be necessary and workers would be paid higher wages, as the authors argued happened in Australia (may be then, but certainly not now).

Pigou is quoted, in the opening of the discussion on pollution, on social costs versus private costs and so on. They give a judicious account of the limitations of GNP as a measure of well being, seeing it as, 'at best, a measure of growth of economic power in the world market' (310). They express a slim hope that enlightenment may prevail: ' The best hope for the anti-pollutionists is to enlist [the widespread sentiment in favour of bringing up healthy children] on their side of the case' (311). They close with a gloomy but not unreasonable conclusion:

> One prediction that can be made with some confidence is that the governments and corporations in the capitalist sphere will be slow and reluctant to heed the warnings of the biologists about the effect on the capacity of the planet to support a life of 'growth' in the wealthy nations, and that the state of the world will certainly get worse before it begins to get better.
>
> (312)

Chapter 2, 'Socialist states', is superficially, the most dated, perhaps redundant part of the book because of the collapse of the USSR and the Eastern European (so-called) socialist states in the 1990s and the transformation of China post-Mao into, in effect, a mixed economy (in outline exhibiting the suggestions Joan Robinson made in her lectures in China in the 1950s, see Chapter 9). Yet it is still well worth reading for it highlights in a simple stark manner, the problems of planning by a single authority: how to decide and plan what to produce and how to achieve it, once it has been decided. These problems, it is claimed, though present in capitalist economies, present themselves in very different forms and so require different analysis and policy.

Employment is not a problem because full employment is assured (jobs or at least employment must be found for all),[10] and the split between the consumption goods and investment goods sectors, the rate at which workers leave agriculture depends 'on the rate at which investment is expanding industry, creating jobs for them' (313).

With international trade, the overriding goal is to export only in order to pay for imports. This makes socialist economies even more nationalistic than capitalist ones. '[Their] trade is controlled by [their] own bureaucrats, while the personnel of [capitalist firms owe their] loyalty to [the businesses concerned rather than to the nations concerned]' (314).

As for inflation, it is mostly suppressed because price setting is centralised so that socialist countries can continually maintain a high and stable level of employment without suffering from inflation.

Taxes are not on incomes of persons but are turnover taxes on commodities and taxes on profits of nationalised industries. Taxes on commodities are less unpleasant to pay, are hard to avoid and do not need huge bureaucracies to collect them. Funds to put the surplus to work are centralised which has something going for it but (shades of Keynes and the arts) 'the monolithic system of finance for cultural life supports the power of obscurantists and philistines in authority to persecute and suppress originality' (316).

The authors admit that alienation at work may be as much a problem in socialist economies as in capitalist economies. 'The greatest problem for all countries in the Soviet sphere is to find some way to get the workers to work ... made all the more difficult by the cynicism ... generated by years of sanctimonious official propaganda' (316). Yugoslavia tried an experiment that was only partly successful since worker-owners were more dedicated to their production and profits than in getting rid of unemployment, poverty and inequality. 'The Chinese', we are told, '[sought] to overcome alienation by political education and by consultation between management, technicians and workers, giving everyone a feeling of concern for production' (317), not a view either author would have accepted uncritically in the years after the book was published.

Next, agriculture is discussed and the way in which the agricultural surplus is extracted is shown to influence greatly how a socialist economy develops. The relative merits of replacing rent by taxation or delivery quotas are discussed. Prices reflect a compromise between relying on confiscation or taxes; labour values have nothing to do with it. (Joan Robinson always had a 'thing' against the labour theory of value (see Chapter 11)). Then follows a section on political prices – prices which do not primarily reflect economic fundamentals – comparing Stalin's mistakes due to his heavy industry obsession/fetish with the Chinese approach which learnt from the Soviet mistakes. 'In China, collectivisation was carried out in a manner that helped the cultivators to help themselves ... brought an immediate benefit to the majority – "the poor and lower-middle peasants". ... The surplus ... is taken from those who can best afford to part with their crops ... cultivators are provided with attractive things to spend money on. ... As industrial production develops, the terms of trade are shifted appreciably in favour of agriculture' (318). It would be interesting to see how they would revise these judgements now, and how also they would modify this rose-tinted conclusion: 'The [Chinese] system is not controlled by profitability or by any one-dimensional criterion of success, but by self-respect, ... by the high level of political consciousness of the workers' (321).

The last chapter is on the Third World, a portmanteau term for those countries that do not fit into the categories of fully developed capitalism or of socialist planning. Here politics dominates, 'for in each of these emergent states, economic policy is involved with the type of society that it is building up' (322), but the authors confine themselves to points where economic analysis is relevant. Adam Smith would approve of their central point; 'the whole development of society depends upon the level of output per head in agriculture' (323), as he would of their point that development is identified with industrialisation and capital accumulation as much in agriculture as in manufactures. These economies are subdivided into three 'different phases ... pre-capitalist development, colonial-distorted development, ... incipient modern development' (323).

First, they discuss landlord and peasant relations where they comment that as landlords enjoy a traditional style of life, they do not worry about productivity but 'indeed [may] be positively hostile to improvements which would raise the living standard of the peasants and make them less abject' (323). So while taxing rent constitutes both a way of collecting the surplus and encouraging productivity, it will not be used by governments dependent on landlord support. Yet '[t]o produce an agricultural surplus without having to rely on the extreme misery of the cultivators, it is necessary to increase productivity, and ... to provide the cultivators with the means and motive to part with a considerable portion of their products' (324). This may be done either by taxation or 'by organising marketing and providing some commodities or services that the rural population want to acquire' (324). Some societies have tried land reforms which help peasants without hurting others but this is a pretty forlorn task; hence, the failure of most land reform schemes.

The increase of capitalist methods in farming depends upon a simultaneous rise in employment opportunities elsewhere and rising incomes with which to buy the rising output of food. Otherwise, prices will not be set at levels which justify the application of capitalistic methods. In any event, it is usually the wealthy classes who benefit most.

The next section, unemployment, starts not unsurprisingly with the concept of disguised unemployment of which Joan Robinson was one of the pioneers (see Robinson, 1936d; 1937b (1947), 60–74). While an increase in aggregate demand in these economies may reduce unemployment a little, the basic reason for unemployment is the lack of capital goods to go with the potential labour force; it is Marxian not Keynesian unemployment. Keynesian policies were meant to mop up excess capacity of existing capital stocks by putting people to work with them, but not to reduce unemployment associated with a lack of capital goods.

In the discussion on underemployment in agriculture, the authors perceptively write:

> So long as there is no other productive work for the cultivators, it cannot ... be called 'uneconomic' for them to crowd on to the land ... for all can share the work and the income instead of some being driven off to live on crumbs in the cities. The waste lies in the lack of alternative employment rather than in the inefficient scale of farming. (327)

Unequal holdings among families is another element of rural underemployment. It requires reorganisation of methods of production, but this is easier said than done.

The section on the choice of techniques reflects the debate Joan Robinson had with Sen and Dobb in the 1950s (see Harcourt, 1995c; 2001a), where she argued for choosing techniques which helped to provide extra employment, both in the short term by making the machines and in the longer term by using them, and larger surpluses per unit of accumulation (see Chapter 9). They put in a plea for intermediate techniques to be used in developing economies rather than investment-using ones which foreign capitalists and/or local ones would regard as likely to offer them greater profits.

In the section on foreign trade, the authors are under no illusion that while foreign exchange is needed, social conditions and class structures may mean that much of it is 'wasted' by being spent on luxury imported consumption goods by the well off. Also, because of their past colonial status, many countries are saddled with export industries either owned by foreign capitalists who remit incomes to their own countries of origin or by locals who ape their behaviour. Moreover, governments may fear to take on developed countries because of the nature of the retaliation they may face.

When manufactures are being developed, the best of possible worlds is continuous exploitation of workers by paying low wages and ploughing back the growing surpluses in further productivity-raising accumulation in a manner akin to Arthur Lewis's original model (Lewis, 1954). 'All the same, workers who are being exploited by capitalists are better off than those who are existing ... in disguised unemployment in the cities and as landless labourers in the countryside' (331).

They highlight the paradox that while 'The [f]ree trade doctrine was all very well when it justified British manufacturers ruining handicrafts in the colonial world ... [i]t does not have so much appeal when the boot is on the other foot' (331). This is a reference to the refusal of developed countries to accept products of developing countries which meet the conditions of (static) comparative advantage because competition from them causes loss of profits and unemployment without any guarantee that capital and labour can find employment in more sophisticated industries in which they have a comparative advantage. As Ha-Joon Chang (2007) has recently pointed out, the authors argue that import-substitution industry helps to save scarce foreign exchange and needs protection until it is well established, the path followed by most, if not all developed nations in the past but now not recommended for developing economies today.

The authors point out that to get a process of accumulation going three ingredients are required: 'finance, the purchasing power available to be spent on investment; saving, the restraint on consumption that permits resources to be used for investment; and imports to supplement the resources available at home' (332). Foreign loans to permit a surplus of imports can be invaluable. The development of financial institutions, 'a local banking system and a market for placements, in which owners of wealth have confidence, is a prerequisite for accumulation in conditions of private enterprise' (333). They identify the problems associated with saving as that of preventing 'an increase in profits from leading to an increase in luxury consumption' (334).

They conclude with yet another paradox: 'countries which most deserve help are those which nationalise their industries, preventing profits accruing to private families who consume them, and which prohibit the import of luxury goods [but such] countries ... are the least likely to receive aid' (334).

There is a pessimistic section on the morning after – foreign loans bring development but not increases in exports so that a large part of new loans is needed to pay off old ones. They also take a rather pessimistic view of population growth, 'a drag on the standard of life even in the most wealthy countries and ... a heavy burden on the poorest' (336). They hope that the rise in population mainly due to the fall in infant mortality will be followed by a fall in the birth rate as people's incomes rise, but they see offsetting tendencies in regimes which regard 'cheap labour as a support for landed property or as an attraction for a rapid expansion of capitalist business' (336), where religious prejudice is used 'to put obstacles in the way of family planning except for the privileged class' (336).

Their conclusion is caustic.

> The orthodox doctrines of the theory of equilibrium and free trade ... disseminated among the intellectuals of the Third World, are not relevant to their problems. ... A different approach ... may enable [them] to see their problems in a clearer light but economics alone cannot tell them where to find the answers.
>
> (336)

The book is an impressively coherent and relevant account of the development and application of an alternative approach to political economy and economics. Why did it fail as an alternative text? King and Millmow (2003) in their survey of reviews of Robinson and Eatwell (1973) argue that the book, aimed at beginners, was consistently judged as too difficult for this audience, that there were no exercises to test understanding, no chapter summaries or summaries of new concepts, that the lack of statistical material and of discussion of contemporary economic institutions meant the abstract theory was more difficult to grasp. Perhaps these responses substantiate our earlier comment (chapter 1) that Joan Robinson was not a strategist. It was less the substantial theoretical approach presented in the book than the manner of presentation, its pedagogical style, that caused it to fail.

The book closes with the hope that what has been provided will illuminate and enlighten its readers. But their natural scepticism does not allow the authors to finish on an optimistic note and the subsequent response, or lack of it, to their book and actual events together have vindicated their pessimism.

11
A Concerned Intellectual's Task: Joan Robinson's Three Popular Books

As we saw in Chapter 4, Maurice Dobb, in a letter to Joan Robinson (JVR, 31 January 1941) stated:

> I feel that the 'poetic' element – shades of meaning inherent as it were in style, construction, emphasis – is important in all economic languages certainly, and perhaps in all languages outside the rarest and most refined discourses of Logical Positivists. This is just what gets lost in translation from one poetic convention into another. And most of it, I suggest, is *not* just irrelevant 'moral' stuff, but is concerned with the *slant* that theory has on reality – with the completeness or incompleteness of the picture of the real world it affords, with the perspective and 'projection' and dimensions it is employing, with what it throws into relief as causally important and what it relegates to the shade. Whether these meanings could or could not ultimately be reduced to a propositional system I don't feel competent to say. But I feel quite sure they usually can't be rendered in half-a-dozen or a dozen simple propositions.
>
> (Dobb's emphasis, JVR/vii/120/12)

This chapter presents Joan Robinson as a political economist who relied on, but also looked beyond, deductive reason for knowledge and understanding. This is apparent from her criticisms of neoclassical economics and its practice, and from her more positive statements. Economics was presented to Joan Robinson as formally independent of and separable from morality. She had to find some way of recognising and reintegrating values into the realm of study. For her, ideology prescribes the 'science'; her own use of the science/ideology divide became, in effect, a rejection of that very dual conception and a call for the recognition of their necessary integration. She explored these possibilities in her three more popular books: *Economic Philosophy* (1962b), *Economics: An Awkward Corner* (1966b) and *Freedom and Necessity* (1970). By expanding the range of her methodology, she made it possible to incorporate values into her discussion. Her popular writing gave her the freedom to explore these issues away from the hostile and often irrelevant criteria of her scientific peers (see Stretton, 1969).

11.1 Economic Philosophy (1962b)

What issues did she identify in *Economic Philosophy* (Robinson, 1962b)? The book was both a study of theory and a study of methodology. She distinguished at the outset between Popperian science and 'metaphysics', accepting falsification as the demarcation. But she did not argue that the ideological dimension to a statement or theory diminished its value as a theory.[1] The practice was that '[a]ny economic system requires a set of rules, an ideology to justify them, and a conscience in the individual which makes him strive to carry them out' (ibid., 18). It is from the ideology that the questions arise. Taking a particular economic system as given, its technical features may be described in a dispassionate way, but it is not possible to describe the system itself without making moral judgements. 'This theme is illustrated by reference to economic ideas in an attempt to puzzle out the mysterious way that metaphysical statements, without any logical content, can yet be a powerful influence on thought and action' (ibid., 25). And so, although she tried to maintain a sharp conceptual distinction between science and metaphysics, she argued here that in practice, in economic theory, both dimensions operate and are interdependent. Economics could aim to be more scientific if it were only aware of its implicit biases and these are what she intends to identify in the course of the book.[2] 'Scientific' referred to the propensity of the discipline to generate refutable hypotheses. Yet she argued that '[e]conomists have not yet established an agreed standard for the disproof of an hypothesis. To make matters worse, this introduces a personal element into economic controversies' (ibid., 28). Joan Robinson used these observations to conclude that sometimes, an hypothesis in economics may be irrefutable.

Having set out her premises, she proceeded to examine the concepts of value and utility. She exposed the value-ridden concepts and arguments which characterised neoclassical theory in its many manifestations. She identified aspects of Keynes's argument too as containing ideological elements, but she saw the fundamental principle of neoclassical economics, *laisser-faire*, as always promoting and justifying the status quo. From its concepts, to its logical structure based on the principles of individualistic maximising and equilibrium, it effectively pre-empted its own conclusions. It justified the production of pollution-causing consumption goods (and she quotes Galbraith, *The Affluent Society* (1958, 186–7): 'The family which takes its mauve and cerise, air-conditioned, power-steered, and power-braked car out for a tour passes through cities that are badly paved, made hideous by litter, blighted buildings, bill-boards, and posts for wires that should long since have been put underground.'(125)). It excused an unequal distribution of income within nations ('the tax system and social services ... are continually pushing against the distribution of income that our economic system throws up. The pressure is haphazard and often ineffective' (128)) and also between nations (exacerbated by rising birth rates in less-developed countries: '"With every mouth God sends a pair of hands." True enough, but he does not send a combine-harvester' (108–9)). It justifies private investment in luxury consumption in the face of poverty, ('[orthodox economists] were wont to excuse the inequality generated by private property in the means of production because it was necessary to make total income greater' (112)). *Laisser-faire* in the twentieth century represented privilege; just as privilege enabled *laisser-faire*, so *laisser-faire* consolidated privilege. The theory built up to justify it was empty of operational concepts and hence could not give rise to policies. Her arguments were not in terms of the falsifiability of theories, although she did dismiss theories if they were irrelevant, but rather she subjected this approach to a rational criticism on its own terms.

Her grounds for criticising the *laisser-faire* approach are therefore varied. She makes several jibes at mathematics in economics, formalisation as confirmation of truth or validity; the pursuit of the method as the subject matter of investigation.[3] The theoretical structure was centred round one particular, stagnant concept: the concept of equilibrium. 'Equilibrium' was inherently static and at best only comparisons of different 'equilibrium' positions could be made. The concept of equilibrium she saw as particularly troubling was when it was acknowledged that the 'position of equilibrium ... is shifted by the very process of approaching it' (ibid., 79). This was a critique of the concept and a critique of the associated method. As we have already seen, this argument became for her a dominant theme in the years to come; she first noted it as an aside in *The Economics of Imperfect Competition* (1933a, 16), possibly given weight by Sraffa's reference to this confusion in 1951, and then it was developed into a more considered critique of the method of using comparisons of different positions of equilibrium to analyse a process of change or accumulation. And, associated with this, she raised the problem of path-dependence and the identity, indeed existence, of long-period equilibrium. Consistent with this was her view that Keynes's theory had enabled history to be introduced into economic theory ('[Keynes] saw the capitalist system as ... a phase in historical development' (71)). This introduced an historical relativism. And the idea that the economy at any point in time is the optimal resolution of all the forces operating clearly overlooks the presence of the economically disempowered. In the *laisser-faire* approach, moral virtue and self-interest were indivisible or at least mutually consistent; Ricardo, Keynes and Kalecki focused on the distribution of income as the basis of their analytical structures. Issues of the distribution of income, crucial to understanding the distribution of political and economic power, could not be accommodated in the orthodox theory except by reference to marginal productivity. She was not arguing that neoclassical economics was flawed because of its ideological dimension, rather, that neoclassical economics *is, first of all,* an ideological construct and has to be seen as such. Its purpose was to justify the status quo. This was not ground for rejecting it but the theorist must be aware of this.

Secondly, it was flawed because it did not work – persistent unemployment in the 1930s had demonstrated that; persistent balance of payments problems revealed the outcome of *laisser-faire* in trade.

Thirdly, it was flawed because its arguments were flawed – witness, for example, consumer interdependence, learning as consumption increases, external diseconomies of consumption, the lack of a conception of capital and the limited scope of static theory in general.

Keynes, she argued, had shifted economic theory away from the constraints of this framework into a more relevant domain in which equilibrium was displaced by material concepts and testable hypotheses, and in which public intervention was legitimised by the new goal of 'full employment'. Joan Robinson quotes Keynes: '[o]ur problem is to work out a social organisation which shall be as efficient as possible without offending our notions of a satisfactory way of life' (ibid., 54). She pursues this theme later in *Freedom and Necessity* (Robinson, 1970).

Joan Robinson often employed irony. She left the formal style of pure theory for an informal, intuitively argued prose. But, for all her irony, she was not entirely negative in this book. She presents Keynesian theory as at least able to generate refutable hypotheses, insofar as any hypothesis in economics can be refuted. And in the area of economic growth, her own theoretical area at that time, she sees that there are many unanswered and challenging questions to be investigated (see Chapters 6, 7 and 8).

11.2 Economics: An Awkward Corner (1966b)

Marx proposed that capitalism contained its own contradictions. Joan Robinson, in *Economics: An Awkward Corner* (1966b), took on this evolutionary aspect of Marx's method and showed the forms that these contradictions took and their resolutions in Britain over the twentieth century. She opens the book with the following declaration: 'It is impossible to understand the economic system in which we are living if we try to interpret it as a rational scheme. It has to be understood as an awkward phase in a continuing process of historical development' (ibid., 11). Her thesis is that *laisser-faire* theory and Bastard Keynesian theory have exacerbated, if not given rise to the dire economic circumstances of recent times (1966), and that Keynesian theory, if properly understood, can generate more appropriate policies to guide the modern capitalist economy. Overwhelmingly,

> [t]he notions of *laisser faire* ... are contradicted by the evident need for planning to maintain 'a high and stable level of employment'. The notion that property confers obligations to justify privilege is contradicted by the separation of ownership from control. ... The notion that governments have only to see fair play between employers and employed is contradicted by the requirements of control over money incomes and prices. The notion that the free play of supply and demand produce a viable system of international trade is contradicted by the payments crises.
>
> (ibid., 14)

She continues this theme in pointing out a contradiction in *laisser-faire* that the ultimate outcome of competition is monopoly; that the competitive process is one of absorbing all the competitors in order to control the market, a process which Rothschild (1947) and Hymer (1976) document. This propensity of competition to create non-competitive forms tends then to restrict output and raise prices. The process of competition itself generates waste in large expenditures on advertising, which raise costs and prices. *Laisser-faire*, then, as a practice, does not necessarily lead to maximum/optimum output and efficiency.

Furthermore, in the process of undertaking public investment, to compensate for the gap in employment left by *laisser-faire* (lack of) policy, the state engages in large expenditures on arms thereby wasting resources and tying up skilled labour.

To Joan Robinson, the most striking anomaly is one of apparent injustice, that the massive accumulation of wealth of the nineteenth and early twentieth centuries could only have occurred with the vastly unequal distribution of wealth and income that prevailed (ibid., 12). With the end of the First World War, this easy accumulation was over. 'An exceptionally large unbalance in international trade has been created by the violent swing of history that swept away the dominating position of Britain in the world economy, leaving unchanged the institutions and attitudes that belonged to it' (ibid., 31). *Laisser-faire* was capable of generating mass unemployment and a balance of payments deficit, and showed no tendency to correct the situation. This downward spiral occurs when competition tightens margins and reduces profits, reduces investment and so productivity growth is slow, costs are higher than they otherwise would have been, effective demand is low and employment declines. With costs higher, exports are less competitive, imports are attractive and the balance of trade moves against Britain. To try and rectify the balance-of-payments deficit by raising interest rates and acting on the exchange rate, will only discourage investment more and exacerbate the downturn. Prior to the war, raw materials had been imported for manufactures which were then exported and a balance had prevailed. But as imperial preferences broke up, the ex-colonies found that they could produce the manufactured goods themselves, more cheaply, and so they outcompeted Britain's manufactures both domestically and abroad. The era of untrammeled accumulation was over. The position of capital revealed that the saving which had justified the unequal distribution of income was in fact now generating unutilised capacity and so was harmful to the process of accumulation, an awkward phase for *laisser-faire* theory to explain.

Since the Second World War, Britain, informed by Keynes, had pursued a full employment policy; in this supported context, *laisser-faire* can be accompanied by full employment and inflation. The free play of supply and demand forces, if it is associated with full employment, can also lead to rising money wages and spiralling of prices. A high rate of inflation makes exports uncompetitive and imports cheaper and so creates a balance-of-payments strain. Once again, *laisser-faire* delivers a problematic outcome far from self-correction.

Joan Robinson argued that Keynes's propositions had been misunderstood. In particular, she again emphasised the historical dimension to his theory. This enabled him to argue in terms of categories which represent current institutional processes, which are open-ended, while neoclassical and 'bastard' Keynesian theory still clung to the static framework in which 'equilibrium' underlay and closed the outcome of all the relationships: 'The institutions and the habits of mind built up during the period when the surplus was being squeezed out survive after they have ceased to be useful and have not yet been replaced' (ibid., 13).

11.3 Freedom and Necessity: An Introduction to the Study of Society (1970)[4]

It is 'the interplay of consciousness with environment, of freedom with necessity, which is the characteristic of human life' (Robinson, 1970, 23). Once again, it is a contradiction that informs her argument.

She saw the study of economy to be a part of the study of the history of civilisations. The book undertakes an historical survey of communities of animals and birds as well as of humans to range over the immense variety of ways in which the fundamentally economic questions of survival had been made manifest and been resolved. Within this vast span lay industrial capitalism, the most recently evolved social construction. She examined many examples of societies and noted 'examples of how economic rationality for a community can be preserved as a by-product of beliefs and emotions in the individual which have no economic meaning at all' (ibid., 29). Institutions outlive their original purposes.

Co-existing with the various forms of capitalism were forms of socialism, not so much the successor of capitalism as an alternative means of industrialising poor, agricultural nations. Joan Robinson sees her subject as a component part of the study of society and as a study of the practice of ideologies. She argues that 'value judgements' are endemic in the social sciences, that it is a self-deception to believe that one is ever purely objective. But, she argues, some notions of morality are universal and it is not impossible for an honest person to understand another whose ideas were formed in totally different traditions. This is suggestive of a view of human nature more fundamental than 'economic man' and abandoned from economics after the eighteenth century.

Her study revealed what she referred to as adaptive and also exploratory behaviour. Some exploratory behaviour was successful in its pursuits of better survival and became adapted and itself subject to pressures for change. It is a dialectical path.[5] The process was theorised differently at different stages of development. So the rationality of the

Scottish enlightenment developed into a 'purely rational' model devoid of any counter force from moral philosophy in the twentieth century. Again, Joan Robinson saw what she was doing in terms of introducing some of the implications and indications of history and time into conceptual and theoretical representations in opposition to the purely static frameworks of orthodox theory.

What she demonstrated in the display of societies was that each faced the same fundamental (economic) need for survival but that many, many solutions had evolved and the pursuit of money-making was only one, and a relatively recent one, of these. The new feature that capitalism legitimised was the elevation of making money for its own sake to a respectable business. Joan Robinson had warned that 'We need to combat, not foster, the ideology which pretends that values which can be measured in terms of money are the only ones that ought to count' (Robinson, 1962b, 137).

A theme of her study of societies was a consciousness of the role of ideology in directing rationality, that is, directing the rules of each society and of their implications for its scientific knowledge. What are the implications of a more egalitarian distribution of income and of wealth,[6] of raising the education level of all, of nationalising transport?

She asks for an awareness of those patterns of values that evolve to explain what is and to preserve its identity. 'The task of the social scientist is to reassert morality over technology', that is, over economics.[7] Currently, she argues, our society is being led by technology in every sphere, including knowledge. The mathematisation of economics is an example of the attempt to take over the study of a field of knowledge by a constraining technique. We have seen in her own survey, non-technical, intellectual feats – revelations about a whole range of basic evolutionary economic practices. It is only in modern times that technology has come to dominate as the moral authority and rationality to refer only to what can be exact and precise and to disallow the imprecise.

11.4 Values and science

'In the general mass of notions and sentiments that make up an ideology, those concerned with economic life play a large part' (Robinson, 1962b, 7).

A recurring theme in these three books is the exploration of the role of values in shaping economic theory and policy. In the first book, Joan Robinson examined the role of ideology in the construction and interpretation of theory; in the second, she examined the contradictions which put into motion a society reflected by that theory and in the third, she examined the evolving process of social change which bears alternative social structures and alternative ideologies. The first book was clearly Popperian in its distinction between science and ideology. In the second and third books, she challenged her earlier methodology and the relationship between, or even acceptance of, these two aspects of knowledge became blurred.[8]

Joan Robinson initially saw that knowledge in science is reached through observation, experiment and refutation, and rational debate. Ethics, one's morality, in contrast, is a pattern of beliefs about appropriate behaviour in a range of situations; it was constituent of one's ideology. She argued that a person comes to develop these beliefs usually early in their life through a psychological process analogous to language acquisition. They learn through the complexity of social interaction and observation within their daily context. The content of this conscience then reflects that individual's interpretation of the beliefs, values and practices of that society in which she/he was brought up. These beliefs refer to the interests of the self, both as an individual and in relation to others.

> The biological necessity for morality arises because, for the species to survive, [there must be egoism and this should be extended to the family] ... the pursuit of self interest is mitigated by respect and compassion for others ... there must be a set of rules to reconcile them. Moreover, there must be some mechanism to make the individual keep the rules when they conflict with his immediate advantage. ... Since the egoistic impulses are stronger than the altruistic, the claims of others have to be imposed upon us. The mechanism by which they are imposed is the moral sense or conscience of the individual.
>
> Robinson (1962b, 10–1)

The implication of this for the social group is as follows: 'A society cannot exist unless its members have common feelings about what is the proper way of conducting its affairs, and these common feelings are expressed in ideology' (ibid., 9). She rejects the proposition that the individual pursuit of self-interest is the fundamental basis for organising social and economic behaviour, and is the singular road to 'freedom'. Rather, her view of human nature is that the individual's sense of morality interacts with her/his self-interest. This bears some affinity with Adam Smith's 'fellow-feeling' or his 'sympathy'. Joan Robinson believed that humans make decisions on a 'rational' basis; that they will be persuaded to alter inappropriate behaviour by appeal to reason. Yet she also sees that morality, acquired during childhood through socialisation, is anthropologically contextual; so too then is rationality. Furthermore, she held the view that there are fundamental aspects of morality which are universal. From this belief in some innate and universal sense of morality, together with the power of logic she could suppose that pursuit of self-interest could be consistent with the social 'good'.

In 1932, Joan Robinson undertook a methodological introspection, which culminated in two pieces of writing. One she published: *Economics is a Serious Subject: the apologia of an economist to the mathematician, the scientist, and the plain man* (see Harcourt (1990a); Kerr with Harcourt (eds.), 2002, vol. V, 24–40). The other was for limited exposure: *A passage from the autobiography of an analytical economist* (see Aslanbeigui and Oakes, 2006). These documents both suggest that she had absorbed the pervasive language and structure of the logical positivists. Making a sharp distinction between 'values' and 'facts', she declared that 'the subject matter of economics is neither more nor less than its own technique' (Robinson, 1932a, 4). Hence, the method pre-empts the problems it will deal with. Economics was a 'box of tools'. The adequacy of a theory was then a matter of the realism of assumptions, the logical coherence of the argument and the congruence of the theory with some observable phenomenon. Her main methodological issue was the choice between the opposing forces of tractable and realistic assumptions. In 1937, in her *Essays in the Theory of Employment*, she included an essay, 'An economist's sermon' (1937b), in which she shows how orthodox economic theory has been used to justify certain moral positions. Her argument is with both the logic of those theories and their political implications and she directly takes a position in support of the poor and unemployed, her economic strategy based on the then, alternative and new, Keynesian theory. Perhaps, this is one of her first polemical pieces. In the same collection is another essay, 'Indeterminacy' in which she observes that an economic theory may be indeterminate because factors 'which cannot easily be fitted into the existing structure of pure economic analysis [such as the position of trade unions or political disturbances] have to be brought into the story' (Robinson, 1937b, 171). The answer to this methodological problem is 'to discover determinate problems on which to work' (ibid.). This, she argued, is necessary for economics to become a science. For many years, she maintained the view of economics as a body of neutral techniques. The economist must dutifully separate out the values inherent in assumptions and theoretical propositions for the unsuspecting reader.

In 1955, she delivered some lectures entitled 'Marx, Marshall and Keynes: three views on capitalism', at the Delhi School of Economics. Here, she compares the differing analyses of the three authors, noting that each addressed a different stage of capitalism and that each author held a different political attitude to capitalism: 'But each has significance for other times, for insofar as each theory is valid it throws light upon essential characteristics of the capitalist system which have always been present in it' (Robinson, 1955; *C.E.P.*, vol. II, 1960, 3). As an economic system, capitalism has certain underlying principles which can be described 'scientifically'. Her strict dual of theory and value seems to be weakening:

> Economic doctrines always come to us as propaganda. This is bound up with the very nature of the subject and to pretend that it is not so in the name of 'pure science' is a very unscientific refusal to accept the facts. ... The element of propaganda is inherent in the subject because it is concerned with policy.
>
> (ibid., 3–4)

She now seems to be arguing that economic theory is the vehicle for ideology; theory is introduced to justify a course of action which will be pursued for ideological reasons. This shift from her earlier approach is evident.

> Economic theory, in its scientific aspect, is concerned with showing how a particular set of rules of the game operates, but in doing so it cannot help but make them appear in a favourable or an unfavourable light to the people who are playing the game. ... This element of propaganda enters into even the most severely technical details of the subject ... to pretend that we are not interested in the evaluation is mere self-deception.
>
> (ibid., 4–5)

Although she had previously embraced the division of economic knowledge into the 'box of tools' and the ideologically tainted, associated propositions, now she sees values entering at all stages of the analysis. She continues to argue that while 'every economic doctrine that is not trivial formalism contains political judgements ... [i]t is folly to reject a piece of analysis because we do not agree with the political judgement of the economist who puts it forward' (ibid., 6). Economics, in the formulation of its propositions and theories, she argued, represents an ideology and it can also provide the means for investigating the implications of that ideology. 'It is the business of the economists, not to tell us what to do, but to show why what we are doing anyway is in accord with proper principles' (Robinson, 1962b, 25). That is, the economist provides an apparently rational basis for pursuing the ideologically determined objectives in ways consistent with the system of values embedded in that ideology. And, indeed, Joan Robinson uses such a criterion of relevance to accept or reject a theory. But she proposes subsequently that '[t]o learn from the economists regarded as scientists it is necessary to separate what is valid in their description of the system from the propaganda that they make, overtly or unconsciously, each for his own ideology' (ibid., 12). At the same time, she reveals her empiricist angle: 'An economic theory at best is only a hypothesis. ... It suggests a possible explanation of some phenomenon and it cannot be accepted as correct until it has been tested by an appeal to the facts' (ibid.). 'To make good use of an economic theory we must first sort out the relations of the propagandist and the scientific elements in it, then by checking with experience, see how far the scientific element appears convincing, and finally recombine it with our own political views' (ibid., 17). Knowledge is still seen as being deconstructed into the material, the purely logical and the subjective. Although still within a positivist and empiricist framework, she is now allowing the economist to take an acknowledged stance.

She continues to present this view. In 'Marxism: religion and science' (1962d; *C.E.P.*, vol. III, 1965) published in the same year as *Economic Philosophy*. She differentiates between 'science', whose propositions can be proven false, and 'ideology'. 'Science' may fall short of adequately describing an actual situation. Here, Joan Robinson is trying to reject the proposition that 'Marxism is a scientific ideology' but she lacks the philosophical background and insight to examine its meanings. Her confusion is apparent.

> It is perfectly legitimate to have schools of thought in a developing subject. A school of thought is distinguished by its method, not by its tenets. Science itself, in a certain sense, is based on faith and on a confident belief that all phenomena will yield to investigation and will turn out to fit into a scheme of natural law.
>
> (ibid., 155–6)

She is revealing her earlier view of the unity of science, extending this to the same epistemological space as economic theory, and at the same time implying that 'science' too is subject to tainting by 'values'. Her translation of Marx's concepts into 'operational' terms perhaps begs the question at which stages 'values' enter the development of knowledge.

By this time, Joan Robinson had adopted the classical reproduction schema as a framework and developed a theory of growth which integrated this schema with Keynes's and Kalecki's principle of effective demand, using class categories and aggregate social relationships (e.g., Robinson, 1956a; 1962e), the outcomes of which may or may not be reconciled. These two analytical structures represented, to her, elements in the economists' 'box of tools' and could be seen as 'scientific' and value-free.

She understood at this stage (Robinson, 1962e) that economic theory comprised a set of propositions which are interrelated in some formal way, to provide a 'value-free' contribution to the 'box of tools', an analysis which has been shown to be logically consistent, a set of implications of these analytical propositions, the choice of which for policy, involves political judgement. She accepted that values will enter the way the economist frames the problem, the choice of concepts and of the relevant relationships, but the structure and the analysis, she argued, are without moral content. The problem she now confronts is that of finding some form of relationship or interaction between fact, value and analysis. Dobb (1973) demonstrates the fallacy of the position as held by Schumpeter and, by implication, by Joan Robinson. Like Schumpeter, she still maintained that there exists a body of core analysis, of formal techniques which are all ahistorical and without ideological content. One outcome of this 'box of tools' view is the increasing formalisation of economic theory which is associated with increasing neutrality and so scientificity. Instead, Dobb (1973) argues that theoretical analysis in economics 'inevitably has a causal story to tell'; it has a subject matter. The logical system is a purely formal structure without economic content – a method without a theory – or a response to initiating problems, affected by the initial 'vision' of the economist. Paradoxically, as she was dismissive of the use of mathematics in economic analysis, her views on the role of ideology in theory were at this time unresolved. Dobb writes ten years after the time Joan Robinson discussed this issue, but he makes his own resolution of the relationship between fact, value and analysis clear:

> economic theory is concerned with economic statements ... it can*not* be separated from the answers to the questions it has framed, and hence from the actual ... shape of the economic *problems* with which

> it is designed to deal. ... it is impossible to claim for it 'independence' of the economic content and meaning of the propositions which *are* ... ideologically conditioned
>
> (Dobb, 1973, 5; emphasis in the original)

Joan Robinson is aware that the single-minded pursuit of detachment leads to irrelevance: this conviction lies behind her focus on the implications of time, or history, in economic theory. But she continues to reveal an ambivalence toward the role of ideology in her economics.[9]

How then does she move beyond her Popperian view of knowledge in science and her depiction of the science/value split?[10] Recall her opening words to *Economics: An Awkward Corner*: 'It is impossible to understand the economic system in which we are living if we try to interpret it as a rational scheme' (Robinson, 1966b, 11). Each society generates its own rationality, she argues; it always seeks to justify itself in its ideology. So, 'rationality' is relative. While some aspects of the society's 'rationality' can be formulated into refutable hypotheses, many other aspects cannot: the role of ideology is left implicit. This dichotomy of science and morality leads to responses limited within its own terms, whereas Joan Robinson was attempting to blur these limits. She was much influenced by Gunnar Myrdal in this depiction.[11] Myrdal (1953) had argued that facts do not organise themselves into concepts and theories just by being looked at; indeed, except within the framework of concepts and theories there are no scientific facts, only chaos. Questions must be asked before answers can be given. 'This implicit belief in the existence of a body of scientific knowledge acquired independently of all valuations is, as I now see it, naïve empiricism' (Myrdal, 1953, vii). Joan Robinson's interpretation of Myrdal revealed a similar view, that values pervade all levels of the analysis, not simply the choice of goals. From the moment the basic concepts are formed, values are part of the process of creating knowledge.

'The task of social science now is to raise self-consciousness to the second degree, to find out the causes, the mode of functioning and the consequences of the adoption of ideologies, so as to submit them to rational criticism' (Robinson, 1970, 122). Joan Robinson always stressed that the theorist must scrupulously understand her/his assumptions. But she illustrated through her own examples in these three books that 'rationality' is not the only way of creating knowledge. Furthermore, '[n]or do I think that purely economic argument can ever finally settle any questions for political and human considerations are always involved in every question and are usually decisive' (Robinson, 1957; *C.E.P.*, vol. II, 1960, 113).

In 1973, she again broached the subject of ideology and its relationship to theory.

> The flow of production taking place in an industrial economy is an extremely complex entity that cannot be represented in any simple measure. It is something which exists. It is *there* in reality. It is not affected by the way we chose to represent it, but various ways of representing it are connected with the various alternative ways of diagnosing its behaviour through time, its distribution between classes and so forth.
>
> (Robinson, 1973a; *C.E.P.*, vol. V, 1979, 255, emphasis in original)

The initial choice of a concept pre-empts its role in the consequent theory and determines the understanding of the given material world; and there is a complicity in the concepts chosen with the problem posed.

In 1977, in 'What are the questions?' (Robinson, 1977c; *C.E.P.*, vol. V, 1979, 1–31) she again addresses the issue of what constitutes economics. 'Discussion of an actual problem cannot avoid the question of what should be done about it; questions of policy involve politics ... [p]olitics involve ideology; there is no such thing as a "purely economic" problem that can be settled by purely economic logic; political interests and political prejudice are involved in every discussion of actual questions' (ibid., 1). Here, she seems to be relinquishing the idea of 'pure' economics: the concepts chosen, the logical structure and the sequence of the analysis. There is a complex interdependence. She notes the economist's need to defer to historical evidence which 'can always be read both ways' (ibid., 2). But once again, the comparison with the natural sciences leads her to focus her theoretical attention on getting the logic right on the one hand and accepting the limits to the 'scientific' status of economics on the other due to the ambiguously interpretable nature of its 'facts'. Her commitment to demonstrating the logical errors in the neoclassical theory illustrate the former domain of economics and her prolific work on China and development issues as well as her interpretations of the British economy illustrate the latter (e.g., Robinson, 1966b).

To maintain this opposition, science versus values, appears to be inconsistent with Joan Robinson's view of the world in these three books, and in later essays, as continually undergoing endogenous and complex change; with the view that theory informs policy and changes the world just as moral systems change it and then evolve from it.

Values also change in response to new situations. 'Science', as that which is established through refutable hypotheses, is only one part of knowledge.[12] The broader scope achieved by acknowledging the role of values, introduces the possibility of improving the process and criteria by which economists assess contending theories. Joan Robinson, eventually, effectively bypassed the science/value dichotomy instead revealing interconnections between systems of thought and morality, opening the possibility for extending the economist's method.

Although she posed the question of the nature of economic reasoning, she remained limited by positivism. Particularly in her later writings, she tried to integrate values into the body of her argument but she did not have the philosophical instruments to guide her thinking, or to give validity to her arguments. Her lingering positivism interfered with and limited her theoretical developments, denying her passionately held views on social justice, a status equivalent to what she saw as the 'scientific' element of political economy. But she always maintained her moral commitment to discover a just society.

Over her lifetime, but particularly in her later years, Joan Robinson abandoned the traditional model of economics. First, she extended the boundaries of the subject. She does so not only by going outside orthodox economics but also goes into anthropology, sociology, history and politics for her material. Secondly, she broaches the subject of ideology and analysis. Thirdly, she is more philosophical than 'scientific' and adopts a number of methodologies. She uses examples or particular situations to illustrate her point, she uses the concrete rather than the abstract. She abandons the purely deductive, mathematical, self-interested, singly driven autonomous being and constructs instead an alternative explanation using reason, intuition, social classes and mutuality between entities who are unequal in their power and hold conflicting interests, their behaviour displaying contradictions and asymmetry. She directs attention to areas of applied study and then establishes a practical approach to study them rather than assume an a *priori* approach. Furthermore, she not only abandons the theory of *laisser-faire*, she also rejects its practice and advocates a social welfare state/planned market economy.

12
Conclusion: Joan Robinson's Legacy

12.1

We stress that this volume is an intellectual biography, a discussion of the development of the ideas, in the main, of one person. However, because Joan Robinson always stressed the need for teamwork in the development of ideas, we have also documented the influence on her, and the contributions of those we could loosely call Joan Robinson and her circle. We have left the discussion of personal, as opposed to intellectual interactions, to a minimum, though we hope we have been able to convey to readers who did not know Joan Robinson personally what an extraordinary person she was.

Between them, the authors have written well over 100 essays on the themes taken up in this volume. The first on Joan Robinson arose from a request to GCH in the 1970s by the late Angus Wilson, at the suggestion of Harold Lydall (Wilson was then University Orator at the University of East Anglia) to send him some background notes on Joan Robinson for the address he was to make as the university was awarding her an honorary degree. The response was an essay, 'Portrait of a Lady', which was never published but which was the basis of the entry on Joan Robinson, commissioned by the *International Encyclopedia of the Social Sciences* for its Volume 18, *Biographical Supplement* (Harcourt, 1979).

The first paragraph of the entry read:

> Joan Robinson is the rebel with a cause *par excellence*. She has been at the forefront of most major developments, some of them revolutionary, in modern economic theory since the late 1920s. Joan Robinson has always believed passionately in her subject as a force for enlightenment and she has coupled this belief with an equally passionate

> hatred of social injustice and oppression. She has thrown in her lot with the wretched of the earth, whether they be the unemployed of the capitalist world in the 1930s, or the poverty-stricken and militarily oppressed of the Third World in the post-war era, or students cheated of the living fire by their professors in the 1970s.

Subsequent reflections and research reinforce our belief that the paragraph is a just evaluation of her life and work. In the same entry, when summing up his impression of Robinson and Eatwell (1973), GCH wrote that it was 'a noble experiment which should not be ignored by the hidebound, the pedestrian and the timid'. He hoped that it would serve to produce the 'generation well educated, resistant to fudging, imbued with the humility and the pride of genuine scientists [making] contributions both to knowledge and to the conduct of affairs that no one need be ashamed of' (Robinson, *C.E.P.*, vol. III, 1965, 6). But whatever the outcome of that particular venture, Joan Robinson herself much more than fulfilled her own modest aim of doing 'a little good here and there to set in the scales against all the harm' (ibid.). We hope readers will agree that we have provided the evidence to vindicate this judgement.

In the rest of this concluding chapter, our aim is, first, to highlight and put into perspective her major contributions and achievements; secondly, to report the assessments of some of her contemporaries and, thirdly, to give a final summing up.

12.2

We hope it has already emerged that Joan Robinson had an incisive mind which allowed her to cut into the heart of the matter, to see the logical fallacy of an intricate theoretical argument or the political realities of a complicated situation. She had the facility, which increased with years – it started from a high base – of distilling the essence of the matter in a few sharp crystal-clear sentences, each one the tip of an iceberg of knowledge and thought. She was able to make sense of technical literature, even though she was virtually innocent of mathematical training, because of a combination of superb intuition with equally superb logical powers. (One of her favourite sayings was, 'As I never learnt mathematics, I have had to think.') These qualities explain why she was an outstanding theoretician. They also explain why her political analysis and judgements were sometimes simplistic and distorted, by-products of that ability to abstract and simplify which marks the good theoretician. Hers was also one of the toughest minds in the trade;

she neither avoided nor minded confrontation. Here is the late Harry Johnson's description of a visit by her to Chicago (not recommended as a place for the timid).

> Once she came to Chicago to talk to my students there; they looked at her and decided, 'Well, we'll certainly show this old grandmother where she gets off' ... They picked their heads up off the floor, having been ticked off with a few well-chosen blunt squelches.
>
> (Johnson, 1974, 30)

Her barbs were spiced with a robust and civilised sense of humour, combined, it must be said, with what the late John Vaizey called 'bleak Cambridge rudeness'.

> They [the professors of M.I.T.] now admit ... that there is no logical reason why the pseudo-production function should be [well behaved]. They just assume that it is so. After putting the rabbit into the hat in full view of the audience it does not seem necessary to make so much fuss about drawing it out again.
>
> (Robinson, 1966c, 308)

'The purpose of studying economics is not to acquire a set of ready-made answers to economic questions, but to learn how to avoid being deceived by economists' (Robinson, *C.E.P.*, vol. II, 1960, 17). 'This model was described as a parable. A parable, in the usual sense, is a story drawn from everyday life intended to explain a mystery; in this case it is the mystery which is expected to explain everyday life' (Robinson, *C.E.P.*, vol. V, 1979, 63). She had the ability to cast off and start anew; she was no respecter of vested interests, certainly not her own, though at any moment of time she would argue fiercely to defend her current position.

An original thinker,[1] Joan Robinson was punctilious in documenting her mentors and sources of inspiration. As we have seen, four close associates held pride of place: Keynes, Piero Sraffa, Michal Kalecki and, over many years, Richard Kahn, whose 'remorseless logic [was] an ideal complement to her innovative enthusiasm' (Eatwell, 1977, 64). In the Foreword to *The Economics of Imperfect Competition* (Robinson, 1933a, v), she wrote:

> Of not all the new ideas, however, can I definitely say that 'this is my own invention'. ... I have had the constant assistance of Mr. R. F. Kahn. The whole technical apparatus was built up with his aid and many of the major problems ... were solved as much by him as by me.

In the Preface to *The Accumulation of Capital* (Robinson, 1956a, vi): 'As so often, it was R. F. Kahn who saw the point that we were groping for and enabled us to get it into a comprehensible form.' Piero Sraffa was the inspiration for at least two of her major contributions: *The Economics of Imperfect Competition* (much of the analysis of which, as we saw, she later rejected: 'to apply the analysis to the so-called theory of the firm, I had to make a number of limitations and simplifications which led the argument astray' (Robinson, 1933a, 2nd edn, 1969, vi), and her contributions to the theory of value, distribution, capital and growth. She said of Sraffa: 'I worked out a theory of imperfect competition, inspired by Sraffa's article [Sraffa, 1926]' (Foreword, 1973e, by Robinson to Kregel, 1973, x). In her 'generalisation of the *General Theory*', especially in considering the meaning of the rate of profits, she said: 'Piero Sraffa's interpretation of Ricardo provided the most important clue and the long-delayed publication of his book *The* [*sic*] *Production of Commodities by Means of Commodities* put into a sharp form the ideas that I had been groping for' (Robinson, 1951–80, vol. IV, 1973, 125). Her debt to Keynes is documented in many places.

As we argued in earlier chapters, it was more and more Kalecki's framework (it derived in turn from Marx via Tugan-Baranovsky) that she adopted in her thinking about distribution, accumulation and growth as processes occurring in historical time. This is masked in *The Accumulation of Capital* but it runs through all her subsequent writings on these themes and is especially reflected in the approach she and Eatwell exposited in their introduction (1973) to modern economics for beginners in the subject.

This sea change in her approach and views started in the mid-1930s. Probably the single most important stimulus was meeting Kalecki for the first time in 1936, a meeting which marked the beginning of their long, close friendship and vigorous intellectual exchanges. Joan Robinson was the greatest champion of the clear-cut case for the independent discovery by Kalecki of the principal propositions of *The General Theory*. Most important for her own subsequent development was her introduction to a framework of analysis which Kalecki used for his solution of the realisation problem within models of the cycle. Increasingly, Joan Robinson came to feel that this framework was more appropriate for understanding the workings of capitalism (and, indeed, at a very basic level, of economic systems generally).

Before she met Kalecki, Joan Robinson reviewed John Strachey's 1935 book (Robinson, 1936a), but she had not then mastered the structure of Marx's ideas. That she eventually did, for Keynesian/Kaleckian issues, is shown most convincingly in her superb account of 'Kalecki on capitalism' in the memorial issue for Kalecki in the Oxford Institute *Bulletin* in 1977 (Robinson, 1977c). There, she shows how the pricing policies of firms, the different saving behaviour of the wage-earners and the capitalists (the latter subdivided into entrepreneurial and managerial decision-makers, on the one hand, and a passive rentier class, on the other), and the dominant importance of profit-making and accumulation, may be combined in a simple short-period model of the determination of employment and distribution to illustrate the possibility of an underemployment rest state. The same structure underlay the analysis of her magnum opus of 1956 and its follow-up in 1962 but it was set out most clearly in 1977.

We shall never know whether in their first discussions Kalecki employed the apparatus of his 1936 review in Polish of *The General Theory* (see Kalecki, *C.W.*, vol. I, 199, 223–32), but certainly his use there of a microeconomic foundation in which imperfect competition was the general case, and pure competition the special case from which to build upwards to the central result of *The General Theory* would have been congenial to her later thoughts and expositions. His critique in his review of the details of Keynes's theory of investment was mirrored in her own subsequent critique, that it was an unholy mass of *ex ante* and *ex post* factors which needed to be separated by taking account of the two-sided relationship between profits and investments. Actual investment helped to create actual profits; expected profits (themselves related to actual profits) helped to determine planned investment. As we have seen, the relationship originally suggested by Kalecki became the substance of her famous banana diagram in Essay 2 of the 1962 *Essays in the Theory of Economic Growth* (1962e, 48). She now presented the arguments in a more digestible form than in the 1956 book.

Of other contemporaries, we should also mention Ester Boserup, Harrod, Kaldor, Myrdal, Pigou and Shove, of whose 'teaching in Cambridge for many years past ... [she wrote] influenced the whole approach to many problems of economic analysis' (Robinson, 1933a, vi).

Of the greats of the past, Joan Robinson was most influenced by Ricardo, Marx, Marshall and Wicksell. She found herself far more and more in tune with the former two than the latter two and, indeed, her lasting contribution to the subject, we venture to predict, will be seen as helping to form a unified system of political economy that is classical-Marxian-cum-Keynesian–Kaleckian in inspiration, directly applicable to the analysis of, and policy prescriptions for, problems of the modern world. She admired Wicksell, not so much for his contributions or approach, as for his candour and honesty, which she contrasted with Marshall's attitudes. 'Unlike Marshall, ... Wicksell is very candid. When he cannot get an answer he admits the difficulty. This I found very helpful; I gave great credit to Wicksell – not for getting an answer but for seeing the problem' (Robinson, *C.E.P.*, vol. IV, 1973, 125). Of Marshall she said: 'The more I learn about economics the more I admire Marshall's intellect and the less I like his character' (Robinson, *C.E.P.*, vol. IV, 1973, 259).

> Marshall had a foxy way of saving his conscience by mentioning exceptions, but doing so in such a way that his pupils would continue to believe in the rule. He pointed out that Say's Law ... breaks down when there is a failure of confidence [but] [t]his was mentioned by the way. It was not meant to disturb the general faith in equilibrium under laissez faire.
>
> (Robinson, 1973c, 2)

'Both [static and dynamic] elements were present in his thinking and he showed great agility in appealing, in each context, to whichever would best suit his purpose of presenting a mollifying picture of the private-enterprise economy' (Foreword, Robinson, 1973e, ix, in Kregel, 1973).

Her first major work was *The Economics of Imperfect Competition* (1933a). In writing the book, Joan Robinson was inspired by Sraffa's 1926 article, his 'sacrilege in pointing out inconsistencies in Marshall ... [who] *was* economics' when she came up to Cambridge in 1922. As she finally came to see it, the inconsistencies related to a deep-seated conflict in Marshall's *Principles* between the analysis which is purely static and the conclusions drawn from it which apply to an economy developing through time with accumulation going on. At the time, as Sraffa saw it and Joan Robinson also, the inconsistencies related to the internal logic of static partial equilibrium analysis, especially the dilemma of reconciling the simultaneous existence of falling supply price and competition, and of when the independence of supply and demand curves could be expected to hold. We have documented above Sraffa's influence through his 1926 article, his 1920s lectures and his contributions to the 1930 *Economic Journal* symposium on increasing returns and the representative firm.

There is evidence, though, that neither Joan Robinson nor Kahn were ever completely on Sraffa's wavelength at this time (see Marcuzzo, 1994; Kerr with Harcourt (eds.), 2002, vol. V). Looking back 40 years later, Joan Robinson stated that her 'aim was to attack the internal logic of the theory of static equilibrium and to refute, by means of its own arguments, the doctrine that wages are determined by the marginal productivity of labour' (Robinson, 1973e, x). There is *some* hindsight integrated into this judgement but overall it is a balanced assessment.[2] At a more general level, Keynes (in his report on the book to Harold Macmillan in November 1932) came closest to the correct assessment at that time. He referred to 'a very considerable development of the theory of value in the last five years', developments to be found in journals and in 'oral discussion at Cambridge and Oxford', and to the fact that there is 'no convenient place' in which may be found

> a clear statement of the nature of modern technique, or a summary of the recent work on the subject. Mrs. Robinson aims at filling this gap ... has done it very well. ... The book will be for a little while to come an essential one for any serious student of the modern theory of value.
>
> (*C.W.*, vol. XII, 1973; Kerr with Harcourt (eds.), 2002, vol. I, 149–51)

In the book, Joan Robinson explored systematically the implications for firms in a competitive environment of facing downward-sloping demand curves for their products, so that the profit-maximising prices and quantities are determined by the intersections of their (*long-period*) marginal-cost and marginal-revenue curves. This analysis illuminated the real world facts (alluded to by Sraffa) that businesspeople felt it was demand conditions rather than rising costs which limited their sales, and that firms could still make profits with plants running well below capacity, facts that were incomprehensible within the framework of the Marshallian–Pigovian theories that preceded it. Kahn's analysis related to the same themes but in a short-period context (Kahn, 1929; 1989).

As we know, Joan Robinson refuted (in the Preface to the second edition (Robinson, 1933, 2nd edn, 1969, vi)) the approach of the book because of her dissatisfaction with the static method, its inability to handle time. She regarded as a 'shameless fudge', the notion that business people could find the 'correct' price by a process of trial and error, because it assumed that the equilibrium position towards which a firm is tending at any point in time is independent of the path it is *actually* taking. Thus, she subjected her own analysis to what she regarded as the most fundamental criticism of the general methodology of analysis by comparison of static equilibrium positions, the critique which she developed in other areas in the ensuing years. She still approved of the section in the book on price discrimination but was distressed that the negative lessons of the book, especially the attack on the marginal productivity theory of wages within the confines of its own theoretical framework, had been ignored while the weaknesses had been frozen into orthodox teaching.

At the same time, as we have seen, Joan Robinson was playing a significant part in the formation and propagation of the Keynesian revolution. The most influential people persuading Keynes both to modify and to expand the analysis in his 1930 *Treatise on Money* (Keynes, 1930) and helping to develop his ideas by both criticisms and contributions, included Harrod, Kahn, Meade, Sraffa and Austin and Joan Robinson. (Keynes and Robertson increasingly fell out intellectually at this time, with Robertson deploring Keynes's attack on Marshall and Pigou, and developing the loanable funds theory of interest determination as a rival to Keynes's liquidity preference theory.) As we have argued, Keynes respected and valued Joan Robinson's contributions and judgement. She herself was important, both for her critical grasp and for her expository powers in making the new theory widely accessible to students and others. Her little book *Introduction to the Theory of Employment* (1937a) is still one of the most lucid accounts that we have of the essentials of Keynes's theory, as are her 'Essays 1935' (Robinson, *C.E.P.*, vol. IV, 1973, part 2), the last version of her 1937 *Essays* (1937b). Furthermore, she was one of the first to extend Keynes's analysis to an open economy.

For Joan Robinson, the central themes of *The General Theory* were the theory of effective demand in which is integrated a theory of money and the interest rate, a theory of the general price level, and an analysis of the impact of an uncertain future on the present which occurs through investment expenditure, so locking Keynes's analysis securely into actual historical time.

Joan Robinson developed Keynesian ideas in at least two directions in the post-war years. First, she had a deep understanding of money and its roles in economic systems, something which is often forgotten but not, as we saw, by Frank Hahn (1972, 205), who quotes with approval her remark that 'Money ... gets the blame for the fact that the future is uncertain', adding that he 'for one, [is] ready to forgive and forget'. As we have seen, she was active in Labour Party circles in, for example, making the case for permanently cheap money, using uncompromising Keynesian arguments (see Howson, 1988). She also played a prominent part in the liquidity preference, loanable funds debates which so split members of the Faculty of Economics and Politics at Cambridge at the time. (Harry Johnson tried to build a bridge – 'Some Cambridge controversies in monetary theory' (1951–2) – only to be criticised by both sides of the debate for his efforts.) Joan Robinson's main concern was with the determination of the rate of interest which gave the title to an influential set of essays (Robinson, 1952a). She emphasised Keynes's insight that in macro analysis, we must always be on our guard against the fallacy of composition. The use of *one*-representative-agent models to analyse systemic behaviour will never do, certainly not in an analysis of the determination of prices in the market for financial assets. There, as Keynes and then Kahn and Joan Robinson argued, the equilibrium rate of interest is the level which brings about at least a momentary if uneasy truce between the bulls and the bears (and bullishness and bearishness). If there were *not* differences of opinion between the two groups, no balance or state of rest, not even momentarily, would be possible.

Her essay is a particularly good example – Kahn's 1931 article on the multiplier is another – of the Marshallian/Keynesian method of looking at parts of the economy in sequence, holding constant or abstracting from what is going on, or least, the *effects* of what is going on elsewhere, for the moment. In this way, Marshall hoped we would get definite, if partial, results and that, if we went right round the economy, we would eventually be able to bring all our results together to give a full, overall picture. That the procedure was inconsistent with his deeper vision that economic processes were akin to systemic interrelated biological processes, he, as well as Joan Robinson and Kahn, seem to have forgotten. This may be one of the reasons why in the end both Marshall and Joan Robinson (but not Keynes nor Kahn?) thought that they had ultimately failed, not from realising that by following the procedure, they were attempting the impossible, but because it was the procedure itself which was at fault.

Though her contributions to the economics of Keynes have been significant, we argued that the most significant step in her thought occurred when she decided to graft Marx onto Keynes (partly through the influence of Kalecki). She herself dated this at 1940, though with Piero Sraffa and Maurice Dobb as colleagues and her interest in generalising *The General Theory*, we argue that her interest was aroused even earlier. 'In 1940, as a distraction from the news, I began to read Marx. ... For me, the main message of Marx was the need to think in terms of history, not of equilibrium' (Robinson, 1973e, x). It was Harrod's book *Towards a Dynamic Economics* (1948), which she reviewed in 1949 (Robinson, 1949b) and which she, Kahn and Sraffa discussed when reading the volume in proof sheets in the Dolomites in early 1948 (see Harcourt, 1993, 60) that really brought this message home. She thus found in Marx what she also found in Keynes (and, fudged, because of its uncomfortable implications, in Marshall). For, as she said of the Keynesian revolution, 'on the plane of theory, the revolution lay in the change from the conception of equilibrium to the conception of history; from the principles of rational choice to the problems of decisions based on guess-work or on convention' and '[o]nce we admit that an economy exists in time, that history goes one way, from the irrevocable past into the unknown future, the conception of equilibrium based on the mechanical analogy of a pendulum swinging to and fro in space becomes untenable' (Robinson, 1973c, 3, 5). Thinking in terms of history also involves always asking what sort of society (and its accompanying institutions) is being examined and what social relationships rule in it. It involves, moreover, distinguishing between theories which deal with logical time and those which deal with historical time. 'Logical time can be traced from left to right on the surface of a blackboard. Historical time moves from the dark past behind it into the unknown future in front' (Robinson, 1977a, 57). Analyses in logical time are at best the flexing of intellectual muscles, sometimes in a framework in which to sort out doctrinal puzzles, usually as a preliminary to the real thing, the analysis of processes occurring in historical time. This approach also implied to Joan Robinson that economics is very much a 'horses for courses' discipline, rather than a general theory into which particular situations may be fitted as special cases.

Her book on Marx (Robinson, 1942b), we argued, is still one of the best introductory pieces to be found, despite its idiosyncrasies and even though, or, perhaps, because in places it contains heresies that continue to infuriate the faithful. Especially is this true of her attitude to the labour theory of value, which hardened over the years. Thus,

> we are told that it is impossible to account for exploitation except in terms of *value*, but why do we need *value* to show that profits can be made in industry by selling commodities for more than they cost to produce, or to explain the power of those who command finance to push around those who do not?
>
> (Robinson, 1977a, 51)[3]

To learn from Marx's ideas, we do not have to remain 'stuck in the groove that led him to them'. Nevertheless the book was not written 'as a criticism of Marx [but] to alert my bourgeois colleagues to the existence of penetrating and important issues in *Capital* that they ought not to continue to neglect' (Robinson, 1977b, 50). It abounds in insights and produces a lucid sketch of the skeleton that sustains Marx's system, a skeleton that is too often obscured by the flesh of Hegel, by polemic and by the lack of time and health to polish and rewrite that characterises much of Marx's own writing. All in all, therefore, it is a constructive and sympathetic critique of Marx's work. The same may be said of her subsequent writings on Marx, attitudes which contrast with the impatience she sometimes shows towards Marxists themselves. Joan Robinson's initial response to Sraffa's 1960 book was to see it as a solution to Marx's transformation problem and to demonstrate the logical flaws in neoclassical theory. Perhaps her more considered view of Sraffa (1960) led her to realise that *a* labour theory of value could form the basis of an analytical system which begins with production. This does not have to be Marx's labour theory of value. At the same time, it is more consistent with Marx's theory than her exchange-based interpretation of the quote above.

The 1942 book and follow-up articles led Joan Robinson into her two main preoccupations of the post-war period: on the positive side, the attempt to provide a 'generalisation of the *General Theory*, that is, an extension of Keynes's short-period analysis to long-run development' (Robinson, 1956a, vi), principally to be found in *The Accumulation of Capital* (1956a) and interpretative books and articles that grew up around and from it: *Exercises in Economic Analysis* (1960a), *Essays in the Theory of Economic Growth* (1962e), *Economic Heresies* (1971) (see Chapter 8). A further influence on the way was Rosa Luxemburg's book (1913), also called *The Accumulation of Capital*, to which Joan Robinson contributed the introduction to the 1951 English edition (Robinson, *C.E.P.*, vol. II, 1960, 59–73). Joan Robinson's own work provides us with a Keynesian–Marxist framework (derived in structure from Kalecki's adaptation of the Marxian schemes of reproductions) with which to interpret the process of growth in capitalist economies and to tackle the grand problems of classical political economy: the possibilities of growth in output per head and the course of the distribution of the national product between broad classes in capitalist societies as capital goods are accumulated over time influenced principally by the nature of the 'animal spirits' of the societies' business people, combined with population growth and technical advances. In this area, she and Kahn share with Harrod and, possibly, with Kaldor and Pasinetti, the most influential contributions from the Keynesian school to the modern theory of economic growth and distribution.

As we argued in Chapter 6, *The Accumulation of Capital* sometimes has been misunderstood. Joan Robinson starts the analysis with an examination of the conditions necessary for steady growth, a search for the characteristics of what she calls Golden Ages. Too often this has been taken for descriptive analysis rather than the careful setting out of logical conditions and relationships, one of the principal purposes of which, as is hinted at by the very name, is to show how unlikely it is that they will ever be realised in fact. 'I used the phrase "a golden age" to describe smooth, steady growth with full employment (intending thereby to indicate its mythical nature)' (Robinson, 1962e, 52). In the subsequent clarifications and expansions of her findings, she has emphasised more the lessons of the later chapters on the short period and the interconnections of short periods over time. She also reiterated what she stated in the original work, that the sections on the choice of technique of production at the level of the economy as a whole occupied more space than their importance (as opposed to their difficulty) warranted. Moreover, they related principally (but in the 1956 book not entirely) to the realm of doctrinal debate associated with the vast literature on the aggregate production function and the marginal productivity theory of distribution rather than to that of positive analysis.

The second strand is associated with her sustained attack on the neoclassical theory of value, production and distribution. This was centred in the theory of capital, mainly because of her celebrated article 'The production function and the theory of capital' (Robinson, 1953–4), which started off the Cambridge controversies in the theory of capital. On the surface, the argument tended to evolve around whether or not it is possible to measure 'capital' as a factor of production, what units to use, is there a unit that is independent of distribution and prices, and what sense, if any, may be made of the proposition that the marginal product of capital equals the rate of profits? But, as Joan Robinson stressed again and again, the argument has not really anything to do with the problem of measuring and valuing 'capital', as opposed to the *meaning* of 'capital', but with the attempt by those she dubbed the 'Bastard Keynesians' to reconstruct 'pre-Keynesian theory after Keynes'.

> It has nothing to do either with measurement or with capital; it has to do with abolishing time. For a world that is always in equilibrium there is no difference between the future and the past, there is no history and there is no need for Keynes.
>
> (Robinson, 1973c, 6)

– or Marx.

> The controversies over so-called capital theory arose out of the search for a model appropriate to a modern western economy, which would allow for an analysis of accumulation and of the distribution of the net product of industry between wages and profits. ... [L]ong-run accumulation became the centre of interest, [so making] it necessary

> to come to grips with concepts of the quantity of capital and the rate of profit in the economy as a whole.
>
> (Robinson, *C.E.P.*, vol. V, 1979, 59–60)

Joan Robinson saw the response to her criticisms as the outcome of an ideological tide that reacted continually against the damaging criticisms of Marx, Keynes and Sraffa, that attempted to create an economic theory which by implication at least tended to support the *status quo*, in particular, democratic capitalist free market institutions and, in at least some influential quarters, a doctrine of *laisser-faire*.

Here, Joan Robinson tried to get too many targets into her sights at one time. The groups most favourably disposed to *laisser-faire* – Milton Friedman, Robert Lucas and the Chicago school, and their burgeoning offshoots elsewhere – were vigorously attacking what *they* took to be the exposed flanks of the American or 'Bastard' Keynesians who were led from MIT and Yale, while Joan Robinson was attacking what she took to be other vulnerable areas. The attacked themselves could, with justice, claim that not only were they staunch advocates and defenders of middle-of-the-road to Leftish Keynesian policies but also that they have provided a considerable amount of the ammunition that over the years has been used to destroy the more grandiose claims that may be made for a free-rein market economy as an efficient allocator of resources and a maximiser of community welfare. As Tobin (1973, 106, n1) remarked, '[Samuelson's] work on the theory of public goods ... is only an outstanding example of the attention modern theorists, in America and overseas, have paid to the allocative failures of *laissez faire*'. Thus, Joan Robinson's simplicity of vision may be faulted in detail but there is, nevertheless, considerable validity in her general argument; hence, the irritation and anger that she aroused, especially in conservative academic and political circles.

In the debates, she was tenacious and consistent, returning again and again to the theme that orthodox equilibrium analysis is incapable of handling the essential facts of a capitalist economy, namely, that it exists in real historical time, that it is investment decisions by capitalist business people (and not the saving decisions of households) which are the dynamic driving force of the economy, that uncertainty and unrealised expectations about the future are inescapable facts of life which *must* find a place in any theory of the development of a capitalist economy over time, that

> interest [is] the price that a businessman pays for the use of finance to be committed to an investment [while] profit [is] the return that

> he hopes to get on it, [and that] wage rates are settled in terms of money [while] the level of real wages depends upon the operation of the economy as a whole.
>
> (Robinson, *C.E.P.*, vol. V, 1979, 59)

An index of her success in these endeavours is that both Samuelson (in the *Quarterly Journal of Economics*, 1975) and Hahn, in a number of places, including his Inaugural Lecture (Hahn, 1973) have either explicitly or implicitly conceded the validity of many of her claims. Tobin, in an otherwise rather pained review of *Economic Heresies* (Robinson, 1971) and the two Cambridges' debates, nevertheless, praised her for her repeated stress on the treatment of expectations and her objection that 'Walrasian general equilibrium, even when enlarged to postulate markets in all commodities in all contingencies at all future dates, is no real solution' (Tobin, 1973, 109). Hicks, having repudiated aspects of those versions of Keynesian theory which were peculiarly associated with him through his 1937 *Econometrica* paper, 'Mr. Keynes and the "Classics"' (Hicks, 1937), took approaches which parallel closely those of Joan Robinson (see, for example, Hicks (1976; 1977)). In addition, along with others, especially Sraffa, Joan Robinson exposed the logical inconsistencies in those versions of neoclassical theory which attempt to provide a theory of distribution which could take the place of classical, especially Ricardian, theory and also, of course, of Marxian theory, criticisms which came to a head in the reswitching and capital-reversing debates of the mid-1960s. The debates themselves were the culmination of earlier discussions concerning whether certain results which were rigorously true of simple one-commodity neoclassical models would continue to be so in more complex heterogeneous capital good models. Joan Robinson ultimately regarded these particular criticisms and results as 'unimportant' (Robinson, 1975c). She rested the weight of her critique on her more general methodological arguments, together with her stress on the indispensable need always to postulate what are the social relationships and institutions of the economy being modelled and at what stage in its history is the analytical story taken up. In her Richard T. Ely Lecture to the American Economic Association Meeting in 1971 (Robinson, 1972), she identified a second crisis in economic theory (the first being its inability to handle the inter-war slump), the lack of a suitable framework with which to tackle the terrible problems of modern economic life: poverty, racism, urban puzzles and pollution, excessive population growth and war.

One of her last words on all this was her comprehensive paper, 'What are the questions?' (Robinson, 1977d). As we have seen, she argued that ideology and economic analysis are indissolubly mixed and that the dominant ideology exerts disproportionate power in the discipline at any moment of time, quoting Benjamin Ward (1972, 29–30) in support (see Chapter 11). She savaged Robbins's definition of economics when it is set in the context of a capitalist economy:

> The question of scarce means with alternative uses becomes self contradictory when it is set in historical time, where today is an ever-moving break between the irrevocable past and the unknown future. At any moment, certainly, resources are scarce, but they have hardly any range of alternative uses.
>
> (Robinson, 1977d, 1320)

She deplored the distinction made in modern economics between micro and macro. One cannot exist without the other, for

> micro questions ... cannot be discussed in the air without any reference to the structure of the economy in which they exist [or] to the processes of cyclical and secular change. Equally, macro theories of accumulation and effective demand are generalizations about micro behaviour. ... If there is no micro theory, there cannot be any macro theory either.
>
> (ibid., p. 1320)

Moreover, the macro setting for orthodox micro theory is a kind of vague Say's Law world which, until very recently anyway, is *not* the macro world that is analysed in *its* own separate compartment.

She made important contributions to the theory of international trade. She was amongst the first to systematically apply the Keynesian mode of thought to the problems of an open economy; she wrote a seminal article on the theory of the foreign exchanges (Robinson, 1937b, 134–58) in which she added considerable sophistication to the Marshall–Lerner conditions by the use of home and away elasticities of demand and supply of exports and imports; and in her Inaugural Lecture *The New Mercantilism* (Robinson, 1966a) and lectures at Manchester University (reprinted in Robinson, *C.E.P.*, vol. IV, 1973, 1–24) she applied her general critiques of orthodox theory to the special area of international trade and suggested alternative avenues of approach. There is also a half-way house paper (Robinson, 1946a; *C.E.P.*, vol. I, 1951) in which she critically exposited the classical theory of international trade as it came down from Marshall, in order 'to try to see what basis it offers for the belief in a natural tendency towards equilibrium' (98)

She returned to this theme in 'What are the questions?', pointing out that Ricardo (in 'the famous story which begins with England and Portugal both producing both cloth and wine') was the first to commit the cardinal sin (in her eyes) of analysing a process going on through time by the comparison of two equilibrium positions. (Ricardo, as a pioneer, was absolved.) It must be said that Samuelson, who, along with Solow, she criticised repeatedly for doing this, courteously but firmly denied it, producing chapter and verse in support (Samuelson, 1975).[4] Furthermore, Garegnani, an influential ally of Joan Robinson and Piero Sraffa in their attack on neoclassical theory, also takes issue with her on this point. He argues that comparisons of long-period positions (not, note, equilibrium ones, for equilibrium is a notion that is intimately related to supply and demand) *are* fundamental to economic methodology. However, the neoclassicals err when they try to incorporate the method with *their* overriding emphasis on the forces of supply and demand. *Their* theories, he argues, then run into insuperable logical difficulties, especially in the depiction of the demand curve for 'capital' and the consequent existence and stability of long-period equilibrium positions (see Garegnani, 1959, 1970, 1976b). That is to say, Garegnani wishes to preserve the tradition that began with the classicals of relating key concepts – for example, natural prices – to persistent and fundamental forces. He feels that Joan Robinson's attack on orthodoxy threatens this tradition too. Joan Robinson wished to retain the key classical concepts but to scrap the method.

In 1981, Joan Robinson delivered the Tanner Lectures on Human Values on the subject of the Arms Race (Robinson, 1982). While her subject referred to the Cold War, her argument was more general and largely addressed the dynamic of the military–industrial complex and the economic justifications for arms expenditure. These Lectures elaborated upon the ideas and arguments about military expenditure which were scattered within her work over a number of years. In the Tanner Lectures, she argued that there were three factors which contributed weight to the continuation and escalation of the arms race. The first of these was the Cold War, the clash of ideologies. Since World War II, she noted, the role of military expenditure had changed from 'defence' to 'deterrence' and, even more, to 'aggressive' expenditure. With a policy of pre-emptive strike in a context of no dialogue or diplomacy, deterrence is overstepped. She saw that both the USA and the UK were prepared to use their nuclear weapons against terrorist groups yet, she believed, only a dialogue could resolve such a clash.

The second factor is that force which is built up first, by the process of research and development, and then by the evolution and consolidation of the structures – research, industrial and bureaucratic – which go to make up the defence industry. The very establishment of the military–industrial complex ensured its own dynamic. Science in progress is difficult to stop and the domestic armaments industry contains its own competitive forces and rivalries. There is as well, the weight of vested interests, incomes earned from the military industry which rely on the continuation of research and contracts. To compound the forces of vested interests, there is the internal competition between the three services for new discoveries, funding and prestige. The complexity of the modern armaments industry, she argues, gives an authority to the military for its singular competence in its own direction and in the nature of national security. The momentum is assisted by exaggerations of threat from 'the enemy'. It is a culture of competition and secrecy and status which is difficult to opt out of, let alone to speak out against. Yet Joan Robinson argued that scientists are trained to think objectively and dispassionately, and many top scientists have spoken out against the arms race. They have been frustrated in their warnings.

The third force which sustains the arms race arises out of the connection between military expenditure and employment policy. Keynes had introduced the possibility of policy intervention to achieve full employment and in much of the post–World War II environment, this had been successfully implemented. '[I]t is precisely the economic success of the military–industrial complex (though it has over-reached itself in Vietnam) that puts the greatest obstacle in the way of any such attempt [to resolve conflict peacefully]' (Robinson, 1970, 86). She argued that the economic factors can be changed; the military sector could be transformed, in principle, by structural adjustment programmes. In 1961, she wrote:

> In USA in 1958, it is estimated that expenditure on what is euphemistically called 'defence' was running at more than 11 per cent of the gross national product and in the UK at nearly 8 per cent, which is about equal in each country to the volume of productive industrial investment. ... [so that] without any extra sacrifice or any greater inflationary pressure than has been experienced, the annual increment of industrial productive capacity could have been about doubled if the arms race had been halted.
>
> (Robinson, 1961; *C.E.P.*, vol. III, 1965, 109; see also 1962c; *C.E.P.*, vol. III, 1965, 114–5)

She felt that this argument was particularly relevant to those developing countries which used their aid for military purposes.

Joan Robinson argued from a short-period position that if a certain flow of finance were to be diverted from civilian to military expenditure, employment falls and cost per unit of employment rises; conversely, a switch the other way should see favourable effects. 'From a long-period point of view the loss due to the arms race is literally incalculable' (Robinson, 1982, 284). In the long run, high military budgets hold back public investment and so inhibit the productivity growth associated with high levels of social investment and, furthermore, incur the additional social and economic costs associated with its absence. She suggested redirecting arms expenditure into research in energy production. But to redirect resources away from armaments and into energy or social infrastructure, for example, 'would involve drastic political changes' (Robinson, 1962c; *C.E.P.*, vol. III, 1965, 115). Those who perpetuate the construction of an 'enemy' and the associated culture of fear are themselves no longer rational in terms of their own or of Keynesian economic analysis: 'The horror, the lack of logic, and the isolation due to rules of secrecy produce strange aberrations of thought' (Robinson, 1982, 262).

Joan Robinson also observed the 'super-power' status of USA, its immense influence over world markets which it wields by virtue of its size. '[W]e are beholden, along with the capitalist world as a whole, to the support which the American economy, and so the world market, has received from theirs' (Robinson, 1962c, *C.E.P.*, vol. III, 1965, 115). This extended to Britain's dependence on US research in the military industry, although she did not acknowledge Britain's associated lack of independence in strategic decision-making and foreign policy.

In 1970, she wrote: 'the shadow of the Cold War still hangs over the scene. On the one side this allows the authorities to override objections to the arms race and on the other side allows the authorities to stifle free discussion for fear that criticism may turn into disloyalty' (Robinson, 1970, 99). In the Tanner Lectures she pointed out that, at that time, the costs of nuclear 'deterrence' were even greater; the culture of fear was still nurtured and even more threatening and the enemy was too disparate to target. Economic rationality for the society was subordinated to the political and economic rationality of the military–industrial complex.

There is a puzzle that often emerges in discussion of Joan Robinson's contributions, namely, the lack of empirical work by her of at least the conventional kind. The answer probably lies in two areas: first, she principally was concerned with fundamental theoretical questions, the necessary setting out of definitions, concepts and logical relationships, the provision of a framework which must precede good empirical work. Second, her close associates over the years – Kahn and, of course, Keynes and Kalecki – were applied economists in the old-fashioned sense *par excellence*. They made it their business to know intimately the institutions, the historical sequences and the orders of magnitude of particular situations, and they had a feel for the limits of particular policy recommendations. Joan Robinson's work, therefore, often was complementary to theirs as was theirs to hers. Moreover, much of her theoretical work was based on Marshallian-type empirical generalisations, that is to say, broad qualitative statements which constitute either the basis for the development of a logical argument or the puzzles that are to be explained by theoretical reasoning.

Joan Robinson's admiration for and extensive writings on the Chinese experiment are well known, probably to a wider audience than those for any of her other works. She was always stimulating, full of insights, putting a complicated and changing scene into a manageable framework. As we noted, her writing in this area contains a leaven of advocacy, a conscious effort to try to offset what she believed to have been the unsympathetic critiques of Chinese policies which emanated from orthodox circles. In addition, she wrote extensively on the theoretical and practical aspects of planning in socialist societies, based on her experience with, and criticisms of, the Russian and Eastern European experiments.

Joan Robinson visited China eight times between 1953 and 1978. Her writings on China may be divided into three phases. The first contains her writings before her third visit in 1963. The initial visits allowed her to gather evidence in support of her views. The first phase ended with her third visit. What she saw (and had seen before) provided her with a laboratory with which to test intuitively her thinking about economic development in backward, overpopulated economies. In the first phase, her ideas were broadly similar to the views of the Right in China, to wit, a high rate of capital accumulation, the establishment of which nevertheless was to be achieved without an intolerable sacrifice of consumption, especially by the less well off; the use of profit-orientated industrial management in order to avoid the inefficiencies and drawbacks of a 'bureaucratic tendency'; the use of prices backed up by moral imperatives; control of population growth; reward for work done and the extraction of the agricultural surplus through gradual collectivisation.

In the second phase, which lasted until 1975, Joan Robinson took a sharp turn left. From the 'Great Leap Forward' (1958–9) to the end of the 'Cultural Revolution' decade (1976), a period of statistical and informational blackout, she argued that the problem of socialist organisation lay in industry, not agriculture. She thought that the communes had resolved the dilemma of organising labour in agriculture, whereas Soviet-type industrial management (even in its reformed decentralised form) was criticised for being motivated by profit and for its hierarchical structure which resulted from differentials associated with intellectual property. The 'Cultural Revolution' provided the possibility to create a cooperative system based on the ideology of serve-the-people. She saw the planning system as plagued not only by inherent bureaucracy, but also by the inequity of the property system. Enthusiasm for the Chinese experiment became advocacy for the Maoist position on economic as well as political issues. She believed the information supplied to her at the time of statistical blackout. Her analysis inevitably was constrained by the quality of the information. Her usual incisiveness returned when she was able to rid herself of its distorting influence.

After Mao's death in 1976, she discovered that the Chinese had not told the truth. This marked the beginning of her third phase. As more information became available, she put some of the record straight. She admitted to having been starry-eyed about the 'Cultural Revolution' and returned to supporting Rightist economic reform. It is possible to salvage from her thinking about and enthusiasm for economic development in China, a set of ideas that differ little from the views of those dubbed the Rightists in the so-called two-line struggle of Mao's China. This set of ideas is now, on the whole, dominant in China itself. We argued that in outline her lectures in China in the 1950s are consistent with it.

Her championing of Kalecki's independent discovery of the main propositions of *The General Theory* is well known from a number of delightfully written and absorbing articles. We mention, especially, Joan Robinson (1976 and 1977c); the latter is also a fine introduction to, and exposition of, Kalecki's analysis of capitalism. Moreover, time is confirming her judgement that '[in] several respects Kalecki's version is more robust than Keynes' (Robinson, 1977c, 10).

Nor did she neglect the involved, concerned intellectual's task of communicating to a wider circle than those within her discipline. As we saw in Chapter 11, she contributed a charming and influential book, *Economic Philosophy* (Robinson, 1962b), to the New Thinkers' Library in 1962. (It is, perhaps, too Popperian for most Marxists' taste). Allen and Unwin twice persuaded her to try her hand at books for a wider audience; she wrote *Economics: An Awkward Corner* (Robinson, 1966b), which diagnosed Britain's economic ills, and *Freedom and Necessity* (Robinson, 1970), which is a model for a challenging introductory course in the social sciences if only the teacher were Joan Robinson.

Last, but certainly not the least, her concern for students and what they are taught was evidenced in a number of areas. Generations of Cambridge undergraduates and research students have paid their tribute to a demanding but devoted supervisor, as a perusal of the prefaces of books by former students would show. She lectured all over the world to students, often at their request, and she never refused an invitation from students, if it was humanly possible for her to get there. Her commitment to the education of undergraduates can be seen in the alternative economics 'textbook', written with John Eatwell (1973) (see Chapter 10).

12.3

Joan Robinson was ill for much of the last decade of her life and deeply distressed about the arms race, as we saw in her Tanner Lectures on this theme (Robinson, 1982). She became more and more pessimistic, even nihilistic, in her last years. Two late papers in 1980 reflected these attitudes. The more optimistic of the two is the joint paper with Amit Bhaduri in the *Cambridge Journal of Economics*. The more pessimistic one is 'Spring cleaning', published after her death as 'The theory of normal prices and the reconstruction of economic theory' in Feiwel (1985).

Bhaduri and Joan Robinson defined the role and application of Sraffa's critique and analysis. His contribution is interpreted not only as a fundamental critique of the neoclassical concept of prices as indices of scarcity within the supply and demand framework, but also as the starting point for thinking in terms of thought experiments about production, distribution and technical change – 'the influence of changes in technology on demand for labour, on accumulation and on effective demand' (111). The results were then to be grafted onto the Keynesian approach, as Joan Robinson saw it, whereby in a Marxian/Kaleckian framework, the laws of motion could be analysed in historical time rather than in the logical time of the Sraffian critique. 'Spring cleaning' was much more radical – a plea to clear out the whole house, not only the attic – and start again.

Joan Robinson died in August 1983. She had had a rewarding period in Autumn/Winter 1982 teaching at Williams College in the US; see Juliet Schor's account in Marjorie Turner's *Joan Robinson and the Americans* (1989, 204–7). On her return to Cambridge in late December, she became depressed and disoriented for the month or so before she had a massive stroke from which she never recovered.

As we noted, in her late years, Joan Robinson used to say of her critics: 'I wish they would stop paying me compliments and answer my questions instead'. For one critic in particular this is a harsh judgement. Paul Samuelson did try to answer them when she was alive and he paid Joan Robinson a fine tribute after her death. He described in Samuelson (1989) how she altered his prior perceptions of a major long-term process:

> What I learned from Joan Robinson was more than she taught. I learned not that the general differentiable neoclassical model was special and wrong but that a general neoclassical technology does not necessarily involve a higher steady-state output when the interest rate is lower. I had thought that such a property generalised from the simplest one sector Ramsey–Solow parable to the most general Fisher case.
>
> (137)

In probably their last ever public exchange (Robinson (1975c), Solow (1975)), Bob Solow (who liked, admired and was irritated by Joan in equal measure), agreed with Samuelson that:

> [m]ore generally, and more important, it is not true, even with all the standard assumptions, that steady states with lower interest rates have higher consumption per worker. [He did] not find the result hard to live with [because it occurred] within the framework of the neoclassical assumptions [so that at worst he had] to kiss a neat generalization good-by[e].
>
> (51–2)

Frank Hahn (1989, 909) remained unrepentant, saying that he did not think she, or rather her writings, would be much remembered though he conceded that she had asked some important questions and that she had deep insight in monetary theory. As we noted, Lawrence Klein (1989) appreciated her all-round abilities, arguing that the first 100 pages or so of *The Accumulation of Capital* were among the best for introducing anyone to our 'miserable subject' (Keynes, *C.W.*, vol. XIV, 1973b, 190), by 'laying bare [its] fundamental aspects' (258). As ever, Ken Arrow (1989) is perceptive and generous and Dick Goodwin, a long-time fan, who always acknowledged the major influence she had been on his thought, described her remarkable economic intuition (unaided, in her case, by trained mathematical facility):

> Once I was giving a paper on a two-sector dynamical model ... of which I said that both sectors would exhibit both motions. She

interrupted me to say that I was wrong: ... only one. I denied this ... But I was bothered and later ... discovered she was right.

(Goodwin, 1989, 916)

As we noted, Luigi Pasinetti's *New Palgrave* entry on Joan (1987) (now republished, slightly revised, in Pasinetti (2007)) is a brilliant account of the person and of the nature of her contributions. Pasinetti particularly emphasises the aspect of teamwork in her contributions, while stressing as well her originality. These characteristics are obvious in both the making of *The Economics of Imperfect Competition* and of *The General Theory*, to which vols. XIII, XIV and XXIX of the *Collected Writings* bear eloquent witness, even though much of the discussion was oral. Pasinetti illustrates the theme in his discussion of the capital theory controversies and the ultimate downplaying of them by Joan Robinson. He writes:

> [A]t this point the works of Joan Robinson merge into those of that remarkable group of Cambridge economists ... who took up, continued and expanded the challenge that Keynes had launched on orthodox economic theory. [They] started a stream of thought which is obviously far from complete. Its basic features ... are clear enough ... [–] a determined effort to shift the whole focus of economic theorizing away from the problems of optimum allocation of given resources ... and move it towards the fundamental factors responsible for the dynamics of industrial societies.
>
> (216)[5]

In his authoritative appreciation of Joan Robinson, the late Sukhamoy Chakravarty (1983) stressed her seriousness, that 'economics was not a 'game' played for its own sake. She was profoundly concerned with [its] social relevance [and] attached much greater importance to the seriousness and integrity of an economist than to her/his ability to solve intellectual puzzles' (1716). Profound as her own answers have been, she also 'left us with a very rich set of questions to which we can devote ourselves profitably for years to come' (1716).

Finally, in the obituary of her for the King's College *Annual Report* in October 1984 – it was drafted by her colleague, close friend and rival, Nicky Kaldor – we read:

> It would be no exaggeration to say that, after Keynes, Joan Robinson would be widely regarded as the most prominent name associated

> with the Cambridge School of Economics. As a teacher she was brilliant ... As a writer she was prolific ... As a controversialist she was sometimes alarming ... She held her views with great conviction yet at the same time she was eager to look at every economic 'fact' and was ready to modify her views if these contradicted some of the assumptions on which she had been working. But behind her somewhat forbidding presence she possessed great warmth and sympathy.

What have we learned from Joan Robinson and what do we think are the most valuable lessons she has for future generations in our profession? First, she taught us always to look at the conceptual basis of our theories. The theories themselves should start off from actual situations, from actual societies with explicit 'rules of the game', institutions, past histories and defined sociological characteristics. In analysing them, we should ask: what are the levels of abstraction at which we wish to argue and what exactly are the sorts of questions we are trying to answer? (In her later years, for example, as we saw, she left us two, sometimes overlapping, agendas, her Ely Lecture, 'The second crisis in economic theory' (1972) and 'What are the questions?' (1977c)). Our aim should be to produce theories which contain the essential elements of the reality from which they start as the basic ingredients, in a sufficiently simplified form to allow us to see clearly the relationships at work and how exactly they intertwine. Moreover, we should always be careful to specify explicitly what sort of analysis is appropriate for the question asked. Perhaps, most of all, as we saw, we should always keep at the back of our heads the injunction that: 'The purpose of studying economics is not to acquire a set of ready-made answers to economic questions, but to learn how to avoid being deceived by economists' (Robinson, 1955; *C.E.P.*, vol. II, 1960, 17).

Let us close by saying that while Joan Robinson could often be harsh and unfair to others, she was quite as hard on herself; she was, most of all, as Dick Goodwin (1989) said, 'a passionate seeker after truth'. Ruth Cohen told us at the Memorial Service in October 1983: 'She was unrelenting in her arguments on matters she was working on ... and often frightening'. As she grew older, as we saw, her writings became more 'tip of an iceberg' in character. Like many great economists who aged, she assumed that readers knew as much as she did about the submerged portion. Future generations ought to follow up the tantalising hints revealed and re-read her works for their wisdom, vigour, insight and sheer intelligence, and for the honesty and courage which they reveal.

She was basically a shy person, though not in the conventional sense; it was, rather, that she had very few words to say outside 'shop' (which nevertheless included a huge number of issues, many of which were outside even her broad boundaries of economics). Moreover, she responded to friendship and she was a warm person who was passionately and often quixotically loyal. She could be very perceptive and kind, and she had been known to apologise, albeit succinctly and gruffly. She could also be too quick to make judgements, often false, of persons and could be unfair, that is to say, she was human! As we noted, she is on record as saying that she was a bad mother but a good grandmother. As ever, she was too harsh in her judgement; the first part is not a judgement her daughters agree with. Nearly the last time GCH saw her, her first grandchild, a splendidly democratic outgoing young Canadian, was chatting to her grandmother in her hospital bed, during her last illness, sure that the close bonds established between them long ago would allow them now to communicate as ever. Joan Robinson was never to see the democratic, just and equitable society she so deeply hoped her discipline would promote. Her own nature, class and upbringing would have made it difficult for her to have been a comfortable member of it. But her immediate family and their children have the attitudes and values which are both necessary prerequisites for creating such societies, and for living comfortably within them.

Notes

1 Introduction

1. It should be noted that Joan Robinson might have been very angry at being so described. Marjorie Turner, in discussing Mary Paley Marshall's reaction to *The Economics of Imperfect Competition* (Robinson, 1933a), points out that Joan Robinson 'thought of her own reputation as being that of an economist and not a woman-economist' (Turner, 1989, 12–13; see also below, 8–9.
2. Luigi Pasinetti brilliantly describes their approaches and interrelationships, and evaluates their collective contributions in his entry on Joan Robinson in *The New Palgrave* (Pasinetti, 1987; see also 2007).
3. The editors of the *Cambridge Journal of Economics*, of which she was a Patron, had been preparing a special issue in honour of her eightieth birthday. Sadly, it had to be a Memorial issue instead (see the special issue of December 1983).
4. For an absorbing account of the Maurice debates and the events and issues surrounding them, see Wilson and Prior (2004, 2006).
5. In private conversation with GCH.
6. It was widely thought at Cambridge, in pre- and post-war years, that Marjorie Tappan-Hollond was responsible for Joan Robinson never being elected to a teaching fellowship at Girton (it was only after Joan Robinson retired that she became an Honorary Fellow of Girton and the Joan Robinson Society, which met on 31 October (her birth date) each year, was started). Marjorie Turner documents that there was mutual personal affection between them and even concern on Tappan-Hollond's part for her former pupil but that she strongly disapproved of Joan Robinson's 'messianic' approach to teaching. (Tappan-Hollond was an ally of Dennis Robertson who never got on well with Joan Robinson; see Turner (1989), 14.)
7. JVR/vii/62/5. Berlin enjoyed their 'intellectual gaiety' but was critical of her understanding of dialectical reasoning.
8. The 'Circus' was a small group of scholars formed by Sraffa in the Michaelmas term of 1930 to discuss *A Treatise on Money* by Keynes (1930); see Chapter 3, n1, 230.
9. But see Chapter 2, n6.

2 *The Economics of Imperfect Competition*

1. Writing to Joan Robinson in October 1936, Sraffa (1936, JVR/vii/431/14–15) thanks her for her letter: 'I shall hang it next to an extract from Sidgwick where, after lecturing Ricardo on how meaningless it is to talk of a quantity of labour, goes on cheerfully himself to talk of quantities of utility.' Only someone 'debauched by economics' could be so 'dotty'.
2. In his report to Macmillan, Keynes wrote that the tone of the 'Introduction', but not of the 'Preface', could be interpreted as pretentious, 'not exactly

pretentious, but ... to have some sort of flavour which might give readers that feeling' (1932; Kerr and Harcourt (eds.) 2002, vol. 1, 150).

3. The background to the writing of the article and a detailed analysis of her arguments are to be found in the manuscript (2007) on the young Joan Robinson by Nahid Aslanbeigui and Guy Oakes. We are indebted to the authors for allowing us to see the manuscript.
4. Evidently Austin Robinson's 'very bright' pupil, Charles Gifford, introduced Joan and Richard Kahn to the book's central concept while Austin himself named it marginal revenue. In the preface to the first edition, after referring to 'the number of explorers ... added to the rapidly growing crowd at the Marginal Revenue Pole' (xiv), Joan Robinson writes that 'the conception of the "elasticity of substitution" provides another example of this kind of coincidence, for Mr J.R. Hicks published his formulation of it in his *Theory of Wages* some time after I first made use of it' (xv). We are indebted to Robert Dixon for reminding us of this.
5. 'No student of monopoly could fail to obtain a firmer or more inclusive grasp on the subject by reading her book, or to be grateful to her for saving the necessity of resorting to inferior or more cumbrous sources' Kaldor (1934a; Kerr with Harcourt (eds.) 2002, vol I, 153).
6. In 1983, Kahn reread his dissertation and was impressed by it 'as a contribution made *at the time*'. He wished he had published it straight away and his advice to young authors with 'striking but incomplete' pieces of work was to publish 'without delay'. See Kahn (1929; 1989, xii, emphasis in the original).
7. There is some evidence that Sraffa did not think pure theory should have to handle time, a view which underlies the construction of the theoretical propositions of his 1960 book.
8. A very early article by Kaldor published in the first issue of the *Review of Economic Studies*, (Kaldor, 1934b) is possibly the earliest statement of the possibility of path-dependence by the (then) younger generation of modern economists.
9. Shove had taken John Hicks severely to task on similar incoherence when he reviewed the latter's *The Theory of Wages* (1932) (Shove, 1933b), so much so that Hicks never issued a second edition or attempted to reply to Shove until well after the end of the Second World War. In 1946, Hicks visited the US for the first time. He found 'rather to [his] distress that [he] was being received, not as the author of *Value and Capital* (1939) ..., of which [he] was ... proud, but as the author of *The Theory of Wages*, of which [he] was not proud at all', but which Schumpeter, for one, thought was a 'good' book. This was so not least because of its (embryonic) Walrasian–Wicksellian approach. This emboldened Hicks to reissue his book with a long commentary responding to Shove's many criticisms (see Hicks, 1963, 311–20).
10. Chamberlin's supervisor at Harvard was Allyn Young who was subsequently to lecture on these themes at the LSE at the end of the 1920s (see Kaldor's lecture notes of Young's lectures in Sandilands (ed.) (1990, 18–114).
11. Keynes in his letter to Ohlin (29 April 1937) implies that neither he nor Joan Robinson thought market structures were relevant for the issues they were tackling. Keynes wrote: 'The reference to imperfect competition is very perplexing. I cannot see how on earth it comes in. Mrs Robinson. ... read my proofs without discovering any connection' (*C.W.*, vol. XIV, 1973b, 190).

3 Joan Robinson and her Circle in the Run-up to and Aftermath of Publication of *The General Theory*

1. In the summer term of 1931, however, there was 'A seminar with other members of the Faculty and the best of the third year students', so May 1931 marked the end of the period of the 'Circus' (Kahn, 1985, 44; *C.W.*, vol. XIII, 1973a, 338–9).
2. Keynes, as editor of the *Economic Journal*, had, of course, asked Sraffa to write the review article which has surely been the role model for effective hatchet reviews ever since.
3. As Robert Skidelsky (1992, 447) put it, 'God ensured that the widow's jar was always full of water however much the prophet Elijah drank from it; by contrast the Danaides of Greek legend had to carry water to the city of Argos in broken jars.' He added: 'These stories suggested to Keynes a striking analogy with the cumulative processes which might be set in train by the emergence of windfall profits and losses.'
4. These ideas came to their fulfillment in Kaldor's greatest theoretical paper, 'Speculation and economic stability' (Kaldor, 1939).
5. In the introduction to her first collection of economic papers, she writes that the article

   > (... written for the first number of the *Review of Economic Studies*, a journal ... founded ... by some of the younger members of the London School of Economics and of the Cambridge Faculty to get together behind the backs of their embattled seniors) ... gives an outline of Keynes's theory as far as it had got in 1933.
   >
   > She adds that she wrote the *Economica* article 'in the summer of 1931 ... attempting to explain Keynes's answer [to] the "buckets-in-the-well theory", that ... when thriftiness increases the demand for capital goods ... rises by an equal amount'. She thought the article to be 'somewhat tedious' now and she never reprinted it, wrongly in our view. She says she never knew why it was not published until 1933, a few months before the *Review of Economic Studies* article came out, leading Paul Samuelson and Lawrence Klein 'to date the birth of *The General Theory* between February and October 1933. [She told] this tale as an awful warning to historians'.
   >
   > (Robinson, *C.E.P.*, vol. I, 1951, viii–ix)

6. We are indebted to Cristina Marcuzzo for this point.
7. As with virtually all North Americans, we believe, Tarshis never did take to Marmite (or Vegemite) and so had to leave his rooms in Trinity until Lerner had eaten his Marmite sandwiches in them (see Harcourt, 1982a; 1982b; Sardoni (ed.), 1992, 361–2).
8. Commenting on what became p. 219 of *The General Theory*, she wrote: '[i]n what sense is there "long-period equilibrium" if investment is still going on? You have stopped [*sic*] rather suddenly ... out of the short period with fixed equipment to which the rest of the book belongs.' After further comments, she concludes: 'I have been working out this long-period stuff ... one needs to bring in several considerations that are not really relevant to your main theme ... the elasticity of substitution is an important factor ... this section is

in a limbo between long and short period; you could make your point without bringing the long period in ... if you do ... a definition of "equilibrium" is essential.'

9. It is still going strong today as Robert Solow's paper (Solow, 2005), at the conference for Frank Hahn's eightieth birthday in 2005 makes clear.
10. As mentioned earlier, the issue had been intended to celebrate her eightieth birthday on 31 October 1983, but sadly she died earlier in the year.
11. We have taken a more favourable view of Keynes's definition and analysis than either David Champernowne or Joan Robinson; for a full discussion of their reasons see Boianovsky (2005).
12. Cristina Marcuzzo and Claudio Sardoni (2005, 185) print an amusing anecdote about the review of Strachey's book. It is to be found in an unpublished paper: 'I accused [Strachey] of presenting the labour theory of value in terms of Say's Law, ignoring Keynes and treating Hayek as representative of academic economics. He replied that it was absurd for someone who had never read Marx to talk about him. We each felt that the other had made a fair point. He began to read Keynes and I read Marx.'

4 Marx in Joan Robinson's Argument

This chapter is based on 'Joan Robinson and Maurice Dobb on Marx' published in *Contributions to Political Economy* (2007) 26, 71–92.

1. The page references to *EME* are to the first edition, published in 1942. Some minor changes were made when it was reprinted in 1947. No further revisions were made until it was republished in 1966 with a new preface. Page references to the later editions are indicated in the text.
2. Her view was confirmed by Sardoni's presentation of the evidence in primary sources (Sardoni, 1987).
3. The lecture has been transcribed from notes in the Dobb papers in the Wren Library archives, Trinity College, Cambridge, by Roy Rotheim.
4. Blankenburg (2007) traces the elements of Sraffa's methodological realism from unpublished notes in his papers in the Wren Library, Trinity College, Cambridge. See also Sraffa's prelude to an argument: 'Up to this point we have confined the enquiry to conditions that can be ascertained by simple observation as opposed to those which can only be discovered by experiment. We have thus kept clear of any marginal quantities, which have no objective existence in the absence of change. We shall in what follows take a step into imaginary experiment' (Sraffa: D3/12/54).
5. Joan Robinson made much of the fact that Marx sometimes used 'C' to represent the stock of constant capital and sometimes used it to represent the flow per unit of time (see *EME*, 8–9). Dobb defended Marx, saying that the two meanings served different explanatory purposes. He continued in the letter just quoted: 'Isn't it the case that *everything* is *both* a stock and a flow according to the way you look at it – according to the time-period under consideration; according as one is conceiving everything as congealed at an instant of time, when everything becomes a stock, or as a continuous process through time? Personally I've always regarded the essential difference between

capital and income as consisting in that between a stock notion and a flow notion, and the notion of a rate of profit on capital as combining the two in a ratio between an income flow and a stock of capital measured over a conventional time-interval' (Dobb's emphasis, JVR\vii\120\20). In his next letter, he reiterated his point that, inevitably, Marx would change the reference with a change in the context and that this was defensible 'if one's conceptual apparatus was to be sufficiently multi-dimensional to tackle the central problems' (JVR\vii\120\23). In an earlier letter, he cited a number of passages of Marx to illustrate how Marx had specified what he meant by 'C' in the rate of profit and in the organic composition of capital, pointing out that Marx sometimes assumed a turnover period of one year to make $c+v$ in the flow sense equal it in the stock sense. See JVR\vii\120\27 and also \14–16 where he presents constant capital '"as an index of the *mass of means of production* set in motion by the labour-power" [ch8 of Pt 2 of Vol 3 [Marx]] – mass, ie, not part worn-out or consumed in a given time-interval' and he then quotes passages to illustrate points where Marx instead referred to the constant capital as a flow (see, e.g., Marx, ibid., p. 61). One significance of this distinction was for the relationship between the profit margin and the rate of profit. The latter uses the stock of capital whereas the former refers to the flow of services of capital consumed in production. She dwells on this 'confusion' by Marx again in Joan Robinson (1953) and then again in Robinson (1978a).

6. This was a reference to the fact that Marx used the rate of exploitation as an aggregate from which the rate of profits on average was then calculated; it was a response to Joan Robinson insisting that Marx always assumed therate of exploitation to be uniform across sectors. In his introduction to the Everyman edition of volume I of *Capital* (1930), G. D. H. Cole wrote: '[t]he theme of *Capital* is not the exploitation of individual labourers by individual capitalists, but of one whole class by another. He who would criticise Marx must begin by accepting or attacking this fundamental concept. It conditions the entire Marxian system' (Cole 1930, xxvii).
7. Much later, Joan Robinson was to write: 'I have always felt that it was a mistake for Marxists to allow themselves to be lured onto the terrain of price theory. ... The Marxists should have said: Do not worry about prices. We will get around to that later. Meanwhile we are interested in the mode of production, the rate of accumulation, and the distribution of income. We have a theory of the share of profit – the rate of exploitation. The *share* of profit is far more important than the *rate* of profit' (Robinson, 1977a, 282, emphasis in original).
8. Donald Harris was to put the ideas of Marx and Joan Robinson together in a sympathetic way (Harris, 1978). See also Chapter 8.
9. Dobb 'translates' the process of history: '[i]n other words, the approach towards the position of medium-long run equilibrium generates forces which shift the equilibrium-position back again in a direction unfavourable (temporarily at least) to wages. And I'm not sure that the second rather than the first interpretation is not really the one more consistent with his approach, with his desire to emphasise discontinuities in the process of economic movements as well as to postulate equilibrium relationships' (JVR\vii\120\22–3). What in modern equilibrium-based theory might be termed path-dependence, Dobb regarded as a process of uneven development of history, of opposing

forces and their resolution in some changed form. Joan Robinson also refers to an example of path-dependence, in *EME*, 70.

10. In 'What are the questions?' (Robinson, 1977c), she criticises 'orthodox economics' for doing exactly that.
11. She came more and more to see the need for a historical context without incorporating the features of its process causally into her analysis. For example, she argued that the subsistence wage theory is circular: she accuses Marx of this circularity. But Marx saw the actual wage always at subsistence because of the reserve army, and that the level of the subsistence wage was independently given, for example, by factory legislation. In Robinson (1954), she recognised Marx's distinction between forces and relations of production. By the time of her 1956 book, she was making use of contradictory forces in her theory of accumulation (see Chapter 6).
12. In 1977, Joan Robinson published two articles with very similar titles and overlapping subjects: 'The labour theory of value' and 'The labour theory of value as an analytical system'. In both of these she was more open-minded in her interpretation of Marx, although inconsistently so, but she nevertheless maintained that 'Sraffa's model says very exactly what it can say and nothing more. On this point Meek was mistaken. He tries to squeeze out of amendments to the equations a historical process of moving from a precapitalist world where *value* prices ruled into capitalism with a uniform rate of profit. To project the transformation problem into history seems very far-fetched' (Robinson, 1977b; *C.E.P.*, vol. V, 1979, 287, emphasis in original).
13. 'Marx divides the net product of industry into two parts: *variable capital* and *surplus*. Variable capital (*v*) is the wages bill. Surplus (*s*), which covers net profit, interest and rent, is the excess of net product over wages. The difference between gross and net product is constant capital (*c*), which consists of plant and raw materials. It is *constant* in the sense that it loses in the process of production, new value added being due to the labour-power purchased by variable capital. ... The total product ... is then represented by $c+v+s$ ... measured in *value*, or *socially necessary labour-time*. ... Marx conducts his argument in terms of three ratios: s/v, the *rate of exploitation*, c/v, the *organic composition of capital*, and $s/c+v$, the *rate of profit*' (*EME*, 7–8, emphasis in original).
14. In her new preface to the second edition of *EME*, written in 1965, Joan Robinson stated: 'Piero Sraffa teased me, saying that I treated Marx as a little-known forerunner of Kalecki. There is a certain sense in which this is not a joke. There are many pointers in *Capital* to a theory of effective demand' (Robinson, 1942b, vi).
15. In some notes made by Sraffa (Sraffa D3/12/16) on the tendency for the rate of profits to fall, he sets out very simply but comprehensively the various conditions and counter-conditions of the processes affecting the rate of profits using terms common to orthodox economic theory, not relying on Marx's language, dated July 1942. It is possible these were responses to Joan Robinson's book or to a discussion with Sraffa of the rate of profits and her dismissal of Marx's tendency for the rate of profits to fall. Joan Robinson complained much later that Sraffa refused to discuss her book (in a letter to Kahn on 1 November 1952: RFK/13/90/4/370) although some cryptic notes referring to it are among Sraffa's papers.

16. It is ironic that her argument against long-period theory is precisely that used by long-period theorists against short-period theory.
17. Kalecki responded: 'p.98: I do not think you are right in assuming that the relative share of wages was *generally* constant. In my *Essays* I emphasised the fact that this may be a kind of historical coincidence. In my Theory of the Long-Run Distribution of the Product of Industry in *Oxford Economic Papers*, I showed that it was not constant in the USA manufacturing industries' (JVR/vii/232/11–2; emphasis in original).
18. He continues: '[t]he assumptions are: (1) the capital equipment is always fully employed (2) prices are stable when money-wages change (3) money-wages are an increasing function [*sic*] of the unemployment (?) percentage. From these assumptions then follows the determination of profits. Wages are at such a level that the resulting profits involve an accumulation of capital which keeps pace with the increase in population after allowing for the falling ratio of labour to capital employed. If wages are, for instance, above this level, capital accumulation will not be sufficient to absorb the increasing population, and the percentage unemployed will rise, which causes a fall of wages to the 'equilibrium' level. If time lags are involved the long-run development may be accompanied by the Marxian cycle as you describe it. True, the peculiar feature of this cycle is that output varies proportionately to the capacity of capital equipment, but from this it does not follow that (as you say on p.103) its period must be longer than that of the "business cycle"' (JVR/vii/232/11–2).
19. Keynes continues: 'At the top of page 214 [*GT*], from which you quote, I said expressly that I am thinking of the unit of labour as "operating in a given environment of technique, natural resources, capital equipment and effective demand." How could I have protected myself more completely and more wordily from your accusation? I never connect the wage unit with real output, and merely remark that, subject to the above assumption as to the given environment, it is "the sole physical unit which we require in our economic system, apart from units of money and of time"' (Keynes, *op. cit.*). Joan Robinson's reply continues: '[a]s for the footnote about you – your defence is precisely the same as the point I am making ie that your units work because capital equipment etc is given, and not because labour is in some sense the only factor of production. I did not make this point merely to nag, but because one of the young bolshy writers had quoted this passage as evidence that you have swallowed the labour theory of value. I always feel badly when criticising such points in the *General Theory*, as I had a good chance to spot them earlier and ought now to forever hold my peace – but I thought this in the public interest. I agree with your general view of Marx. He was a terrific intuitive genius but not at all a clear head' (Joan Robinson in JMK/CO/8/246–8).
20. Araujo and Harcourt (1993, 2001a) examine the correspondence between Joan Robinson, Shove and Dobb on this issue. They show that it is possible to have growth maintained with positive net investment and the normal rate of profits being received in the Marshallian system.
21. In correspondence, in 1973, Jerzy Osiatynski suggested to Joan Robinson that she focuses too much on the relation between Marxian values and prices of production, to the exclusion of the social and political aspects of the Law of Value (JVR/vii/326).
22. Steedman, I. (1977) *Marx After Sraffa*, London: New Left Books.

5 Joan Robinson and Socialist Planning in the Years of High Theory

This chapter has been published in the *Cambridge Journal of Economics* (2007) 31, 4, 489–505 and contains minor alterations here.

1. 'I had some vague hope that [economics] would help me to understand poverty and how it could be cured' (Robinson, 1978d, ix).
2. As we saw in Chapter 4, she was to become during this period a scholar of Marx, appreciating aspects of his approaches. She was also later to depict herself as a 'left-wing Keynesian' (1953; *C.E.P.*, vol. IV, 1973, 264).
3. Sraffa argues that the Marshallian industry supply curve is logically compatible with partial supply and demand analysis only for two very exceptional cases, namely, for the case of decreasing returns, when the totality of a factor of production is employed in the production of a single commodity, and for the case of increasing returns, where these are external to the firm and internal to the industry (Sraffa, 1926, 539).
4. 'The credit for introducing the conception of imperfection in the market into the corpus of the classical theory of value is largely due to Professor Sraffa' (Kahn, 1929, 156; 1989, 85).
5. She was not oblivious to the fallacies that involved. She warned Keynes, in commenting on his proofs for *The General Theory*: '[m]onopolistic practices on the part of the employers reduce real wages to given employment and so cause "unemployment" in just the same way as inferior techniques or natural resources. Putting them in here is likely I think to give a wrong impression, many people fall into the simple error of thinking that monopoly reduces output as a whole in the same direct way as it reduces output of one commodity' (JMK/L/R/144).
6. The inconsistency between the two branches of her theoretical approach was resolved by Kalecki's version of the theories of effective demand, and of value and distribution in his review of Keynes's *General Theory* (Kalecki, 1936, also by Targetti and Kinder-Has (trans. and eds.) 1982). Starting with the marginal revenue and marginal cost curves of an individual firm, independently of market structure, he deducts raw materials and the use of equipment to reach marginal value-added and marginal labour cost curves with which he demonstrates the proposition that investment determines the level of output and employment, and at the same time establishes the division of the product between wages and profits and between consumption and investment. Although the review was not translated into English until 1982, Joan Robinson would possibly have discussed with Kalecki his points of difference with Keynes's theory. See, for example: 'Kalecki produced a more coherent version of *The General Theory*, which brought imperfect competition into the analysis and emphasised the influence of investment on the share of profits.' (*C.E.P.*, 1973, vol. IV, 97; see also 1969, viii). And as we have seen, she ran a discussion class on Kalecki (1939a) during 1940. In 1958, in retrospect of *The Economics of Imperfect Competition*, she wrote: 'Keynes was not much interested in price theory, but the two streams [value and distribution and output and employment] of thought were combined by Michal Kalecki (*Essays in the Theory of Economic Fluctuations* (1939a)). He showed that the determination of

gross profit margins is the key to the distribution of the product of industry between wages and profits, and is therefore highly relevant to the problem of effective demand and the level of employment' (*C.E.P.*, vol. II, 1960, 241). Joan Robinson had read Kalecki's manuscript and he acknowledges her for her criticisms (see also Harcourt (2006b, ch. 2, 3).

7. Joan Robinson's failure to understand Sraffa's critique is suggested in his comments to her in a letter prior to *EIC*. 'On the whole, on the question of the a priori reasoning, as far as it goes, you accept the criticism; and on the question of fact you have not produced the evidence. I am therefore unable, in the name of whatever school I am supposed to be identified with, to acknowledge defeat.' (31 May 1931) (JVR/vii/431/1–3).
8. The two strands offer two different theories of output, and, implicitly, hold two different theories about the distribution of income between wages and profits. The theory of effective demand was based upon a theory of demand for money that was different to that implicit in the value theory of imperfect competition. The two strands gave completely different accounts of employment.
9. '[T]he theory of employment was, of course, far more important, both for analysis and for policy than anything concerned with the theory of individual prices' (*C.E.P.*, vol. II, 1960, 241). The practice of drawing policy conclusions from an inappropriate model did not seem to occur to her as being invalid although it was partly on these grounds that she criticised *laisser-faire*.
10. 'The general practical moral of Marshallian teaching was the defence of *laisser-faire*' (Robinson, 1980; 1985, 157).
11. The perfect competition to which she referred was closer to Marshall's 'free competition', a competitive market without perfect foresight or knowledge. See Joan Robinson (1934) where she explored the relevance of freedom of entry, of number of firms, of normal profits or of frictions, for perfect competition.
12. Her contempt for *laisser-faire* was accompanied by her uncritical assumption that production and distribution based on a 'rational' plan would in some way be 'better'. Her use of 'efficiency' tended to shift from the optimal allocation of resources based on a given income distribution to an optimal allocation of goods based on needs.
13. GCH suggests, further, that she had an implicit critique of the equilibrium method as well as the intimated path dependency in *EIC* (King and Harcourt, 1995, 35–6).
14. Kalecki's 'Political aspects of full employment' (1943) was published around the same time.
15. '[E]stablish Socialism – remove the profit principle – and the inventor will have a free hand. The mechanisation of the world, already rapid enough, would be, or at any rate could be enormously accelerated' (George Orwell, 1937, 192).
16. Perhaps Keynes did understand Harrod because, in his Galton lecture, he suggests reducing the propensity to save and increasing the capital to output ratio to avert declining employment (see Harcourt (2002)).
17. His 'Theory of the Business Cycle' was published in 1936–7; in 1938, she read the proofs of *Essays in the Theory of Economic Fluctuations*.
18. Kalecki (1939a). See Sylos Labini (1985, 61–2) and Sardoni (1984, 460).

19. Clark also advised giving the NIB control over the export of capital, offering support schemes for new inventions, requiring of borrowers that they pay trade union (TU) wages and observe TU conditions, and supervising investment of funds by insurance companies and savings banks. The NIB was part of a scheme to transfer ownership and control of capital and land to public authority.
20. In a review of Dobb's (1948) *Soviet Economic Development since 1917*, entitled 'The theory of planning', Joan Robinson (1949b) is impressed with the 30 years of Soviet progress and remarks that its 'grand moral' is for undeveloped nations (*C.E.P.* vol. I, 1951, 181).
21. See also Lange (1936) and Dobb (1941) for different views on this.
22. She seemed to assume an endogenous money supply and no constraints from international flows.
23. Kaldor, in his Mattioli Lectures (Kaldor, 1984; 1996) and also Kalecki, reached similar conclusions (see, for example, Kalecki, 1991, 143 *et seq.*).
24. James Meade's reply was that only very small adjustments to relative wages would be needed to induce large shifts of labour out of declining industries and to newly emerging fields. He agreed that it would be unwise to bring on significant distributional shifts of income in an attempt to induce labour to move. See also Reddaway (1959).
25. Although, see King (2001, n. iv), for a qualification of these policies.
26. The USSR, Nazi Germany and Japan were excluded from this network, a sizeable proportion of global economic activity.
27. Keynes, at the end of the war, doubted the wisdom of the proposed central role in the international settlement system of the US dollar and instead proposed a neutral currency unit, Bancor. Joan Robinson also doubted that the US would make available foreign loans to offset its predicted chronic surplus on its balance of trade.

6 The Making of *The Accumulation of Capital*

1. Indeed, as far as analysing types of technical progress were concerned, she laid the foundations for her subsequent arguments with Roy Harrod before the war (see Robinson, 1938; 1949b, *C.E.P.*, vol. I, 1951, 155–74).
2. As we saw, Piero Sraffa teased her that she seemed to regard 'Marx as a little-known forerunner of Kalecki' (see Robinson, 1942b; 1966, vi).
3. In these endeavours, he in turn was influenced by Gramsci.
4. Evidently, the pamphlet caused 'great offence ... to Marxists and to Walrasians'. Joan Robinson 'did not think that the offence was caused by errors in it' (248) (to which she drew attention when introducing the essays in 1973b, 247–8).
5. I (GCH) was a graduate student at Cambridge in the 1950s when the 1956 volume was published. I locked myself up with it for a term and then emerged to read a paper on it to the research students seminar (chaired by Piero Sraffa and Robin Marris) over two successive weeks, with Joan Robinson coming to a third session to answer queries. She chided us for mainly ignoring the big picture, for being concerned rather with the nitty-gritty of technical analysis. Unfortunately, I mislaid the paper during one of my subsequent moves – I would dearly love to find it in order to see, over 50

years on, what I think of my evaluation now. (I was told that Joan Robinson herself formed a good opinion of the paper based on second-hand reports on it to her.)

6. The same approach may be adapted to an understanding of the workings of a planned democratic socialist society. This aspect was developed even more by Kalecki than by Joan Robinson.
7. The table of contents contains seven books: 'Introduction', 'Accumulation in the long run', 'The short period', 'Finance', 'The rentier', 'Land', 'Relative Prices' and 'International Trade'. Book II 'Accumulation in the long term', has as well three sections: 'Accumulation with one technique', 'The technical frontier' and 'Accumulation with technical progress'. There are 37 chapters in all, followed by 'Notes on various topics', 'Diagrams' and 'The value of invested capital', written by David Champernowne and Richard Kahn. By the third edition, the volume was 444 pages long.
8. In her superb introductory chapter, the ideal source for all who want to know what our discipline is about, who want 'a truly masterful statement of economic principles, especially principles of macroeconomics' (Klein, 1989, 258), she stressed the importance of specific rules of the game in characterising different modes of production.
9. Robert Dixon (17 March 2007) commented to us that there is also an implicit assumption 'that the propensity to save out of profits is 1. (Or at least that savings rates are given)'.
10. She defines neutral technical progress on p. 133: '[a] neutral relationship between the two spectra means that, with the superior technique, labour per unit of output and capital in terms of labour time per unit of output are reduced in the same proportion over the whole range of techniques, so that the real-capital ratio is the same with Beta-plus as with Beta technique, the same with Alpha-plus as with Alpha and with Gamma-plus as with Gamma.'
11. Though Salter's book on these themes was not published until 1960, the dissertation on which it was based was examined in 1955 and its results were already well known in Cambridge at that time.
12. In her world, even competitors are price-makers who act together, not collusively, but because they know that all their rivals are experiencing similar conditions, for example, a rise in costs.
13. In the sense that only after GCH had worked out his results did he realise that they looked familiar – so he re-read Worswick's paper and found two identical paragraphs in it.

7 The Choice of Technique in the Economy as a Whole and the Cambridge–Cambridge Debates in the Theory of Capital: Joan Robinson's Role

1. It was refuted by Garegnani (1976a), Sato (1976) and Laibman and Nell (1977).
2. At the end of the English version of her contribution to the *Revue* symposium, she quoted:

   He who is convinced against his will
   Is of the same opinion still.

`She adds: '[it] is high time to abandon the mainstream and take to the turbulent waters of truly dynamic analysis' (Robinson, 1977a; 1978d, 125).

3. Less noticed was Abba Lerner's 1953 article which is an extremely clear discussion of the issues within the contexts of Austrian, Knightian and Keynesian theories.
4. 'Time is unlike space in two ... striking respects. In space, bodies moving from *A* to *B* may pass bodies moving from *B* to *A* but in time ... one-way traffic is always in force ... in space the distance from *A* to *B* is of the same order of magnitude ... as the distance from *B* to *A*; in time, the distance from to-day to to-morrow is twenty-four hours ... the distance from to-day to yesterday is infinite' Joan Robinson (1953–4, 85; *C.E.P.*, vol. II, 1960, 120).
5. Apart from the appropriateness of this unit for her immediate purposes, Joan Robinson had earlier on in correspondence with Keynes, agreed with him on its general suitability as a unit of measurement in economic analysis.
6. Equation (4) is also implied by the equality of equation (1).
7. For a more full discussion and evaluation of Champernowne's article, see Harcourt (1972, 29–34).
8. For a fuller discussion and evaluation of Swan's arguments, see Harcourt (1972, 34–9). See also Peter Swan's ANU Inaugural Trevor Swan Distinguished Lecture on 'Trevor Winchester Swan AO' for the correspondence between Joan Robinson and Swan on his article and on his 1964 paper, 'On Golden Ages and production functions'. She felt they were 'coming much closer together' by the time of the second paper. Swan himself, we understand, rather gave up working on these issues in despair.
9. Christopher Dougherty (1972) argued that Pasinetti was not attacking the Fisherian theory of the rate of profits but 'any [including Solow's] suggestion that a "Fisherian" concept of the rate of return could be used to resurrect John Bates Clark's parable of the determination of the rate of profit[s]' (1324). The latter is implied in Solow's analysis despite his declared desire to get away from it and use only the Fisherian social rate of return on investment.
10. For a full discussion of this three-way debate between Dougherty, Pasinetti and Solow, see Harcourt (1976) and Sardoni (1992 (ed.), 151–6).
11. This was the strategy she followed in the narrative of her 1956 book (see Chapter 6 of this volume).
12. As we saw, Joan Robinson published the draft of the version in English of her contribution (which was in French) in vol. V of her *C.E.P.* (1979, 59–70), with the title, 'The meaning of Capital'.
13. We are indebted to Harvey Gram who sent us copies of the letters.

8 After *The Accumulation of Capital*: Defence and Development

1. She gave her Inaugural Lecture, *The New Mercantalism* (1966a), in October 1965 to a packed Lady Mitchell Hall, resplendent in a long deep-blue gown probably designed by her elder daughter, Ann. Austin, to whose chair she had succeeded in 1965, was not able to be present but he sent a splendid bouquet of flowers which was presented to her at the lecture. *Economic Heresies* was the first fruit of her 'retirement' – she was 67, the official retirement age at Cambridge, in 1970.

2. Some examples:

   'The non-monetary theory, that real forces tend to establish equilibrium, ... reaches its apotheosis in the doctrine that money is the only thing that matters' (76).

   'The General Theory is a "monetary theory" only in the sense that relationships and institutions concerned with money, credit and finance are necessary elements in the "real" economy with which it is concerned' (96).

   'The distinction between "demand–pull" and "cost–push" is not very useful when applied to the market for goods but ... has an important meaning when applied to the market for labour' (92).

   'An inflationary economy is in the situation of a man holding a tiger by the tail' (95).

   'The determination of firms to grow by reinvesting profits was characteristic of capitalism from the start; ... if it were not the case, capitalism would never have happened' (102).

   'Where competition is vigorous, there must be a tendency towards monopoly, which is often held up at the stage of oligopoly when a few powerful firms prefer armed neutrality to the final battle for supremacy' (102).

   'The modern development of conglomerates provides clear evidence that it is financial power, rather than technical economies of scale, that permits firms to continue to grow when they are already large' (102).

3. Michael Ambrosi (2003) shows how correct Keynes could be in his insightful analysis of the relationship between the structure of *The General Theory* and Pigou's 1933 book.
4. While it is correct that Salter gave much space to a purely competitive analysis in his book, he did sketch what happens when market structures are imperfectly competitive so that Joan Robinson has overstated the case on p. 129, n21.

9 Joan Robinson's Views on Development Economics as Political Economy

1. This section is based on Pervez Tahir's monograph, *Making Sense of Joan Robinson on China*, which he wrote when he was the 1990 Joan Robinson Memorial Lecturer at the Faculty of Economics and Politics, University of Cambridge. The authors are most grateful to Rachel Murphy and Peter Nolan for their comments on a draft.
2. It is ironic that what he warned could happen if his suggestions were not followed did in fact happen just after he died, as Josef Steindl noted ruefully in his wonderful portrait of Kalecki in the *Journal of Post Keynesian Economics* in 1981: 'Half a year after Kalecki's death (1970) Gomulka was forced out of office by masses of workers taking to the streets to demonstrate against insufficient real earnings and widespread scarcities of everyday consumer supplies. Kalecki's logic had come back with a vengeance' (Steindl, 1981, 592–3).
3. Peter Nolan, in personal conversation, reminds us that Joan Robinson never departed from her view that full human potential could not be realised in

the capitalist mode of production because of the essential nature of wage labour but that moral incentives – 'save the people' – could allow it to happen. Rachel Murphy, in conversation, reminds us of the irony that Mao wanted to minimise Soviet mistakes and human costs by obliterating a system of planning and management!

4. Joan Robinson's approach on surplus mobilisation and the choice of techniques in developing economies is similar to that of Kalecki. See Kalecki (1955; 1976, 55).
5. Maurice Dobb (eg 1954) with the USSR in mind had argued for the use of techniques which maximised the surplus over wage costs but not the total output per period.
6. See Chapter 11 (195–6) where she explains what she sees as the role of a moral code in any society.
7. Ten years on, during the 'Cultural Revolution', she came to believe that people could be saints and serve each other selflessly. In another ten years, she reverted to her original position that the moral method cannot run a complex economy.
8. She tended, however, to minimise the significance of these problems when they arose later during the rush towards collectivisation.
9. Robinson and Eatwell (1973) had organised their discussion of the Third World similarly to capture the interdependency between the different aspects of the issues (see Chapter 10).
10. Tahir (1990a) credits Joan Robinson as the original author of 'disguised unemployment' in 1936 (see Robinson, 1937b, 60–74). In 1943, Rosenstein-Rodan (1943) used the concept in the context of underdevelopment. Joan Robinson had originally associated it with urban, industrialised economies (Robinson, 1978c, 93–4).
11. The first and second stages are the exploitation of the extractive industries and the exporting of manufactures to the Third World, 'partly through setting up assembly works close to markets and exporting components under the guise of "import-saving" investment' (ibid., p. 143).

10 *An Introduction to Modern Economics*: A light that Failed?

1. The people concerned are named and thanked in Acknowledgements (xv).
2. GCH was a member of the group who read the drafts.
3. Gurley had been a most respected mainstream economist but then was radicalised by, amongst other events, the Vietnam War and became a scholar of Marx and of Chinese economic development.
4. JLE told GCH (23 October 2007) that he wrote the HET section, JR, the policy section. The middle section, 'Analysis', was written half and half between them. We do not think that this division of labour could be deduced from reading the book – perhaps each author left their distinctive marks on presentation in the subsequent revisions of the original drafts.
5. There was a surge in the literature at this time on analysis and ideology; see, for example, Stretton (1969), Dobb (1973, 1975), Harcourt (1972, Ch. 1). GCH was subsequently clobbered by Bliss (1975, Ch. 15).

6. We mentioned in Chapter 8 that Joan Robinson's Inaugural Lecture in 1965 was on 'The New Mercantilism'.
7. For a defence of Marx's insights and procedures, see Harcourt and Kerr (1996), Harcourt (2001a) and Harcourt (2006a).
8. This view has much in common with Keynes's criticism of Russell, Wittgenstein and Ramsey that '[t]he gradual perfection of [their] formal treatment [of logic] had been ... to empty it of content ... to reduce it ... to mere dry bones ... to exclude not only all experience, but also most of the principles, usually reckoned logical, of reasonable thought' (Keynes 1933b; *C.W.*, vol. X, 1972, 338).
9. This was not always the desired reaction. Lionel McKenzie once showed GCH his page-by-page selection from his copy of the book of what he took to be either distortion or misunderstanding of orthodox propositions, about which he was furious. Or, perhaps, it is what they expected!
10. 'The revolution was made in the name of the working class; the principal benefit that they have got from it is a guarantee against unemployment' (314).

11 A Concerned Intellectual's Task: Joan Robinson's Three Popular Books

Economic Philosophy (1962b), *Economics: An Awkward Corner* (1966b) and *Freedom and Necessity* (1970) are the three important books of Joan Robinson.

1. The controversial nature of values in economic theory was not new in Joan Robinson's mind. In 1937, in her *Introduction to the Theory of Employment* (1937a), she included a chapter of reflections on the nature of controversy, concluding the book with the observation that this book was itself free of controversy.
2. Clarence Ayers wrote to her (17 October 1963):

> [c]ertain items in your *Economic Philosophy* astonished and dismayed me. In particular ... your apparent dismissal of value judgments as having no general intellectual validity. ... Thus my position ... is that we do in fact make value judgments (of good and bad, right and wrong) and define values on the basis of knowledge and understanding of facts
>
> (JVR/vii/46)

3. Logical structures of this kind have a certain charm. They allow those without mathematics to catch a hint of what intellectual beauty means. This has been a great support to them in their ideological function. In the face of such elegance, only a philistine could complain that the contemplation of an ultimate stationary state, when accumulation has come to an end, is not going to help us very much with the problems of today.

   (ibid., p. 61)

4. Tahir (1990b) notes that Joan Robinson chose the title of her book from a quote from Mao: 'the leap from the kingdom of necessity to the kingdom of freedom is gradually achieved in a long-term process of recognition' (218).
5. She stated:

> [b]ut I want you to think about me dialectically. The first principle of the dialectic is that the meaning of a proposition depends on what it denies. Thus the very same proposition has two opposite meanings according to whether you come to it from above or from below
>
> (JVR, i/16.3/11–2).

6. She was particularly intolerant of forms of wealth such as land and shares which allowed their owners an income for no effort.
7. Examples of the manner in which technology, in the guise of economics, had dominated over morality were the presentation of an argument for improved health services in terms of lost production due to sickness, or the construction of human capital as a concept.
8. 'When two economic theories differ in their ideology the most important distinction between them lies in the sphere of political action, but the best sport that they offer is to trace the difference in their ideologies to its roots in a difference in the logical structure of the systems' (JVR/i/16.1).
9. In all this I should emphasise that economic theory, in itself, preaches no doctrines and cannot establish any universally valid laws. It is a method of ordering ideas and formulating questions. For this reason, I should pay a good deal of attention to method. ... None of these tells us anything about causation. ... To find causal relations we want to know how individuals behave and how the behaviour of various groups reacts on each other

   (Robinson, *C.E.P.*, vol. III, 1965, 5).

10. 'To pretend to have none [values] and to be *purely objective* must necessarily be either self-deception or a device to deceive others' (Robinson, 1970, 122) (emphasis in the original).
11. In reviewing *Asian Drama* (Gunnar Myrdal, 1968), she observed that '[a]t one level the book is an essay in the methodology of the social sciences' (JVR/ii/11).
12. Perhaps she heeded the opinion of a much earlier correspondent, Allen Flanders.

> The strongest impression your book [*An Essay on Marxian Economics*] left in my mind was the confirmation of previous conclusions that economics has advanced to a very small extent as a science. Is it perhaps not a mistake to consider it as a science, or at least only as a science. Is it not like politics an art? In all human relationships there are so many factors at play that we can only judge the probable effects of certain causes by a kind of intuition which is, however, based upon accumulated experience.
>
> (JVR/vii/140; 2 October 1942)

12 Conclusion: Joan Robinson's Legacy

1. We are comforted by the following observations of Robin Matthews (letter to G C H, 27 April 1987) who was a colleague of Joan Robinson from the late 1940s on.

> In some ways her originality was more as a synthesiser than as an originator. The collection of elements on which the brew was concocted was

> an unusual one: Marshall (in a very large helping), Marx, Keynes, Shove, Sraffa and Kalecki [we would add Pigou], to say nothing of Richard Kahn's contributions. Therein lay much of the originality ... The hallmarks [of her style] were clarity carried to the point of homeliness ... of one anxious to convince. Her lack of mathematical background ... sometimes led her to misunderstand opponents but it did not matter much as far as her own contributions were concerned. Her indefatigable worrying away at problems, with occasional help from friends, was usually enough to get her to the answers.

2. This was not the view expressed in Harcourt (1979; 1982b, 350). Later criticisms of this view by Paul Flatau (2001) have convinced us of the veracity of the statement in the text.
3. Nevertheless it may be argued that even if she did not believe in the labour theory of value, she ended up using it (see Harcourt, 1991, 484).
4. But see our support of her position in Chapter 8.
5. This is the major theme of Pasinetti (2007), in which he outlines the way forward.

References

Ambrosi, G. M. (2003) *Keynes, Pigou and Cambridge Keynesians. Authenticity and Analytical Perspective in the Keynes-Classics Debate*, Houndmills, Basingstoke, Hants: Palgrave Macmillan.

Araujo J. and G. C. Harcourt (1993) 'Accumulation and the rate of profits: reflections on the issues raised in the correspondence between Maurice Dobb, Joan Robinson and Gerald Shove' and 'An addendum', *Journal of the History of Economic Thought*, 15, 1–30; reprinted in Harcourt (1995b) and Kerr with Harcourt (eds.) (2002), vol. II, 239–67.

Arrow, K. J. (1989) 'Joan Robinson and modern economic theory: an interview' in Feiwel (ed.) (1989b), 147–35.

Asimakopulos, A. (1969) 'A Robinsonian growth model in one-sector notation', *Australian Economic Papers*, 8, 41–58; reprinted in Kerr with Harcourt (eds.) (2002), vol. III, 119–36.

—— (1970) 'A Robinsonian growth model in one-sector notation. An amendment', *Australian Economic Papers*, 9, 171–6; reprinted in Kerr with Harcourt (eds.) (2002), vol. III, 137–43.

—— (1984) 'Joan Robinson and economic theory', *Banco Nazionale del Lavoro Quarterly Review*, 37, 381–409; reprinted in Kerr with Harcourt (eds.) (2002), vol. V, 440–65.

—— (1991) *Keynes's General Theory and Accumulation*, Cambridge: Cambridge University Press; section on 'Robinson on the accumulation of capital', 166–87; reprinted in Kerr with Harcourt (eds.) (2002), vol. III, 144–63.

Aslanbeigui, N. and G. Oakes (2006) 'Joan Robinson's "secret document": a passage from the autobiography of an analytical economist', *Journal of the History of Economic Thought*, 28, 413–26.

—— (2007) 'The young Joan Robinson', mimeo.

Barens, I. (ed.) (2005) *Political Events and Economic Ideas*, Cheltenham: Edward Elgar.

Barna, T. (1957) 'Review of Joan Robinson (1956a)', *Economic Journal*, 67, 490–3; reprinted in Kerr with Harcourt (eds.) (2002), vol. III, 30–3.

Berg, M. (ed.) (1990) *Political Economy in the Twentieth Century*, New York, London: Philip Allan.

Berrill, K. (ed.) (1964) *Economic Development with Special Reference to South East Asia*, London: Macmillan.

Bhaduri, A. (1969) 'On the significance of recent controversies on capital theory: A Marxian view', *Economic Journal*, 79, 532–9; reprinted in Kerr with Harcourt (eds.) (2002), vol. IV, 117–24.

Bhaduri, A. and J. Robinson (1980) 'Accumulation and exploitation: An analysis in the tradition of Marx, Sraffa and Kalecki', *Cambridge Journal of Economics*, 4, 103–15.

Bliss, C. J. (1975), *Capital Theory and the Distribution of Income*, Amsterdam: North Holland; New York: Elsevier.

Boianovsky, M. (2005) 'Some Cambridge reactions to *The General Theory*: David Champernowne and Joan Robinson on full employment', *Cambridge Journal of Economics*, 29, 73–98.

Brown, M., K. Sato and P. Zarembka (eds.) (1976) *Essays in Modern Capital Theory*, Amsterdam: North Holland.
Cairncross, A. (1993) *Austin Robinson: the life of an Economic Advisor*, Basingstoke: Macmillan; New York: St Martin's Press.
Cambridge Journal of Economics, (1983) Special Memorial Issue for Joan Robinson, September/December, 7 (3/4), Oxford University Press for the Cambridge Political Economy Trust.
Chakravarty, S. (1983) 'Joan Robinson: An appreciation', *Economic and Political Weekly*, 18, 1712–6.
Chamberlin, E. H. (1933) *The Theory of Monopolistic Competition. A Reorientation of the Theory of Value*, Cambridge, MA: Harvard University Press.
Champernowne, D. G. (1953–4) 'The production function and the theory of capital: a comment', *Review of Economic Studies*, 21, 112–35; reprinted in Kerr with Harcourt (eds.) (2002), vol. III, 233–63.
Chang, Ha-Joon (2007) *Bad Samaritans. Rich Nations, Poor Policies and the Threat to the Developing World*, London: Random House Business Books.
Chossudowsky, E. M. (1943) 'Review of Joan Robinson (1942b)', *Economica*, IX, 389–92.
Clower, R. W. (1961) 'Review of Joan Robinson (1960a)', *American Economic Review*, 51, 701–2; reprinted in Kerr with Harcourt (eds.) (2002), vol. III, 164–5.
Cohen, R. (1983) 'Address' at the Memorial Service in King's College Chapel, 29 October.
Cohen, A. J. and G. C. Harcourt (2003) 'Whatever happened to the Cambridge Capital Theory controversies?', *Journal of Economic Perspectives*, 17, 199–214.
Cole, G. D. H. (1930) 'Introduction' to Marx (1930).
Dardi, M. (1996) 'Imperfect competition and short-period economics' in Marcuzzo, Pasinetti and Roncaglia (eds.) (1996), 29–35; reprinted in Kerr with Harcourt (eds.) (2002), vol. I, 355–61.
Davidson, P. (1972), *Money and the Real World*, London: Macmillan (2nd edn, 1978).
Dobb, M. H. (1932) *On Marxism Today*, London: Hogarth Press.
—— (1935) 'A criticism of some trends in modern economic theory', an unpublished lecture delivered to the Economics Society, Copenhagen, transcribed from notes archived in the Dobb Papers, Wren Library, Trinity College, Cambridge by Roy J. Rotheim, Skidmore College, Saratoga Springs, New York.
—— (1937, 1940) *Political Economy and Capitalism*, London: George Routledge and Sons.
—— (1941) 'A review of the discussion concerning economic theory in its application to a socialist economy', *Revue de la Faculte des Sciences Economique de l'Universite d'Istanbul*, 155–167.
—— (1948) *Soviet Economic Development since 1917*, London: Routledge and Kegan Paul.
—— (1951) *Some Aspects of Economic Development. Three Lectures*, Delhi: Ranjit Printers and Publishers.
—— (1954) 'A note on the so-called degree of capital-intensity of investment in under-developed countries', *Economie Appliquee*, VII, 3; reprinted in Dobb (1955).
—— (1955) *On Economic Theory and Socialism*, London: Routledge and Kegan Paul.

—— (1973) *Theories of Value and Distribution Since Adam Smith*, Cambridge: Cambridge University Press.

—— (1975), 'Revival of political economy: an explanatory note', *Economic Record*, 51, 357–9.

Dougherty, C. R. S. (1972) 'On the rate of return and the rate of profit', *Economic Journal*, 82, 1324–50.

Duesenberry, J. S. (1949) *Income, Saving and the Theory of Consumer Behaviour*, Harvard: Harvard University Press.

Durbin, E. (1985) *New Jerusalems. The Labour Party and the Economics of Democratic Socialism*, London: Routledge and Kegan Paul.

Eatwell, J. L. (1977) 'Portrait: Joan Robinson', *Challenge*, 20, 64–5.

—— (1983) 'The long-period theory of employment', *Cambridge Journal of Economics*, 7, 269–85; reprinted in Kerr with Harcourt (eds.) (2002), vol. II, 40–63.

Eatwell, J., M. Milgate and P. Newman (eds.) (1987) *The New Palgrave: A Dictionary of Economics*, vol. 4, Q to Z, London: Macmillan.

Edwards, C. (1933) 'Review of Joan Robinson (1933a)', *American Economic Review*, 23, 683–5; reprinted in Kerr with Harcourt (eds.) (2002), vol. I, 160–2.

Ellis, H. S. (1948) *A Survey of Contemporary Economics*, Philadelphia: Blakiston Co.

Fay, C. R. (1942) 'Review of Joan Robinson (1942b)', *Cambridge Review*, June 13.

Feinstein, C. H. (ed.) (1967) *Socialism, Capitalism and Economic Growth: Essays presented to Maurice Dobb*, Cambridge: Cambridge University Press.

Feiwel, G. R. (ed.) (1985) *Issues in Contemporary Macroeconomics and Distribution*, London: Macmillan.

—— (ed.) (1989a) *The Economics of Imperfect Competition and Employment. Joan Robinson and Beyond*, London: Macmillan.

—— (ed.) (1989b) *Joan Robinson and Modern Economic Theory*, London: Macmillan.

Ferguson, C. E. (1969) *The Neoclassical Theory of Production and Distribution*, Cambridge: Cambridge University Press.

—— (1972) 'The current state of capital theory: a tale of two paradigms', *Southern Economic Journal*, 39, 160–76; reprinted in Kerr with Harcourt (eds.) (2002), vol. IV, 271–95.

Findlay, R. (1963) 'The Robinsonian model of accumulation', *Economica*, 30, 1–12; reprinted in Kerr with Harcourt (eds.) (2002), vol. III, 72–84.

Flanders, A. (1943) 'Marxian and modern economics: review of Joan Robinson (1942b)', *Socialist Commentary*, January.

Flatau, P. (2001) 'Some reflections on the "Pigou–Robinson" theory of exploitation', *History of Economics Review*, Winter, 1–16.

Galbraith, J. K. (1948) 'Monopoly and the concentration of economic power' in Ellis (ed.) (1948), 99–128.

—— (1958) *The Affluent Society*, Boston: Houghton Mifflin.

Galloway, L. and V. Shukla (1974) 'The neoclassical production function', *American Economic Review*, 64, 348–58; reprinted in Kerr with Harcourt (eds.) (2002), vol. IV, 315–30.

Garegnani, P. (1959) 'A problem in the theory of distribution from Ricardo to Wicksell', unpublished PhD dissertation, Cambridge University.

—— (1970) 'Heterogeneous capital, the production function and the theory of distribution', *Review of Economic Studies*, 37, 407–36, and 'A reply', 439; reprinted in Kerr with Harcourt (eds.) (2002), vol. IV, 19–59.

—— (1976a) 'The neoclassical production function: comment', *American Economic Review*, 66, 424–7.
—— (1976b) 'On a change in the notion of equilibrium in recent work on value and distribution' in Brown, et al. (eds.) (1976), 25–45.
—— (1996) 'The long-period theory of aggregate demand in a 1936 article by Joan Robinson', in Marcuzzo, Pasinetti and Roncaglia (eds.) (1996), 67–74; reprinted in Kerr with Harcourt (eds.) (2002), vol. II, 64–72.
Gibson, B. (ed.) (2005) *Joan Robinson's Economics. A Centennial Celebration*, Cheltenham, Gloucestershire, UK; Northampton, MA, USA: Edward Elgar.
Goodwin, R. M. (1967) 'A growth cycle' in Feinstein (ed.) (1967), 54–8.
—— (1989) 'Joan Robinson – passionate seeker after truth' in Feiwel (ed.) (1989b), 916–7.
Gram, H. (2005) 'Expectations and the capital controversy' in Gibson (ed.) (2005), 109–22.
Gram, H. and V. Walsh (1983) 'Joan Robinson's economics in retrospect', *Journal of Economic Literature*, 21, 518–50; reprinted in Kerr with Harcourt (eds.) (2002), vol. V, 365–406.
Gurley, J. G. (1974), 'Review of Joan Robinson and John Eatwell (1973)', *Economic Journal*, 84, 447–50; reprinted in Kerr with Harcourt (eds.) (2002), vol. V, 305–7.
Hahn, F. H. (1972) 'Review of Joan Robinson (1971)', *Economica*, 39, 205–6; reprinted in Kerr with Harcourt (eds.) (2002), vol. V, 18–20.
—— (1973) *On the Notion of Equilibrium in Economics. An Inaugural Lecture*, Cambridge: Cambridge University Press.
—— (1989) 'Robinson–Hahn love–hate relationship: an interview' in Feiwel (ed.) (1989b), 895-910.
Harcourt, G. C. (1963) 'A simple Joan Robinson model of accumulation with one technique: a comment', *Osaka Economic Papers*, 9, 24–8.
—— (1969) 'Some Cambridge controversies in the theory of capital', *Journal of Economic Literature*, 7, 369–405.
—— (1972), *Some Cambridge Controversies in the Theory of Capital*, Cambridge: Cambridge University Press.
—— (1976) 'The Cambridge controversies: old ways and new horizons – or dead-ends?', *Oxford Economic Papers*, 28, 25–65; reprinted in Sardoni (ed.) (1992), 130–65.
—— (1979) 'Robinson, Joan' in Sills (ed.) (1979), 663–7.
—— (1982a) 'Occasional portraits of the founding post-Keynesians: Lorie Tarshis (or, Tarshis on Tarshis by Harcourt)' in Harcourt (1982b), 362–75.
—— (1982b), *The Social Science Imperialists*, P. Kerr (ed.), London: Routledge and Kegan Paul.
—— (ed.) (1985) *Keynes and his Contemporaries*, Houndsmills, Basingstoke, Hants: Macmillan.
—— (1990a) 'Joan Robinson's early views on method', *History of Political Economy*, 22 (3), 411–27; reprinted in Kerr with Harcourt (eds.) (2002), vol. V, 24–40.
—— (1990b) 'On the contributions of Joan Robinson and Piero Sraffa to economic theory', in Berg (ed.) (1990), 35–67.
—— (1991) 'R.F. Kahn: a tribute', *Banco Nazionale del Lavoro Quarterly Review*, 176, March, 15–30; reprinted in Harcourt (1993), 51–65.
—— (1993) *Post-Keynesian Essays in Biography. Portraits of Twentieth Century Political Economists*, Basingstoke, Hants: Macmillan.

—— (1994) 'Kahn and Keynes and the making of the *General Theory*', *Cambridge Journal of Economics*, 18,11–23; reprinted in Harcourt (1995b), 47–62.

—— (1995a) 'Some reflections on Joan Robinson's changes of mind and the relationship of them to Post-Keynesianism and the economics profession' in Harcourt (1995b), 107–119, and in Marcuzzo, Pasinetti and Roncaglia (eds.) (1996), 317–29.

—— (1995b), *Capitalism, Socialism and Post-Keynesianism. Selected Essays of G.C. Harcourt*, Aldershot, UK; Brookfield, US: Edward Elgar.

—— (1995c, 2001a) 'Lorie Tarshis, 1911–1993: an appreciation', *Economic Journal*, 105, 1244–55; reprinted in Harcourt (2001a), 114–30.

—— (1995d, 2001a) 'Joan Robinson, 1903–1983', *Economic Journal*, 105, 1228–43; reprinted in Harcourt (2001a), 91–113.

—— (1997a) 'Edward Austin Gossage Robinson 1897–1993', *Proceedings of the British Academy*, 94, 707–31; reprinted in Harcourt (2001a), 131–56.

—— (1997b) 'Pay policy, accumulation and productivity', *Economic and Labour Relations Review*, 8, 78–9; reprinted in Harcourt (2001b), 263–75.

—— (1998, 2001a) 'Two views on development; Austin and Joan Robinson', *Cambridge Journal of Economics*, 22, 367–77; reprinted in Harcourt (2001a), 306–22.

—— (2001a) *50 Years a Keynesian and Other Essays*, Hampshire: Palgrave Macmillan.

—— (2001b) *Selected Essays on Economic Policy*, Hampshire: Palgrave Macmillan.

—— (2002) 'Review of J. Toye (2000)', *Economic Journal*, 112, 391–3.

—— (2006a) 'Paul Samuelson on Karl Marx: were the sacrificed games of tennis worth it?' in Szenberg, Ramrattan and Gottesman (eds.) (2006), 127–41.

—— (2006b) *The Structure of Post-Keynesian Economics. The Core Contributions of the Pioneers*, Cambridge: Cambridge University Press.

Harcourt, G. C. and P. Kerr (1996) 'Marx, Karl Heinrich (1818–83)' in Warner (ed.) (1996), 3388–95; reprinted as 'Karl Marx, 1818–83' in Harcourt (2001a), 157–68.

—— (eds.) (2002) *Joan Robinson, Archive Edition*, Hampshire: Palgrave Macmillan.

Harcourt, G. C. and P. A. Riach (eds.) (1997) *A 'Second Edition' of The General Theory*, 2 vols, London: Routledge.

Harris, D. (1975) 'The theory of economic growth: a critique and reformulation', *American Economic Review, Papers and Proceedings*, 65, 329–37.

—— (1978) *Capital Accumulation and Income Distribution*, Stanford, CA: Stanford University Press.

Harris, J. P. and M. P. Todaro (1970) 'Migration, employment and economic development: a two sector analysis', *American Economic Review*, 60, 126–42.

Harrod, R. F. (1930) 'Notes on supply', *Economic Journal*, vol. 40, 232–41.

—— (1931) 'The law of decreasing cost', *Economic Journal*, 41, 566–76.

—— (1936) *The Trade Cycle. An Essay*, Oxford: Clarendon Press.

—— (1937) 'Review of Joan Robinson (1937b)', *Economic Journal*, 47, 326–30; reprinted in Kerr with Harcourt (eds.) (2002), vol. II, 11–14.

—— (1939) 'An essay in dynamic theory', *Economic Journal*, 49, 14–33; reprinted in Kerr with Harcourt (eds.) (2002), vol. III, 7–24.

—— (1942) '"Economic man": review of Joan Robinson, *Essay on Marxian Economics*', *The Observer*, 19 July 1942.

—— (1948) *Towards a Dynamic Economics. Some Recent Developments of Economic Theory and their Application to Policy*, London: Macmillan.

Hawtrey, R. G. (1937) 'Review of Joan Robinson (1937b)', *Economic Journal*, 47, 455–60; reprinted in Kerr with Harcourt (eds.) (2002), vol. II, 5–10.
Hayek, F. A. von (1931a) *Prices and Production*, London: George Routledge and Sons.
—— (1931b) 'Reflections on the pure theory of money of Mr. J.M. Keynes', *Economica*, XI, 270–95.
—— (1931c) 'A rejoinder to Mr. Keynes', *Economica*, XI, 398–403.
—— (1932a) 'Reflections on the pure theory of money of Mr. J.M. Keynes, Part II', *Economica*, XII, 22–44.
—— (1932b) 'Money and capital: a reply', *Economic Journal*, 42, 237–49.
Helleiner, G. K. (1980) 'Review of, Joan Robinson (1978c)', *Canadian Journal of Economics*, 13, 515–17.
Hicks, J. R. (1932) *The Theory of Wages*, London: Macmillan.
—— (1937) 'Mr. Keynes and the "Classics": a suggested interpretation', *Econometrica*, 5, 147–59.
—— (1939) *Value and Capital. An Inquiry into Some Fundamental Principles of Economic Theory*, Oxford: Clarendon Press.
—— (1963) *The Theory of Wages*, London: Macmillan (2nd edn).
—— (1976) 'Some questions of time in economics' in A. M. Tang, F. M. Westfield and J. S. Worley (eds.) (1976), 135–51.
—— (1977) *Economic Perspectives: Further Essays on Money and Growth*, Oxford: Clarendon Press.
Howson, S. (1988) '"Socialist" monetary policy: monetary thought in the Labour Party in the 1940s', *History of Political Economy*, 20(4), 543–65.
Hymer, S. (1976) *The International Operations of National Firms: A Study of Direct Foreign Investment*, Cambridge, MA: MIT Press.
'Increasing returns and the representative firm: a symposium', *Economic Journal* (1929–30), 40, 76–116.
Jackson, T. A. (1943) 'Some flowers for Marx's grave', *The Plebs*, May.
Johnson, H. G. (1951–2) 'Some Cambridge controversies in monetary theory', *Review of Economic Studies*, 19, 90–104.
—— (1962) 'A simple Joan Robinson model of accumulation with one technique', *Osaka Economic Papers*, 10, 28–33.
—— (1974) 'Cambridge in the 1950s: memoirs of an economist', *Encounter*, 62, 28–39.
Kahn, R. F. (1929, 1989) *The Economics of the Short Period*, Basingstoke, Hants: Macmillan.
—— (1931) 'The relation of home investment to unemployment', *Economic Journal*, 41, 173–98.
—— (1937) 'The problem of duopoly', *Economic Journal*, 47, 1–20.
—— (1959) 'Exercises in the analysis of growth', *Oxford Economic Papers*, 11, 143–56; reprinted in Kahn (1972) and in Kerr with Harcourt (eds.) (2002), vol. III, 41–53.
—— (1972) *Selected Essays on Employment and Growth*, Cambridge: Cambridge University Press.
—— (1985) 'The Cambridge Circus (1)', in Harcourt (ed.) (1985), 42–51.
Kaldor, N. (1934a) 'Mrs Robinson's *Economics of Imperfect Competition*', *Economica*, 3, 335–41; reprinted in Kerr with Harcourt (eds.) (2002), vol. I, 152–9.
—— (1934b) 'A classificatory note on the determinateness of static equilibrium', *Review of Economic Studies*, 1, 122–36.

—— (1939) 'Speculation and economic stability', *Review of Economic Studies*, 7, 1–27.
—— (1954) 'The relation of economic growth and cyclical fluctuations', *Economic Journal*, 64, 53–71.
—— (1955–6) 'Alternative theories of distribution', *Review of Economic Studies*, 23, 83–100.
—— (1957) 'A model of economic growth', *Economic Journal*, 67, 591–624.
—— (1959a) 'Economic growth and the problem of inflation: Part I', *Economica*, 26, 212–26.
—— (1959b) 'Economic growth and the problem of inflation: part II', *Economica*, 26, 287–98.
—— (1961) 'Capital accumulation and economic growth', in Lutz and Hague (eds.) (1971), 177–222.
—— (1984) 'Joan Robinson, 1903–1983', *Annual Report*, King's College, Cambridge, 32–34; reprinted in Kerr with Harcourt (eds.) (2002), vol. V, 487–9.
—— (1996) *Causes of Growth and Stagnation in the World Economy*, Cambridge: Cambridge University Press.
Kaldor, N., J. Robinson, A. A. Evans, E. F. Schumacher and P. L. Yates (eds.) (1943) *Planning for Abundance*, London: National Peace Council; Peace Aims Pamphlet no. 21.
Kaldor, N. and J. A. Mirrlees (1962) 'A new model of economic growth', *Review of Economic Studies*, 29, 174–92.
Kalecki, M. (1936) 'Pare uwag o teorii Keynesa' [Some remarks on Keynes's theory], *Ehonomista* 3; reprinted in J. Osiatynski (ed.) (1990) *Collected Works of Michal Kalecki, vol I: Capitalism, Business Cycles and Full Employment*, Oxford: Clarendon Press. (also translated and edited by Targetti and Kinder-Hass (1982)).
—— (1939a) *Essays in the Theory of Economic Fluctuations*, London: Allen and Unwin.
—— (1939b) 'Money and real wages', published in Polish (trans. 1966); in *Collected Works of Michal Kalecki, vol II* (1991).
—— (1943) 'Political aspects of full employment', *Political Quarterly*, vol. 14, 322–31.
—— (1955), 'The problem of financing Indian economic development', *Indian Economic Review*, 2, 1–22.
—— (1968) 'Trend and business cycles reconsidered', *Economic Journal*, 78, 263–76; reprinted in Kalecki (1971), 165–83.
—— (1971) *Selected Essays on the Dynamics of the Capitalist Economy, 1933–1970*, Cambridge: Cambridge University Press.
—— (1976) *Essays on Developing Economies*, Sussex: Harvester Press.
—— (1990–7) *Collected Works of Michal Kalecki*, 7 vols, J. Osiatynski (ed.), Oxford: Oxford University Press.
Kerr, P. (2004) 'Joan Robinson on post-war Britain's prospects', *Contributions to Political Economy*, 23, 1–8.
—— (2008) 'Joan Robinson and Ethics' in *Handbook on Economics and Ethics*, I. Van Staveren and J. Peil (eds.), Cheltenham: Edward Elgar.
Kerr, P. in collaboration with G. C. Harcourt (eds.) (2002) *Joan Robinson: Critical Assessments of Leading Economists*, 5 vols, London and New York: Routledge.
Keynes, J. M. (1926) 'The end of laissez-faire', *C.W.*, vol. IX, 1972, 272–94.
—— (1930) *A Treatise on Money*, 2 vols, London: Macmillan, *C.W.*, vols V–VI, 1971.

—— (1931a) 'The Pure Theory of Money. A reply to Dr. Hayek', *Economica*, XI, 387–97.
—— (1931b) *Essays in Persuasion*, *C.W.*, vol. IX, 1972.
—— (1932) 'Keynes's reader's report to Macmillan', *C.W.*, vol. XII, 1973, 866–68; reprinted in Kerr with Harcourt (eds.) (2002), vol. I, 149–151.
—— (1933a) 'The means to prosperity', *C.W.*, vol. IX, 1972.
—— (1933b) *Essays in Biography*, *C.W.*, vol. X, 1972.
—— (1936) *The General Theory of Employment, Interest and Money*, London: Macmillan, *C.W.*, vol. VII, 1973.
—— (1937) 'The general theory of employment', *Quarterly Journal of Economics*, 51, 209–23; reprinted in *C.W.*, vol. XIV, 1973, 109–23.
—— (1945) 'The concept of a capital budget', *C.W.*, vol. XXVII, 1980.
—— (1973a) *The General Theory and After. Part I Preparation*, *C.W.*, vol. XIII.
—— (1973b) *The General Theory and After, Part II: Defence and Development*, *C.W.*, vol. XIV.
—— (1979) *The General Theory and After. A Supplement*, *C.W.*, vol. XXIX, London: Macmillan.
King, J. E. (1998) '"Your position is thoroughly orthodox and entirely wrong": Nicholas Kaldor and Joan Robinson, 1933-83', *Journal of the History of Economic Thought*, 20, 411–32.
—— (2001) 'Labour and unemployment' in Pressman and Holt (eds.) (2001).
—— (2005) 'Planning for abundance: Nicholas Kaldor and Joan Robinson on the Socialist reconstruction of Britain' in Barens (ed.) 206–34.
—— and G. C. Harcourt (1995) 'Talking about Joan Robinson: Geoff Harcourt in conversation with John King', *Review of Social Economy*, LIII, 31–64.
—— and A. Millmow (2003) 'Death of a revolutionary textbook', *History of Political Economy*, 35:1, 105–34.
Klein, L. R. (1989) 'The economic principles of Joan Robinson' in Feiwel (ed.) (1989b), 258–63; reprinted in Kerr with Harcourt (eds.) (2002), vol. V, 218–23.
Kregel, J. A. (1973) *The Reconstruction of Political Economy: An Introduction to Post-Keynesian Economics*, London: Macmillan.
—— (1976) 'Economic methodology in the face of uncertainty: The methods of Keynes and the post-Keynesians', *Economic Journal*, 86, 209–25.
Kregel, J. A. (1983) 'The microfoundations of the generalisation of *The General Theory* and "bastard Keynesianism": Keynes's theory of employment in the long and the short period', *Cambridge Journal of Economics*, 7, 343–61; reprinted in Kerr with Harcourt (eds.) (2002), vol. II, 15–39.
Laibman, D. and E. J. Nell (1977) 'Reswitching, Wicksell effects and the neoclassical production function', *American Economic Review*, 67, 878–88; reprinted in Kerr with Harcourt (eds.) (2002), vol. IV, 331–47.
Lancaster, K. (1960) 'Mrs. Robinson's dynamics', *Economica*, 27, 63–9.
Lange, O. (1936) 'On the economic theory of socialism', *Review of Economic Studies*, IV, 1, 53–71.
Lerner, A. (1944) *The Economics of Control: Principles of Welfare Economics*, London, New York: Macmillan.
—— (1953) 'On the marginal product of capital and the marginal efficiency of investment', *Journal of Political Economy*, 59, 1–14.
—— (1957) 'Review of Joan Robinson's *The Accumulation of Capital*', *American Economic Review*, 47, 693–9; reprinted in Kerr with Harcourt (eds.) (2002), vol. III, 34–40.

Levhari, D. (1965) 'A nonsubstitution theorem and the switching of techniques', *Quarterly Journal of Economics*, 79, 98–105.

Levhari, D. and P. A. Samuelson (1966) 'The nonswitching theorem is false', *Quarterly Journal of Economics*, 80, 518–19.

Lewis, W. A. (1954) 'Economic development with unlimited supplies of labour', *Manchester School of Economic and Social Studies*, 22, 139–91.

Lutz, F. A. and D. C. Hague (eds.) (1961) *The Theory of Capital*, London: Macmillan.

Luxemburg, R. (1913; 1951) *The Accumulation of Capital* (English edn), London: Routledge and Kegan Paul.

Malthus, T. R. (1798) *An Essay on the Principles of Population, as it affects the future improvement of society. With remarks on the speculations of Mr. Godwin, M. Condorcet, and other writers*, London: printed for J. Johnson, in Saint Paul's Church Yard.

Marcuzzo, M. C. (1994) 'At the origin of imperfect competition: different views' in Vaughn (ed.) (1994), 63–78.

—— (2005) 'Robinson and Sraffa' in Gibson (ed.) (2005), 29–42.

—— (2002) 'The writings of Joan Robinson' in Volume I *Joan Robinson, Archive edition*, G. C. Harcourt and P. Kerr (eds.), Hampshire: Palgrave Macmillan, xxxii–lxxiii.

——, L. L. Pasinetti and A. Roncaglia (eds.) (1996) *The Economics of Joan Robinson*, London and New York: Routledge.

—— and A. Rosselli (eds.) (2005) *Economists in Cambridge. A study through their correspondence 1907–1946*, London and New York: Routledge.

—— and C. Sardoni (2005) 'Fighting for the Keynesian revolution: the correspondence between Keynes and J. Robinson', ch. 6 in Marcuzzo and Rosselli (eds.) (2005), 174–95.

Marglin, S. (1973) 'Review of Joan Robinson (1971)', *Economic Journal*, 83, 535–8; reprinted in Kerr with Harcourt (eds.) (2002), vol. V, 21–3.

Marx, K. (1909a) *Capital. A Critique of Political Economy*, Volume II, *The Process of Circulation of Capital*, edited by Friedrich Engels translated from the 2nd German edition by Ernest Untermann, Chicago: Charles H. Kerr and Co.; London: Swan Sonnenchein.

—— (1909b) *Capital. A Critique of Political Economy*, Volume III; *The Process of Capitalist Production as a Whole*, translated by Ernest Untermann, Chicago: Charles H. Kerr and Co.; London: Swan Sonnenchein.

—— (1930) *Capital. A Critique of Political Economy*. Volume I, *A Critical Analysis of Capitalist Production*, with an Introduction by G. D. H. Cole, Everyman's Library, London: J. M. Dent.

Matthews, R. C. O. (1954–5) 'The saving function and the problem of trend and cycle', *Review of Economic Studies*, 22, 75–95.

McMurrin, S. M. (ed.) (1982) *The Tanner Lectures on Human Values*, Salt Lake City: University of Utah Press.

Meade, J. E. (1936) *An Introduction to Economic Analysis and Policy*, London: Oxford University Press.

—— (1958) 'Comments by J.E. Meade on Joan Robinson (1960a)', King's College Archives, Cambridge, RFK/16/3/64–72; reprinted in Kerr with Harcourt (eds.) (2002), vol. III, 169–81.

—— (1993) 'The relation of Mr. Meade's relation to Kahn's multiplier', *Economic Journal*, 103, 664–5.

Mill, J. S. (1848) *Principles of Political Economy, With Some of their Applications to Social Philosophy*, 2 vols, London: John W. Parker.

Morrison, H., T. W. Agar, B. Wootton, C. E. M. Joad, J. Robinson and G. D. H. Cole (1944) *Can Planning be Democratic? A Collection of Essays for the Fabian Society*, London: Routledge.
Myrdal, G. (1953) *The Political Element in the Development of Economic Theory*, London: Routledge and Kegan Paul.
—— (1968) *Asian Drama. An Inquiry into the Poverty of Nations.* 3 vols. New York: Twentieth Century Fund, Pantheon Books.
Nuti, M. (1969) 'The degree of monopoly in the Kaldor–Mirrlees growth model', *Review of Economic Studies*, 36, 257–60.
Orwell, G. (1937) *The Road to Wigan Pier*, London: Victor Gollancz (Penguin (1962)).
O'Shaughnessy, T. (1988) 'Robinson and Eatwell on the long-period theory of employment', Cambridge; in Kerr with Harcourt (eds.) (2002), vol. II, 73–99.
Pasinetti, L. L. (1966) 'Changes in the rate of profit and switches of techniques', *Quarterly Journal of Economics*, 80, 503–17.
—— (1969) 'Switches of technique and the "rate of return" in capital theory', *Economic Journal*, 79, 508–31.
—— (1974) *Growth and Income Distribution: Essays in Economic Theory*, Cambridge: Cambridge University Press.
—— (1987) 'Robinson, Joan Violet (1903–83)', in J. Eatwell, M. Milgare and P. Newman (eds.) (1987), 212–17.
—— (2007) *Keynes and the Cambridge Keynesians: A Revolution in Economics to be Accomplished*, Cambridge: Cambridge University Press.
Pigou, A. C. (1933) *Theory of Unemployment*, London: Macmillan.
Pressman, S. and R. P. F. Holt (eds.) (2001) *A New Guide to Post Keynesian Economics*, London: Routledge.
Ramsey, F. P. (1928) 'A mathematical theory of saving', *Economic Journal*, 38, 543–9.
Reddaway, W. B. (1959) 'Wage flexibility and the distribution of labour', *Lloyd's Bank Review*, 13, 54, October, 32–48.
Reddy, A. K. N. (1973) 'Towards an Indian science and technology', *Journal of Scientific and Industrial Research*, 32, 207–15.
Robertson, D. H. (1956) *Economic Commentaries*, London: Staples Press.
—— (1957) *Lectures on Economic Principles, vol I*, London: Staples Press.
Robinson, E. A. G. (1931) *The Structure of Competitive Industry*, Cambridge: Cambridge University Press; revised edition 1953.
—— (ed.) (1965) *Problems in Economic Development*, London: Macmillan.
—— (1967) *Economic Planning in the United Kingdom: Some Lessons*, Cambridge: Cambridge University Press.
Robinson, J. (1932a) *Economics is a Serious Subject: The Apologia of an Economist to the Mathematician, the Scientist and the Plain Man*, Cambridge: W. Heffer & Sons.
—— (1932b) 'Imperfect competition and falling supply price', *Economic Journal*, 42, 544–54.
—— (1933a) *The Economics of Imperfect Competition*, London: Macmillan (2nd edn, 1969).
—— (1933b) 'A parable of saving and investment', *Economica*, 13, 75–84.
—— (1933c) 'The theory of money and the analysis of output', *Review of Economic Studies*, 1, 22–8; reprinted in *C.E.P.*, vol. I (1951), 52–8.

—— (1934) 'What is perfect competition?', *Quarterly Journal of Economics*, 49, 104–20; reprinted in *C.E.P.*, vol. I (1951), 20–34.
—— (1935) 'A fundamental objection to laissez faire', *Economic Journal*, 45, 580–2; reprinted in *C.E.P.*, vol. I (1951), 49–51.
—— (1936a) 'Some reflections on Marxist economics' (a review of Strachey, 1935), *Economic Journal*, 46, 298–302.
—— (1936b) 'Review of R.F. Harrod, *The Trade Cycle*', *Economic Journal*, 46, 691–3; reprinted in *C.E.P.*, vol. I (1951), 59–61.
—— (1936c) 'Mr. Keynes and Socialism', *Left Review*, 2, 853.
—— (1936d) 'Disguised Unemployment', *Economic Journal*, 46, 225–37; reprinted in Robinson (1937b), 60–74.
—— (1937a) *Introduction to the Theory of Employment*, London: Macmillan (2nd edn, 1969).
—— (1937b) *Essays in the Theory of Employment*, Oxford: Basil Blackwell (2nd edn, 1947).
—— (1937c) 'The economic system in a socialist state', *Cambridge Review*, 58, 289–90.
—— (1938) 'The classification of inventions', *Review of Economic Studies*, 5, 139–42.
—— (1941) 'Marx on unemployment', *Economic Journal*, 51, 234–48.
—— (1942a) 'Industry and the state', *Political Quarterly*, 13, 400–06.
—— (1942b) *An Essay on Marxian Economics*, London: Macmillan (2nd edn, 1966).
—— (1943a) *Private Enterprise or Public Control*, London: Association for Education in Citizenship.
—— (1943b) 'Abolishing Unnecessary Poverty' in Kaldor et al. (1943).
—— (1943c) 'Planning', *Fabian Quarterly*, 36, January, 4–8.
—— (1943d) 'Planning full employment I. The need for a constructive approach', *Times*, 22 January 1943; reprinted in *C.E.P.*, vol. I (1951), 81–8.
—— (1943e) 'Planning full employment II. Alternative solutions to the dilemma', *Times*, 23 January 1943; reprinted in *C.E.P.*, vol. I (1951), 81–8.
—— (1943f) *The Future of Industry*, London, Common Wealth: Frederick Muller.
—— (1943g) *The Problem of Full Employment*, London: Workers Educational Association.
—— (1943h) 'The World We Want', series of broadcasts by BBC, October–November 1943; BBC Written Archives Centre, Reading.
—— (1943i) 'The international currency proposals', *Economic Journal*, 53, 161–75.
—— (1944a) 'Budgeting in the postwar world', in Morrison et al, 75–94.
—— (1944b) 'The currency plan', *Socialist Commentary*, June 9, 246–50.
—— (1944c) 'Review of H.B. Larry, *The United States in the world economy*', *Economic Journal*, 54, 430–7; reprinted in *C.E.P.*, vol. I (1951), 206–13.
—— (1945a) 'Are cartels either desirable or necessary?', BBC broadcast, January 1945, BBC Archives.
—— (1945b) 'The economics of full employment' reviewing *Six Studies in Applied Economics*, prepared at the Oxford Institute of Statistics, *Economic Journal*, 55, 77–82; reprinted in *C.E.P.*, vol. I (1951), 99–104.
—— (1946a) 'The pure theory of international trade', *Review of Economic Studies*, XIV, 98–112; reprinted in *C.E.P.*, vol. I (1951), 182–205.

—— (1946b) 'Obstacles to full employment', lecture to Nationalokonomisk Forening, Copenhagen, 6 December 1946; reprinted in *C E.P.*, vol. I (1951), 105–14.
—— (1949a) 'The theory of planning; a review of *Soviet Economic Development since 1917*, by Maurice Dobb' in *Soviet Studies*, I, October 1949, 60–4; reprinted in *C.E.P.*, vol. I (1951), 175–81.
—— (1949b) 'Mr. Harrod's dynamics', *Economic Journal*, 59, 68–85.
—— (1951–80) *Collected Economic Papers*, 6 vols., London: Macmillan; Oxford: Basil Blackwell.
—— (1951a) 'Introduction' to Rosa Luxemburg (1951) *The Accumulation of Capital*, London: Routledge and Kegan Paul; reprinted in *C.E.P.*, vol. II (1960), 59–73.
—— (1951b) 'Marx and Keynes' in *C.E.P.*, vol. I (1951), 133–45.
—— (1952a) *The Rate of Interest and Other Essays*, London: Macmillan.
—— (1952b) 'The model of an expanding economy', *Economic Journal*, 62, 42–53; reprinted in *C.E.P.*, vol. II (1960), 74–87.
—— (1953) *On Re-reading Marx*, Cambridge: Students' Bookshop; reprinted in *C.E.P.*, vol. IV (1973), 247–68.
—— (1953–4) 'The production function and the theory of capital', *Review of Economic Studies*, 21, 81–106; reprinted in *C.E.P.*, vol. II (1960), 114–31.
—— (1954) 'The labour theory of value', *Science and Society*, Spring; reprinted in *C.E.P.*, vol. II (1960), 49–58.
—— (1955) 'Marx, Marshall and Keynes,' *Delhi School of Economics Occasional Paper No. 9*; reprinted in *C.E.P.*, vol. II (1960), 1–17.
—— (1956a) *The Accumulation of Capital*, London: Macmillan (2nd edn, 1965; 3rd edn, 1969).
—— (1956b) 'India 1955: unemployment and planning', *Capital* (Calcutta), Annual Supplement, December; in *C.E.P.*, vol. III (1965), 182–91.
—— (1957a) 'What remains of Marxism?' in *C.E.P.*, vol. III (1965), 158–66.
—— (1957b) 'Population and development' in *C.E.P.*, vol. II (1960), 107–13.
—— (1957c) 'Notes on the theory of economic development', in *C.E.P.*, vol. II (1960), 88–106.
—— (1958), 'Some reflections on the philosophy of prices', *Manchester School of Economic and Social Studies*, 26, 116–35.
—— (1959) 'A comment', *Oxford Economic Papers*, 11, 141–2.
—— (1960a) *Exercises in Economic Analysis*, London: Macmillan.
—— (1960b), 'The philosophy of prices', in *C.E.P.*, vol. II (1960), 27–48.
—— (1961) 'Prelude to a critique of economic theory', *Oxford Economic Papers*, 13, 53–8; reprinted in *C.E.P.*, vol. III (1965), 7–14.
—— (1962a) 'Review of H.G. Johnson, *Money, Trade and Economic Growth* (1962)', *Economic Journal*, 72, 690–2; reprinted in *C.E.P.*, vol. III (1965), 100–02.
—— (1962b) *Economic Philosophy*, London: Watts and Co.
—— (1962c) 'Latter-day capitalism' *New Left Review*, July–August, 2, 37–46; reprinted in *C.E.P.*, vol. III (1965), 113–24.
—— (1962d) 'Marxism: religion and science', *Monthly Review*, 14, 423–35; reprinted in *C.E.P.*, vol. III (1965), 148–57.
—— (1962e) *Essays in the Theory of Economic Growth*, London: Macmillan (2nd edn, 1963).
—— (1963) 'Findlay's Robinsonian model of accumulation', *Economica*, 30, 408–11; reprinted in *C.E.P.*, vol. III (1965), 48–51.

—— (1964a), 'Solow on the rate of return', *Economic Journal*, 74, 410–7; reprinted in *C.E.P.*, vol. III (1965), 36–47.

—— (1964b) 'The final end of laissez-faire', *New Left Review*, Summer; reprinted in *C.E.P.*, vol. III (1965), 139–47.

—— (1966a) *The New Mercantilism. An Inaugural Lecture by Joan Robinson*, Cambridge: Cambridge University Press; reprinted in *C.E.P.*, vol. IV (1973), 1–13.

—— (1966b) *Economics: An Awkward Corner*, London: Allen and Unwin.

—— (1966c) 'Comment on Samuelson and Modigliani', *Review of Economic Studies*, 33, 307–8.

—— (1967a) 'Growth and the theory of distribution', in *Annals of Collective Economy*, vol. XXXVIII, 3–11; reprinted in *C.E.P.*, vol. V (1979), 71–5.

—— (1967b) 'Smoothing out Keynes' a review of Robert Lekachman, *The Age of Keynes', The New York Review of Books*, 26 January; reprinted in *C.E.P.*, vol. V (1979), 178–83.

—— (1970) *Freedom and Necessity. An Introduction to the Study of Society*, London: George Allen and Unwin.

—— (1971) *Economic Heresies: Some Old-fashioned Questions in Economic Theory*, London: Macmillan.

—— (1972) 'The second crisis of economic theory', *American Economic Review*, 62, 1–9; reprinted in *C.E.P.*, vol. IV (1973), 92–105.

—— (1973a) 'Ideology and analysis'; a contribution to the Festschrift for Eduard Marz, Europaverlags A.G. Wien; in *C.E.P.*, vol. V (1979), 254–61.

—— (1973b) 'Introduction' to "Essays 1953"'; in *C.E.P.*, vol. IV, (1973b), 247–8.

—— (ed.) (1973c) *After Keynes*, Oxford: Basil Blackwell.

—— (1973d) 'What has become of the Keynesian revolution?' in Robinson (ed.) (1973c), 1–11

—— (1973e) 'Foreword' to Kregel (1973), ix–xiii.

—— (1974) 'History versus equilibrium', London: Thames Polytechnic; reprinted in *C.E.P.*, vol. V (1979), 48–58.

—— (1975a) 'Review of L.L. Pasinetti, *Growth and Income Distribution*', *Economic Journal*, 85, 397–9.

—— (1975b) 'Introduction 1974: Reflections and reminiscences', in *C.E.P.*, vol. II, 1960 (2nd edn, 1975), Oxford: Basil Blackwell, iii–xii.

—— (1975c) 'The unimportance of reswitching', *Quarterly Journal of Economics*, 89, 32–9; reprinted in *C.E.P.*, vol. V, (1979), 76–89.

—— (1976) 'Michal Kalecki: a neglected prophet', *New York Review of Books*, 4 March, 28–30.

—— (1977a) 'The labour theory of value as an analytical system', paper given to the Conference of the Economic Section of the Academy of Sciences of Montenegro; reprinted in *C.E.P.*, vol. V, (1979), 289–97.

—— (1977b) 'The labour theory of value', a review of *Studies in the Labour Theory of Value* by Ronald Meek (2nd edition), 1976, *Monthly Review*, December 1977, 50–9; reprinted in *C.E.P.*, vol. V, (1979), 280–8.

—— (1977c) 'Michal Kalecki on the economics of capitalism', *Bulletin of the Oxford Institute of Economics and Statistics*, February, 39, 7–17; reprinted in *C.E.P.*, vol. V (1979), 184–96.

—— (1977d) 'What are the questions?', *Journal of Economic Literature*, 15, 1318–39; reprinted in *C.E.P.*, vol. V, (1979), 1–31.

—— (1977e) 'The meaning of capital, *C.E.P.*, vol. V (1979), 59–70.

—— (1978a) 'The organic composition of capital', *Kyklos*, 31, 5–20; reprinted in *C.E.P.* vol. V (1979), 262–74.
—— (1978b) 'Formalism versus dogma: review of Steedman, *Marx After Sraffa* (1977)', *Contemporary Asia*, 8; reprinted in *C.E.P.* (1979), 275–9.
—— (1978c) *Aspects of Development and Underdevelopment*, Cambridge: Cambridge University Press.
—— (1978d) *Contributions to Modern Economics*, Oxford: Basil Blackwell.
—— (1979) 'Who is a Marxist' in *C.E.P.*, vol. V (1979), 248–53.
—— (1980, 1985) 'Spring cleaning', mimeo, Cambridge; published as 'The theory of normal prices and the reconstruction of economic theory' in Feiwel (ed.) (1985), 157–65
—— (1982) 'The Arms Race', in McMurrin (ed.) (1982), 257–89.
—— (2004) 'British Balance of Payments', a talk to the British Council; reprinted in Kerr, (2004), 1–8.
—— and K. A. Naqvi (1967) 'The badly-behaved production function', *Quarterly Journal of Economics*, 81, 579–91.
—— and J. Eatwell (1973) *Introduction to Modern Economics*, Maidenhead: McGraw-Hill.
Rogers, C. (1997) 'The existence of a monetary long-period unemployment equilibrium', in Harcourt and Riach (eds.) (1997), vol. I, 324–42.
Rosenstein-Rodin, P. (1943) 'Problems of industrialisation of Eastern and South-Eastern Europe', *Economic Journal*, 53, 202–11.
Rosselli, A. (2005) 'An enduring partnership. The correspondence between Kahn and J. Robinson', in Marcuzzo and Rosselli (eds.) (2005), 259–91.
Rothschild, K. (1947) 'Price theory and oligopoly', *Economic Journal*, 57, 299–320.
Said, E. (2006) *On Late Style*, London: Bloomsbury.
Salter, W. E. G. (1960) *Productivity and Technical Change*, Cambridge: Cambridge University Press (2nd edn, 1966).
—— (1965) 'Productivity growth and accumulation as historical processes' in E. A. G. Robinson (ed.) (1965), 266–91.
Samuelson, P. (1962) 'Parable and realism in capital theory: the surrogate production function', *Review of Economic Studies*, 29, 193–206.
—— (1966) 'A summing up', *Quarterly Journal of Economics*, 80, 568–83.
—— (1975) 'Steady-state and transient relations: a reply on reswitching', *Quarterly Journal of Economics*, 89, 40–47; reprinted in *C.E.P.*, vol. V (1979), 83–7.
—— (1989) 'Remembering Joan' in Feiwel (ed.) (1989), 125–43.
Sandilands, R. F. (ed.) (1990) 'Nicholas Kaldor's notes on Allyn Young's Lectures, 1927–29', *Journal of Economic Studies*, 17, 1–170.
Sardoni, C. (1981) 'Multisectoral models of balanced growth and Marxian schemes of expanded reproduction', *Australian Economic Papers*, 20, 383–97.
—— (1984) 'Some ties of Kalecki to the 1926 "Sraffian Manifesto"', *Journal of Post Keynesian Economics*, 6/3, 458–65.
—— (1987) *Marx and Keynes on Economic Recession*, Brighton: Wheatsheaf Books.
—— (ed.) (1992) *On Political Economists and Modern Political Economy. Selected Essays of G.C. Harcourt*, London and New York: Routledge (No.4 in Routledge Library Editions – Economics, 2003).
Sardoni, C. and P. Kriesler (eds.) (1999) *Keynes, Post-Keynesianism and Political Economy. Essays in Honour of Geoff Harcourt*, vol. 3, London and New York: Routledge.

Sato, K. (1976) 'The neoclassical production function: comment', *American Economic Review*, 66, 428–33.

Schumpeter, J. (1934) 'Review of Joan Robinson (1933a)', *Journal of Political Economy*, 42, 249–57; reprinted in Kerr with Harcourt (eds.) (2002), vol. I, 163–70.

—— (1954) *History of Economic Analysis*, London: George Allen and Unwin.

Shove, G. F. (1933a) 'Review of Joan Robinson (1933a)', *Economic Journal*, 43, 657–61; reprinted in Kerr with Harcourt (eds.) (2002), vol. I, 171–5.

—— (1933b) 'Review of Hicks (1932)', *Economic Journal*, 43, 460–72.

—— (1944) 'Mrs Robinson on Marxian Economics', *Economic Journal*, 54, 47–61; reprinted in Kerr with Harcourt (eds.) (2002), Vol. II 225–38.

Sills, D. L. (ed.) (1979) *International Encyclopaedia of the Social Sciences, Biographical Supplement*, vol. 18, New York: Free Press.

Skidelsky, R. (1992), *John Maynard Keynes, vol 2: The Economist as Saviour 1920–37*, London: Macmillan.

Solow, R. M. (1956a) 'The production function and the theory of capital', *Review of Economic Studies*, 23, 101–8.

—— (1956b) 'A contribution to the theory of growth', *Quarterly Journal of Economics*, 70, 65–94.

—— (1957) 'Technical change and the aggregate production function', *Review of Economics and Statistics*, 39, 312–20.

—— (1963) *Capital Theory and the Rate of Return*, Amsterdam: North-Holland.

—— (1970) 'On the rate of return: reply to Pasinetti', *Economic Journal*, 80, 423–8.

—— (1975) 'Brief comments', *Quarterly Journal of Economics*, 89, 48–52.

—— (2005) 'The elasticity of substitution is only 73 years old but here are a few thoughts anyway', Cambridge: mimeo.

Sraffa, P. (1925) 'Sulle relazioni fra costo e quantita prodotta', *Annali di Economia*, (Milan) II, 277–328.

—— (1926) 'The laws of returns under competitive conditions', *Economic Journal*, 36, 535–50.

—— (1930) '"A criticism" and "A rejoinder" in "Increasing returns and the representative firm: a symposium"', *Economic Journal*, 40, 89–92, 93.

—— (1932a) 'Dr. Hayek on money and capital', *Economic Journal*, 42, 42–53.

—— (1932b) 'A rejoinder', *Economic Journal*, 42, 249–51.

—— (1936) 'Letter from Piero Sraffa to Joan Robinson, 27 October 1936'; reprinted in Kerr with Harcourt (eds.) (2002), vol. III, 292.

—— (1960) *Production of Commodities by Means of Commodities. Prelude to a Critique of Economic Theory*, Cambridge: Cambridge University Press.

—— (1962) 'Production of commodities: a comment', *Economic Journal*, 72, 477–9.

Sraffa, P. with the collaboration of M. H. Dobb (eds.) (1951) 'Introduction' to *The Works and Correspondence of David Ricardo*, vol. 1, published for the Royal Economic Society, Cambridge: Cambridge University Press.

Steedman, I. (1977) *Marx after Sraffa*, London: New Left Books.

Steindl, J. (1981), 'A personal portrait of Michal Kalecki', *Journal of Post Keynesian Economics*, 3, 590–6.

Strachey, J. (1935) *The Nature of Capitalist Crisis*, London: Victor Gollancz.

Stretton, H. (1969) *The Political Sciences. General Principles of Selection in Social Science and History*, London: Routledge.

Swan, P. L. (2006) 'Trevor Winchester Swan AO', Australian National University Inaugural Trevor Swan Distinguished Lecture, ANU, pp. 27.

Swan, T. W. (1956) 'Economic growth and capital accumulation', *Economic Record*, 32, 334–61.
—— (1964) 'Of Golden Ages and production functions' in Berrill (ed.) (1964), 3–16.
Sylos Labini, P. (1985) 'Sraffa's critique of the Marshallian theory of prices', *Political Economy: Studies in the Surplus Approach*, 1, (2), 51–71.
Szenberg, M., L. Ramrattan and A. Gottesman (eds.) (2006) *Samuelsonian Economics and the Twenty-first Century*, New York: Oxford University Press.
Tahir, P. (1990a) 'Some aspects of development and underdevelopment: critical perspectives on Joan Robinson', unpublished Ph.D. dissertation, University of Cambridge.
—— (1990b) 'Making sense of Joan Robinson on China', mimeo, Cambridge.
—— (1999) 'Joan Robinson: a neglected precursor of internal migration models', in Sardoni and Kriesler (eds.) (1999), 312–33.
Tahir, P., G. C. Harcourt and P. Kerr (2002) 'On Joan Robinson and China' in Kerr with Harcourt (eds.) (2002), vol. V, 267–80.
Tang, A. M., F. M. Westfield and J. S. Worley (eds.) (1976) *Evolution, Welfare and Time in Economics. Essays in Honour of Nicholas Georgescu- Roegen*, Lexington Heath: Lexington Books.
Targetti, F. and B. Kinder-Has (1982) 'Kalecki's review of Keynes' *General Theory*', *Australian Economic Papers*, 21, 244–60.
Tobin, J. (1973) 'Cambridge (U.K.) versus Cambridge (Mass)', *Public Interest*, 31, 102–9.
Toye, J. (2000) *Keynes on Population*, Oxford: Oxford University Press.
Triffin, R. (1941) *Monopolistic Competition and General Equilibrium Theory* (1941), Cambridge, MA: Harvard University Press, 36–49; reprinted in Kerr with Harcourt (eds.) (2002), vol. I, 362–73.
Turner, M. (1989) *Joan Robinson and the Americans*, Armonk, New York: M. E. Sharpe.
Vaughn, K. I. (ed.) (1994) *Perspectives on the History of Economic Thought, vol. X: Method, Competition, Conflict and Measurement in the Twentieth Century*, Aldershot: Edward Elgar.
Veblen, T. (1908) 'Professor Clark's economics', *Quarterly Journal of Economics*, 22, 147–95; reprinted in Kerr with Harcourt (eds.) (2002), vol. III, 281–91.
Ward, B. (1972) *What's Wrong with Economics?*, New York and London: Basic Books.
Warner, M. (ed.) (1996), *International Encyclopaedia of Business and Management*, London: Routledge.
Whitaker, J. K. (1989) 'The Cambridge background to imperfect competition' in Feiwel (ed.) (1989a), 169–96; reprinted in Kerr with Harcourt (eds.) (2002), vol. I, 176–202.
Wilson, T. and R. Prior (2004, 2006) 'Maurice, Sir Frederick Barton (1871–1951)', *Oxford Dictionary of National Biography*, Oxford: Oxford University Press.
Wong, S. (2006) *The Foundations of Paul Samuelson's Revealed Preference Theory. A Study by the Method of Rational Reconstruction* (revised edition), New York: Routledge.
Worswick, G. D. N. (1959) 'Mrs Robinson on simple accumulation: a comment with algebra', *Oxford Economic Papers*, 11, 125–42; reprinted in Kerr with Harcourt (eds.) (2002), vol. III, 54–71.
—— (1962) 'Review of Joan Robinson (1962e)', *Economic Journal*, 73, 295–7; reprinted in Kerr with Harcourt (eds.) (2002), vol. III, 182–4.

Index